MUSIC WAS
NOT ENOUGH

MUSIC WAS
NOT ENOUGH

by

BOB WILBER

Assisted by
Derek Webster

NEW YORK
OXFORD UNIVERSITY PRESS
1988

© Bob Wilber 1987

First published in 1987 by
The Macmillan Press Ltd
London
England

Published in 1988 in the United States by
Oxford University Press Inc
200 Madison Avenue
New York
NY 10016

ISBN 0–19–520629–0

Typeset by
Wessex Typesetters
(Division of The Eastern Press Ltd)
Frome, Somerset
in 10/12pt Caledonia

Printed in Great Britain by
Anchor Brendon Ltd
Tiptree, Essex

Dedicated to my wife, Pug,
who has made everything I've ever dreamed of
(including this book)
possible

Contents

Prologue

This is the story of an angry man.

I looked into the mirror on my 50th birthday. I didn't like what I saw. Gazing back at me was the mild mannered, easy-going Bob Wilber the jazz world knew, but the real Bob Wilber was an angry and frustrated man, wondering why he felt that way. I went over my usual targets, my list of scapegoats: my parents who hadn't prepared me for the rough and tumble of life; the unsupportive, uncaring public who had destroyed my self-confidence; the short-sighted, greedy, insensitive critics, agents and producers who hadn't appreciated what I had to offer. Talking to myself in the mirror on that momentous day, I was able to say for the first time, "Wait a minute, Wilber. Who is really to blame for your lack of success? You are, my friend, so stop blaming everybody and everything else. You haven't dealt effectively with life, and only you can do something about it. So get busy man, move!"

On that grey March day, the beginning of my 50th year, I took stock of my life. I knew in my heart that it was really my own fault I hadn't attained the goals I had sought when I first started playing jazz. I was well aware of the fact that I had made my life far more difficult than it ought to have been. What had become of the much talked about protégé of Sidney Bechet, the curly-haired teenage clarinet player, leader of the Wildcats, the youngest American to appear at the first postwar International Jazz Festival in Nice, France? He didn't even rate a listing in the *Dictionnaire du jazz*, published in France in the 1960s. A lack of self-confidence, an inability to deal with people both at business and social levels, and a mild and almost self-apologetic demeanor in a world that demanded dynamism and charisma were real and painful problems that had combined to bring me to a point where I neither felt good about myself nor liked the person I had become.

I had been an insecure, shy lad, dominated by an over-achieving father and protected by a loving and caring mother, a combination not exactly conducive to producing an aggressive and assertive character. At the age of 13 I had taken up the clarinet, and I immediately made an astounding discovery: I could play jazz! Crudely, perhaps, but well enough to earn the appreciation of fellow jazz fans in my home town, and I felt I had finally achieved something. I was flattered by their interest in me. They were all a couple of years older than I, in my sister Mary's class at school; they were people I admired and looked up to. When they started inviting me to jam sessions, referring to me as "Kid Wilber," their great new find on clarinet, I was elated. I had been accepted by these older, smarter, sophisticated guys. I belonged! I convinced myself that music was the true answer to my problems and would provide all the happiness and self-esteem that I hadn't felt up till then. From that point onwards, all my attention was focused on music. Music was the thing: to hell with boy scouts, sports, studies – and who needed girls, anyway? The normal, healthy progression into adulthood became stunted and suspended by my obsession. Looking back, I realize what had happened: I had found something I could do better than my father. Music was an addiction, and my dependence on it as a hiding place from the world was total.

I had discovered jazz. It seemed to me to celebrate the very joy of being alive. How different from the rest of my life! I felt stifled in the staid environment of Scarsdale, the suburb of New York City where my family lived. I was fascinated by the backgrounds and life styles of the musicians I admired so much – Louis, Bix, Benny, Fats and the Hawk. I became acutely aware of how difficult the struggle to gain recognition had been for these jazz greats, and contrasted it with the security and affluence of my own life. The comparisons troubled me. It is not difficult to appreciate how the poverty and deprivation of Louis Armstrong's childhood presented barriers that for most people would have proved well-nigh insurmountable. It says a lot for Louis's resilience and character that he overcame them in the way that he did. It is much more difficult to understand how a privileged childhood, in which I had seemingly been surrounded by love and had wanted for nothing, could have produced problems that in their own way were just as severe as those facing a boy growing up in the back alleys of New Orleans. Yet that was the situation in which I found myself.

I was filled with the excitement of learning about jazz. I wanted to tell the whole world about this wonderful music, to persuade everybody to love it as much as I did. The more involved I became, the stronger those feelings grew, yet I felt frustrated. Scarsdale seemed to be the very antithesis of that exciting world I had discovered. The calm, orderly gentility of the place was in such contrast to the kaleidoscopic color and excitement in the world of jazz. The town assumed a mantle of grayness, and like Dorothy, I dreamed of escaping to my own land of Oz, where life would be one long continual jam session. I loved the title of Ma Rainey's blues *The world is jazz crazy and so am I*. Unfortunately the world wasn't jazz crazy – it was just me and a few of my buddies. My poor parents didn't know how to deal with their rebellious offspring. A firm hand on my shoulder coupled with parental advice might have helped temper my enthusiasm with a more realistic view of life, but I probably wouldn't have listened anyway: like all young rebels, I knew best. Nothing would deter me from immersing myself totally in jazz. I embarked on the long path that led up to that look in the mirror, when I faced the fact that music had not provided the answer to all of life's problems – that indeed, music was not enough.

Part I. Aspirations

ONE

Early years

I made my entrance into the world on 15th March 1928 to join my sister Mary Margaret, my mother Mary Eliza and my father Allen Sage Wilber, a partner in the publishing firm of F. S. Crofts, a small company specializing in college textbooks. At that time we were living on Sullivan Street, just south of Washington Square in Greenwich Village, New York City. I was little more than a year old when Dad took us all out to California to visit my mother's parents, to show them their new grandson and to attend to some publishing business. He had planned to leave his family with his in-laws for a few weeks while he visited colleges in the Midwest. Shortly after leaving California he was shocked to receive a telephone call from his wife's sister, Margaret, telling him that Mary Eliza had been taken seriously ill. He returned immediately by train, only to learn that she had died less than 12 hours after Margaret had talked to him. His grief must have been particularly intense because his wife had no history or indication of illness at all. Many years later a close friend of the family told me that my father came back from California to announce in an almost stoic manner that his wife had died "riddled with cancer." From that day onwards my father was never to mention the subject again until shortly before his death, some 55 years later.

Looking back, I often wonder what it was that could have allowed Dad to display to the world such an unemotional façade despite the deep grief that must have been within him. I often wonder, too, about my mother and how she had successfully concealed not only from family and friends but also from her dear husband the fact that she was suffering from cancer. She may not have known what it was, but it is hard to believe she had no inkling that something was wrong. I suppose that even then, at that formative stage, I was subconsciously receiving my first lesson in the art of disguising one's true feelings. If only my father had allowed his grief to pour out, how much more honest and open would our future relationship have been.

Dad returned to New York with his two young, motherless children. I remember little of life on Sullivan Street other than a succession of nannies and governesses, one of whom treated us very badly until Dad found out and dismissed her. He eventually engaged the services of Miss Breed, who was a kindly, genteel, professional nanny, and life was very happy with her. In later years I found out that one of our Sullivan Street neighbors at that time was John Hammond, fresh out of college and already beginning to make a name for himself as a dedicated promoter of jazz. In fact, John's apartment was the one next to ours, and I have often wondered if the first jazz I ever heard was from John's phonograph next door as I lay in my crib.

In 1931 we moved to a lovely large apartment in Gramercy Park, between Third and Park avenues. Gramercy Park is now, as it was then, a London-style park square ringed by charming and beautifully kept houses dating from the mid-1800s and recalling the elegance and gentility of a bygone age. I attended kindergarten at Friends Seminary, a Quaker school just a few blocks away. Our family were not Quakers; Dad hailed from a long line of Presbyterians. His father and his uncle, a twin brother, had both been ministers, whilst his mother was the organist in her husband's church. Curiously enough, my mother's father, grandfather Clark, was also a Presbyterian minister, along with *his* twin brother, Edward. We've had no more ministers in the family since – nor any more twins for that matter!

I first became aware that there was a new lady in my father's life when Mary Margaret and I were introduced to Miss Margaret Alder. As a young woman from an upper-middle-class background, she had graduated from Wellesley College in 1920 and was employed as a lay-out artist for the magazine *Review of Reviews*. She was very kind to my sister and me, and clearly wanted to get to know us. In November 1933 she married my father and became the only mother I have ever really known. This beautiful, gracious lady is still alive and well at the age of 89. The marriage took place at my stepmother's home in Montclair. It was a very grand affair, and when at school on Monday morning we children were asked what we had done over the weekend, I proudly announced that I had attended my parents' wedding! The teacher could hardly suppress a smile.

After the marriage we continued to live in Gramercy Park. That winter, Dad, while watching his two young children attempting to slide down the two-foot high incline around the statue of Edwin Booth on their new Christmas sleds, decided that it was about time he gave his family a country environment. He rented a house in Scarsdale and so set the scene for all the factors that had such a profound effect upon my life.

Scarsdale is a suburban community to the north of New York, from which people in business commute some 40 minutes to the city by train each day. It is a community of wealth and privilege, of country clubs and gracious socializing, an Ivy League enclave. During the time I was growing up there, the population was predominantly WASP (white Anglo-Saxon Protestant). After the war, as Scarsdale grew, many people of Jewish background moved up from the city; recent years have seen an influx of Japanese families as more executives with Japanese corporations maintain offices in New York. To this day, there are very few black people living in Scarsdale. When we moved there in 1934 it was a very desirable environment in which to grow up, and I can remember being very happy; my father's affluence provided us with everything children could want. Dad was an achiever. He had graduated from the University of Kansas a Phi Beta Kappa, gone to business school and entered the publishing world with Macmillan in 1913, eventually forming his own company with a colleague, Fred

Crofts. There was seemingly little he couldn't do. He was a marvelous raconteur, a talented amateur musician, a tennis player, golfer, swimmer, athlete, skier and skater. He was very active in town affairs and was president of the Town Club, the principal men's organization in Scarsdale. All in all, he was a highly respected member of the community. I don't recall exactly when the thought first entered my mind, but it began to dawn on me that it was going to be difficult to follow in his footsteps, and as I grew older this feeling became stronger.

But in truth, it was from my father that I developed my interest in music. During his days at college, ragtime was at its height and Dad had become a fairly proficient pianist in that idiom. He was also an *aficionado* of the Broadway musical theater, and our home was always full of sheet music. During his early days in New York, his room-mate was a theater critic for a newspaper and Dad was able to get free passes to all the plays, often seeing them on opening night. He grew to know and love the melodies of Berlin, Gershwin and Kern in that golden era of the Broadway musical. In later years he loved to recollect the evening at college when he attended a concert by the Yale University Glee Club and the intermission pianist was a young Yale student named Cole Porter. His interest was transmitted to me each evening when he used to play the piano after a hard day's work. I can see him now, his hands flying over the keyboard, and my mother tapping her feet or dancing round the room. The first jazz record I can remember hearing was Duke Ellington's Victor recording of *Mood Indigo*, which Dad had purchased shortly after its release. As the record was issued early in 1931, that would put my age at only three, yet I can still remember as if it were yesterday: the mysterious sound of the high muted trumpet and trombone, the mournful low-register clarinet and the solemn, steady "plonk, plonk, plonk" of the banjo.

Mary Margaret and I were brought up with firmness and kindness, but in retrospect I feel something was missing. The death of Mary Eliza had been a traumatic shock for Dad and it seemed as if, in order to protect himself from any further hurt, he concealed his deepest feelings from the outside world. There was nevertheless a gentle warmth about him and a serenity that filled our home, a calmness that allowed no acknowledgement of sadness, grief, pain, anger, rage or frustration as having any part in life. Yet there was no doubt of his fondness for his new wife, nor of hers for him. He was a man of total self-control, and he endeavored to raise us in the same image. Unseemly displays of feeling were frowned upon; no outbursts of anger were permitted, voices were never raised, and we were taught at all times to make the best of any situation. Throughout my childhood I never saw or heard any member of my family cry. I never heard my parents quarrel or even raise their voices to one another, and I never heard or saw them make love. I saw nothing but this calm gentility. It seemed as if normal reactions between a husband and wife had to be concealed from me to prevent any possible harm to my psyche, and as a result my life had a gray unrealness about it. In later years, when contact with my family consisted of get-togethers at ceremonial occasions (such as Thanksgiving, 4th of July, Christmas and occasional family holidays in Florida or the Caribbean) with everybody on their best behavior and observing all the social graces, this same feeling of grayness seemed always to be present.

Mine was such a privileged childhood with so many nice things about it. My grandparents' old Victorian mansion in Montclair was always a fascination to me. My stepmother's parents were known as Dada and Auntie Cew. Dada was a big, dignified, stately man who had had a very successful career with US Steel, starting in his teens as an office boy and working his way through the ranks until eventually he attained the position of treasurer and vice-president of the company. My memory of Auntie Cew was that she was a very gracious lady who ran a tight ship and was very much in charge of the staff, household schedules and social arrangements. It was all very Victorian. They didn't have cocktails and wines because that wasn't part of their life style, but after the main course at dinner finger bowls would always be brought out into which we dipped our fingers before drying them off on our linen napkins. When I first stayed there, I was always puzzled because every once in a while, during the course of the meal, Madison the butler would appear from out of the kitchen to perform some specific task. I could never figure out how he knew when to come in, but one day I discovered that there was a button beneath the beautiful Turkish rug that covered the floor under the dining table, and every time my grandmother pressed it with her foot a bell rang in the kitchen. Once I knew that, I used to crawl under the table to press the button. Shortly after my parents' marriage I developed the measles, and, to avoid my sister catching it from me, I was taken to Montclair to stay with Dada and Auntie Cew. My mother tells me that after we had been there for a week or so her father asked her, "Daddy girl, what are you going to do about that new young man of yours? He just sits up there in bed and sings all the time."

Madison also acted as the chauffeur. He used to wash and polish the family Packard to perfection each afternoon. He was a black man, and a great fan of Bill Robinson. He fancied himself as a tap-dancer, and I used to plead with him, "Teach me how to tap dance, Madison. Please."

"Take a walk, son, take a walk," he would say. Every once in a while, though, Madison would unbend and show me a few steps that I would try to copy.

Another family house I loved to visit was the one at Prouts Neck, a fashionable resort community on the coast of Maine. Holiday House, as it was known, was owned by Auntie Mum, Auntie Cew's sister. My grandparents used to spend the summers there, with Dada working in New York during the week and commuting to Prouts Neck each weekend. Auntie Mum used to take in genteel boarders, people with very good references. Although it was a means of making money, these weren't just any people: they practically had to be friends of the family to be acceptable.

At school I had plenty of opportunity as far as music was concerned. In fifth grade we had a music appreciation group on Friday afternoons, when we would listen to a radio show for children hosted by Walter Damrosch over station WNYC. He played excerpts from the classics and explained them to his young audience in a patient, gentle way. The teacher had the idea of getting everyone to participate in a recital for our final class of the year. Most of the kids played piano, violin or some other instrument, but it was all classical. My pal Bob Delahanty and I were crazy about the swing music we heard Bob's teenage brother and sister, Tom and Ruth, and their friends playing on the phonograph every afternoon after school. Bob had an old set of drums, complete with maroon temple blocks; there was a tropical picture on the bass drum, which had a light inside. He had them set up in the alcove next to the enclosed porch where the teenagers gathered every afternoon. I had a tin flute and we'd try to play along with the records (*Sing, sing, sing* was one of our favorites) until Tom would chase us outside. That spring we decided that our contribution to the recital would be a duet performance of one of our favorite records, Glenn Miller's *In the Mood*. We knew every note of the arrangement, from the first bar to the last, and we gave a three-minute performance. I played on my tin flute, or imagined I did, every single note, including the Al Klink–Tex Beneke tenor battle and the Johnny Best trumpet solo, and our act received the loudest applause of the program.

Aside from a few musical pals, I was something of a loner at school. I wasn't into athletics or sports and I was very shy as far as girls were concerned. The friendships I did have developed through music. In junior high school, when I took up the clarinet, I was discovered by these guys in my sister's class who were into collecting records, playing jazz and going to places like Nick's and Jimmy Ryan's to listen to live music. They became my circle of friends. Our gang – Lou Levi, Geoff Gould, Bill Robbins, Tom Alley and myself – was considered an odd-ball group because we thought of nothing but music, and were therefore different. It was not that our fellow students disliked us, but we were not the usual run-of-the-mill teenagers. In fact I was quite popular at social gatherings because of my ability to play a little boogie-woogie on the piano. Boogie-woogie was very popular in the early 1940s. By sitting hunched over the keyboard at parties, pounding away at *Yancey Special* or *Pinetop's Boogie* – my two big pieces – I could avoid confronting that knotty, seemingly insoluble problem of how to deal with girls. On one occasion we came up with the idea of putting on some musical entertainment during the lunch hour. Any opportunity to play was a plus for us, so when the Student Council accepted our proposal we jumped at the chance. We started playing in the auditorium to kids wandering in after their meal, but after a while some wise guy started to throw pennies at us. The other students thought this was a great idea, and soon we were being pelted with coins thrown not only at our feet but also at our bodies and faces. In their own way they were poking fun at us and emphasizing that we were different.

I recall another occasion when I was singled out for some discriminatory treatment. I was about 13 at the time. One day in the locker room, while my attention was engaged by a group of boys, one of their number slipped a match between the sole and upper of my shoe and lit it. I soon felt the heat and realized I had been given a "hot foot" – a prank that appealed to the schoolboy sense of humor. My immediate reaction was one of anger, but strangely enough I felt paralyzed, unable to express my feelings. Although I certainly would have been justified, I felt incapable of striking back and obligated to pause and consider whether the pranksters had in some way been justified. It seems absurd, but I couldn't ignore an inner voice that said, "Hold on – maybe they're right, perhaps you did something to deserve this treatment." This incident stuck in my memory because it was indicative of a problem I have had all my life: not feeling I have the right openly to express anger or indignation.

It was around this time, in 1941, that my parents took me to Café Society Uptown in New York City. Dad had become intrigued by recordings of Teddy Wilson's piano playing, and so one night he took the family to hear Teddy. The group consisted of Big Sid Catlett on drums, Benny Morton on trombone, Edmond Hall on clarinet, Emmett Berry on trumpet and John Williams on bass. What a marvelous band! Little did I know I would have the opportunity to play with all those wonderful musicians one day! Café Society was an elegant place, with long blue drapes behind the bandstand. The musicians were immaculately attired in cream dinner jackets. It was a nightclub that offered a complete evening out, with dining, dancing and a floor show. Not only was there Teddy's band but also a very funny comedian named Jimmy Savo. In addition, the program included the Delta Rhythm Boys singing beautiful rhythmic spirituals and an intermission group, Bill Coleman and his trio. As if all that were not enough, Hazel Scott was playing piano and singing. It was a marvelous collection of talent and an unforgettable evening for me. Incidentally, Café Society was run by Barney Josephson, who until recently ran the Cookery, the club in Greenwich Village where Alberta Hunter made her sensational comeback.

Back at school, my musical interests were still developing, but by this time I had progressed from tin flute to clarinet. I was in the Boy Scouts when I started on clarinet. My ambition was to be in the school marching band because it seemed so glamorous with the fancy uniforms. It would also give me the opportunity of traveling to the other high schools with the football team and watching all the games. When I went to see the band director, he gave me a trumpet and told me to try it over the weekend. I couldn't get a sound out of it, however, so the next Friday he gave me a clarinet. By Sunday I was confidently playing *Row, row, row your boat*. This was it! The band director was Willard Briggs, an excellent clarinetist and my first teacher.

My initial interest was in such musicians as Glenn Miller, Benny Goodman and Harry James, but through the record collections of my friends I discovered the great black bands of the swing era, plus the music of New Orleans, Kansas City and Chicago. This was right at the beginning of that period when early jazz recordings were first reissued on a systematic basis. Most of this music had laid buried and all but forgotten throughout the swing era, but those reissues represented new and exciting discoveries for me. I listened to Louis Armstrong, Jelly Roll Morton, Sidney Bechet and the Chicagoans such as Eddie Condon and Frank Teschemacher, and what I heard moved me intensely. The more I listened, the more excited I became. This music seemed to contain something that was flesh and blood and reality. By this time I was being allowed by my parents to go into New York City on Sunday afternoons to attend the jam sessions run at Jimmy Ryan's by Milt Gabler. I saw and felt the excitement of the crowds, the music, the whiskey, the smoke, people in love and people fighting. The whole thing represented reality to me, and as I grew more involved, the more jazz became the most important thing in my life. It was hard to feel that I wasn't loved or was neglected, because we had everything we wanted; to feel unhappy would appear to be ungrateful, but I was unhappy in many ways and jazz offered an escape from an environment I didn't like and an alternative to the problems of growing up.

In the film *The Wizard of Oz* you saw Dorothy passing from the real world of black and white into the fantasy world of technicolor. This is exactly what I felt when I traveled into the city on the New York Central railroad. Even the name of the branch line that Scarsdale was on, the Harlem Division, had an exciting appropriateness to it. There was a magic line between Scarsdale and New York, and every time the train approached the 125th Street station in Harlem I crossed the line and passed from black and white into color, and vice versa. Duke Ellington, who once described his first view of Harlem as being "like a scene from *Arabian Nights*" was once asked what the title "Harlem Airshaft" referred to. He explained it this way: "So much goes on in a Harlem air shaft. You hear fights, you smell dinner, you hear people making love. You hear intimate gossip floating down. You hear the radio. An air shaft is one great big loudspeaker. You see your neighbor's laundry. You hear the janitor's dog. The man upstairs' aerial falls down and breaks your window. You smell coffee. A wonderful thing, that smell. An air shaft has got every contrast. One guy is cooking dried fish and rice and another guy's got a great big turkey. You hear people praying, fighting, snoring. Jitterbugs are jumping up and down, always over you, never under you."

By this time, 1943, I was well and truly under the spell of those wonderful recordings of Sidney Bechet and his New Orleans Feetwarmers. One of the things that particularly impressed me was the piano playing of Willie "the Lion" Smith, and the way he complemented the horns so beautifully on numbers like *Georgia Cabin*, *I'm comin' Virginia* and *Limehouse Blues*. A school chum of mine, Arthur Ecker, who aspired to be a pianist, somehow got his parents to arrange for Willie to come out to Scarsdale every Sunday afternoon to give him lessons. I know Arthur will forgive me if I say that he was not much of a pianist, but his parents really enjoyed having Willie up from New York. At the conclusion of Arthur's lesson, Mr and Mrs Ecker and their friends would gather in the living room with a round of drinks and Willie would entertain them. He loved to perform and could mesmerize any audience. Our gang got wind of this development and we strong-armed Arthur into inviting us over after his lesson. We couldn't pass up a chance to play with the great Willie Smith and be coached by him – "the Lion" was our professor! This arrangement became a regular weekly happening and we loved it. I arranged with Willie to come out to my home for a session, and in honor of the occasion Dad stocked up on cigars, brandy and milk. Willie loved brandy, but because of stomach trouble, probably caused by too much bath-tub gin, he had to dilute it with milk. At the last minute Willie had to cancel and never did get out to our house. That supply of cigars and brandy sat in the cupboard for quite a while, until eventually the cigars went moldy and had to be thrown away. Dad never smoked cigars. He associated them with low-class politicians and therefore considered that they were not for genteel folk.

That year I took a summer vacation job, working as a hotel bell-boy in Prouts Neck. Figuring that I was now a man, I started smoking, despite the nausea I experienced. I managed to save most of my wages and tips, and when I returned home to Scarsdale I bought a second-hand alto saxophone. I thought it was a beautiful instrument, and when I blew my first note I expected to hear a mellifluous sound, something like that produced by Johnny Hodges. What a terrible disappointment! The screech that came out sounded like a rooster having its neck wrung. I was so devastated I sold the horn and never worked up the courage to try the alto again until the mid-1970s.

One memorable experience I had was in that same year, 1943, when I was 15 years old. On January 23rd, Duke Ellington gave a concert at Carnegie Hall in which he gave the première of his first extended major work, *Black, Brown and Beige*. It was a black-tie affair with the proceeds going to the Russian War Relief Fund. Somehow Dad had managed to obtain tickets and he took my mother, my grandmother, my sister and me. We sat in the middle of the orchestra stalls and listened, enthralled, to the Ellington band in all its glory. Barney Bigard had left by this time and had been replaced by Chauncey Haughton, but all the other regulars were there – Ben Webster, Rex Stewart, Lawrence Brown, Johnny Hodges, Juan Tizol, Harry Carney. It was a marvelous concert, and I remember particularly how much my grandmother Gonka enjoyed it. She had been a church organist all her life and was then in her 80s. During one of Tricky Sam Nanton's plunger solos she turned excitedly to me and said, "He's trying to tell us something." Clearly the message of this music had even reached her! It was a very thrilling sight in those days to see musicians dressed so sharply. There was this marvelous elegance about the band as they came out in gray tuxedos with burgundy cummerbunds, their instruments shined till the brass sparkled. The Duke was dressed in black tie and tails, and after the intermission he reappeared in white tie and tails. He was such a glamorous, marvelous man, and so impressive to me as a kid. I loved the elegance and glamor of both the scene and the music, and I still love it. I deplore the current attitude of so many musicians with their scruffy dress, unkempt hair, and dirty jeans. I feel that the way they look is reflected in the way they play – with a lot of clinkers and wrong notes and a "who cares anyway" attitude. The Ellington gentlemen, however, were very proud of their music, and their dress and manner reflected this tremendous pride in what they were doing.

Meanwhile, back at school, our group of jazz lovers was getting more and more ambitious. We had formed a hot club while in 11th grade. The members used to meet in the music department once a week after school hours and listen to records and hold jam sessions. We came up with the idea of having a concert at the end of the school year and inviting New York professionals up to play. We managed to assemble a fine group of all-star musicians, including Art Hodes on piano, Pops Foster on bass, Danny Alvin on drums, Wilbur De Paris on trombone, Sterling Bose on cornet and Rod Cless and Mezz Mezzrow on clarinets. I invited Eddie Condon, who sent a very charming letter regretting his inability to attend. His signature was very wavy and I couldn't understand why he had signed it that way, but in later years he told me that it had probably been signed on "the morning after the night before." The group played a rousing set, and then our jazz band joined them for a grand finale. The whole program was a tremendous success and our jazz gang became heroes among the student body.

My closest friend in school was Denny Strong. In 1944 his family moved to Scarsdale from North Carolina. When I found out Denny and his brother Charlie were jazz fans and had an extensive record collection, I received them into our little jazz fraternity with open arms. They were particularly welcome because some of the older fellows had graduated and left for the armed services. Their mother was a pianist. Denny played drums and Charlie played trombone and bass. Denny was not a great drummer, but he was a very intelligent and perceptive jazz fan. The first soprano sax I played was one that Denny picked up in a hock shop. I was intrigued with it because by then I was fascinated by Sidney Bechet. In later years Denny loved to recall his first meeting with Sidney. A chubby, bespectacled, shy little fellow, it was not easy for him to approach the great Bechet, whom he espied one night standing by the jukebox at Ryan's, smoking a cigarette between sets. Having just finished reading an article on Bechet's recent engagement at Jazz Ltd in Chicago, where the band included Dick Wellstood and a drummer from Boston named Bob Saltmarsh, Denny sidled warily up to Sidney. Pointing to the write-up, he exclaimed nervously, "I'm Denny Strong. I'm a friend of Bob Saltmarsh." Sidney slowly turned towards him, took a long drag on his cigarette, and, looking down at Denny's moon-shaped face staring up at him through thick lenses, intoned cryptically, "He don't play no fuckin' drums."

Denny and I used to go to the jam sessions at Ryan's each Sunday afternoon with the permission of our parents, but we were getting the urge to expand our listening activities. One Friday night we planned to go to the movies in the neighboring town of White Plains, but at the last moment we decided to take the train into the city to hear some jazz. We planned to catch the 1 a.m. train from New York to Scarsdale, then walk back to our homes, and nobody would be any the wiser. When we arrived at Grand Central Station we went straight downtown to Nick's in the Village, where we listened to Brad Gowans, Pee Wee Russell, Chelsea Quealey, Charlie Queener, Bob Casey and Joe Grauso. From Nick's we took the subway up to 52nd Street to Ryan's, where we soaked up the sounds of Zutty Singleton and his trio, with Joe Eldridge on alto and Don Frye on piano. Although we were only kids, they used to let us in these places providing we didn't try to order booze. By slowly nursing a Coke, we could just about afford the tariff.

From Ryan's we moved next door into the Onyx Club to hear Billie Holiday singing with the Al Casey trio, with Pete Brown on alto. Billie was sensational. She came out wearing an off-the-shoulder evening gown with a white gardenia in her hair. She was the most beautiful woman I had ever seen.

We were so mesmerized by Billie that we forgot completely about the time. We looked at our watches. It was ten minutes to one, so we ran all the way back to Grand Central Station. We arrived, out of breath, to find we had just missed the last train to Scarsdale. After the first few panic-stricken moments we decided there was nothing we could do about it. As the next train would be the "milk" train at 6 a.m., the only sensible thing to do would be to head back to 52nd Street!

This time we went to Kelly's Stables, between Sixth and Seventh avenues. It was about two o'clock; things were quiet, and the place was practically empty. The waiter showed us to a table right in front of the bandstand, where we sat and listened to the band. After a while a striking figure in a double-breasted pin-stripe suit came striding up the aisle and onto the stand. There he was – the famous Coleman Hawkins! He picked up his tenor as one of the guys in the band asked, "Whadya wanna play, Bean?" In a deep, mellifluous voice that sounded so much like his huge saxophone tone, he replied, "Body – one, two." Denny and I sat there goggle-eyed, less than three feet away from the great man, as he went through his intricate improvisations on *Body and Soul*. We were in seventh heaven – he was one of our idols. But we were too scared to say anything to him – he was such an awesome figure.

By that time everything was beginning to close down on the Street, so we headed back to Grand Central. We were getting sleepy by now, so we found a couple of empty benches, curled up and went to sleep. The next thing I was aware of was waking to the hustle and bustle of people hurrying by on their way to work. We took that first train to Scarsdale and made our separate ways to our respective homes. I opened the front door, took off my shoes and began to tip-toe upstairs.

"Is that you, son?" It was my father awaiting my return. I had to go into their bedroom to confront my parents and sheepishly confess to what we had done. They felt badly about my having deceived them, but they were understanding because they knew how much I cared about jazz. It had been the first time I had gone into New York on my own at night; all my previous visits to hear jazz had been on Sunday afternoons. But the excitement and glamor of the Street at night was something else again, and had been an unforgettable experience.

It perhaps occurred to my father that this was an appropriate time for certain facts to be made clear to me, and an incident took place which illustrated the lack of communication between us. I was going through my sexual awakening at that time, with wet dreams, fantasies, masturbation, all the things normal to boys of that age. One morning I came down from the third floor where I slept, and there on the newel post at the bottom of the stairs was a condom. My immediate reaction was one of shock. It was as if I had been discovered in the act of doing something dreadful. They must be trying to tell me something, but what? There was no communication at all, just that condom, not even in its wrapper, sitting there on the post. I was too embarrassed to ask my parents what it was all about, and my father never saw his way clear to explaining. It was obviously his way of trying to communicate with me about a subject he couldn't bring himself to talk about. His strange way of dealing with the delicate subject made me too embarrassed to ask him what it meant, and undoubtedly contributed to the sexual inhibitions that plagued me for years. It was not until the last few years of Dad's life that we could really speak to each other with any degree of openness or frankness.

I was now approaching the point where the question of the next stage in my education had to be considered. There was great pressure from my parents to go to college and follow the normal path of the typical young person from Scarsdale – Ivy League college, law or medical school, and so on. My father even took me along on business trips to Princeton and Yale, where, because of his work in the text-book business, he knew the administrators and professors. I feel sure that if I had wanted to, I would have had little difficulty in getting into an Ivy League school. Going into one of the dormitories at Princeton and climbing up those stone steps that had been hollowed out by the feet of countless generations of students, it all seemed so old and musty to me; I just couldn't picture myself there. I felt the same thing about Yale. Again there was the sense of being overwhelmed by the weight of tradition, which wouldn't allow for the freedom and excitement I felt from jazz. I knew it wasn't what I wanted. I had an obsession with jazz and I was determined to pursue it. Eventually I went up to the Eastman School of Music in Rochester, which in a way pleased Dad because his company published the Eastman Music School Series. It was a compromise. Although most of my studies were in music, I had to take English, history and some athletics – I suppose in order to ensure that my development wasn't too one-sided.

I spent only one term there. It was cold and inhospitable, and, worse still, there was no jazz. My only close friend was a young high-school student named Pepper Adams, who later became famous as a baritone saxophonist. He lived near the school and had a good collection of records. I used to spend a lot of time at Pepper's house listening to jazz, and this helped to fill the void. When I came home for Christmas, I stunned my parents by telling them I intended to finish out that semester, but after that I wasn't going back. They didn't know what to do with me. I had refused to go to an Ivy League college to get the kind of liberal arts education that they wanted for me, we had compromised on a music school and now I was telling them I didn't even want that. Perhaps owing to their bewilderment they seemed incapable of giving me advice or guidance. At that stage in my life I needed it more than anything else. Much as I might have resisted, I think that some sort of direction was what I really wanted at heart, and I missed it. We made some sort of attempt to thrash out the problem: "Well, son, what do you want to do with your life?"

"I want to study jazz."

"How do you study jazz, son?"

"I've got to hang around 52nd Street where all these great guys are playing. I want to spend time at Nick's in the Village and get to know those musicians better. I'm going to rehearse and get gigs with our band. That's what I'm going to do. That's what I've got to do. I've got to play jazz."

So that's what I did. I finished the first semester at Eastman and came home. I was still living at home, running around with Denny Strong, Johnny Windhurst, Dick Wellstood, Charlie Traeger, Eddie Hubble and Eddie Phyfe. They were all as totally immersed in jazz as I was. Charlie Traeger was going to Columbia University, as was Dick Hyman, a pianist from Westchester, not a regular member of our group. I think the reason Charlie and Dick were going to college was because their parents insisted. In retrospect, I don't think there was any reason why I couldn't have gone to college and still been around the New York jazz scene; there was really nothing incompatible in the two activities. Dick Wellstood was another guy like me, growing up in Greenwich, Connecticut, and very much of a rebel. I can remember parties at Wellstood's house when his mother was away. We would be there in the evening with all sorts of people milling around, drinking beer and listening to records. Out of the cupboards would come all the pots and pans and glasses, and we'd have a jam session that sounded like an African tribal orgy. It was really wild, with people passing out on the lawn. The terrible din would continue until the neighbors called the police. Greenwich, Connecticut, is, like Scarsdale, an upper-middle-class suburban community. It was escapades such as these that prompted Dick's poor mother to say to me one day, "Bob, what on earth are we going to do with Richard?"

Dick was a wild character, but he was very funny. He got some cards printed and went down to Julius's bar – just round the corner from Nick's – where he would hand out cards to the customers. The card read "Can you help me meet Joe Sullivan?" Joe was Dick's idol on piano before he discovered James P. Johnson. We had a crazy gang, including the trombonist Eddie Hubble and the drummer Eddie Phyfe. Hubble was another wild guy. Our new trumpet player, John Glasel, had been picked by the Junior High School Social Committee to have the band for their junior high prom. This was a big thing for John who, being two years younger, was still in junior high himself. He was the bandleader, but he used the rest of us who were all in senior high. We set up little cardboard music stands on the platform on which we put sheets of paper to make it look as if we had music. As we played, all the kids were dancing round with the chaperones looking on. Eddie had been drinking and he was in an obstreperous mood. He sat there playing and suddenly he kicked his music stand and sent it flying across the dance floor. After the set he wandered off into the night and was later picked up by the police. Poor John – this was his first job as a leader, and Eddie had loused it up!

Hubble and Windhurst were great buddies. They were into foreign cars, and at one time they had an old Pierce Arrow convertible with isinglass windows. It was an interesting car because it had independent suspension on all four wheels. When it turned a corner, the chassis turned first and the body followed. As a result it could turn corners at tremendous speed without overturning. Eddie and Johnny were constantly tearing around Westchester at high speeds and were frequently chased by police on motor-cycles with sirens wailing. Just as they were about to be overtaken they would turn a corner at high speed, leaving the poor cop to skid into the ditch. Their next car was a Rolls with an open cockpit for the chauffeur. Later on, when they were short of money, they sold it to Brad Gowans. Brad used to get Pee Wee Russell to work on the car with him after they'd finished work at Condon's in the early hours of the morning. They stripped off the original body of the Rolls and replaced it with a racing body made of sheet metal. For some inexplicable reason the original steering wheel was not to Brad's liking, so he fashioned an alternative one by bending a piece of metal tubing into something resembling a circle.

On one occasion Brad was hired to play in the band at the annual Princeton reunion weekend. Driving up in the Rolls, Brad arrived an hour late for the job. By this time all the alumni were well into their beer and not at all happy that the trombonist hadn't showed. As Brad drove up he heard the band playing and decided to make a spectacular entrance. Unfortunately, as he drove the Rolls under the marquee, his bumper caught on a guy wire and the whole tent came tumbling down. The gentleman of the class of 1895, all of them around 75 years of age, were in no mood for such frivolity, and after they'd extricated themselves from the yards of canvas they took Brad outside and thrashed him to within an inch of his life. As he lost most of his teeth, his playing was seriously curtailed for the next few months.

We used to roar around the county and into New York in the Pierce Arrow and the Rolls, almost freezing to death in the winter. Among the jazz fraternity we came to be known as the "Westchester Kids." It was an exciting time, searching out places to jam all over Westchester, up to Greenwich, down to Nick's, and all points in between. Condon's club had just opened. Its first customer was Eddie Hubble, who got there at four o'clock in the afternoon and hung around until opening time. He also bought the first drink served at the club – illegally served because he was under age! As for myself, I was concerned with only one thing – blowing my horn. When I see pictures of myself in those days, I realize just how much of a rebel I really was. My hair was wild, sticking up all over the place; I never combed it – in fact I don't think I even owned a comb. I was totally into playing, oblivious of everything around me except music. Our whole crowd was like that. Our Bible was Mezz Mezzrow's *Really the Blues*, and we immersed ourselves in it. We imagined we were the new Austin High School Gang. We loved the stories of Pee Wee Russell and Bix Beiderbecke living by the side of Hudson Lake, shaving with the aid of a piece of broken glass propped up against the side of their old car. We read about Pee Wee keeping a gin bottle by the side of his bed, and how the first thing he did each morning was to reach down for a swig. Clarinetist Bob Fowler was a great admirer of Pee Wee and, naturally, he also had to have his bottle of gin by the bed. Bob died very tragically in an automobile accident in 1946 and it was in his memory that I composed my first recorded composition, *Blues For Fowler*. Once, we were asked to play a concert at the old Webster Hall on 11th Street (it's now the Ritz Ballroom, a palace of rock-and-roll). Mutt Carey was in town from the West Coast, and it was the only occasion I ever got to play with him. But the big excitement was that the man himself, the author of our bible, the Mighty Mezz, was going to be there. We had to show Mezz how hip we were, and, although we'd never tried marijuana,

Denny had heard that if you smoked catnip in a pipe it smells just like gage – nobody called it "pot" in those days. As soon as we saw Mezz, who was engaged in deep conversation with a friend at the end of a long table, we sat down at the other end and Denny got out his pipe. After he blew a few mighty puffs in Mezz's direction we all sat and waited for a reaction. Imagine Denny's chagrin to see Mezzrow suddenly pause in mid-sentence and, lifting his nose to sniff the air, exclaim loudly, "Who the hell is smokin' that cat-nip?" We were just jazz-crazy kids, very similar to Condon, Teschemacher, Freeman and the McPartland brothers in the 1920s.

My poor parents, in an almost desperate attempt to restore me to sanity, insisted that I went to White Plains three times each week to attend a typing school. They figured that, since I would probably never get any other type of gainful employment, at least I might become a secretary or some such thing. Their pitiable attempt to rescue their doomed offspring was not a success, and to this day I still don't know one end of a typewriter from the other.

The guys I have mentioned so far were those who took jazz the most seriously, but we were just the tip of the iceberg. There were at least 30 to 40 other young musicians jamming around the Westchester area, and naturally there were girls hanging around, too. Some of the fellows had their own girls, but I was so damned shy and unsure of myself that I just concentrated on the music. If there were any girls who had their eye on me, I was completely unaware of the fact. These feelings of sexual inadequacy were not helped when I compared myself with my father, who was quite a ladies' man. In truth, I desperately needed an area in which I could do something as well as he. I found it in music, in which I knew I really could outshine him. I was thrilled when two of our gang, Eddie Hubble and Johnny Windhurst, got a job at Ryan's working with Red McKenzie's Candy Kids. We were all excited about them being on the Street – that was where we all wanted to be.

TWO

Out on my own

I finally got tired of living in Scarsdale, and I managed to talk my parents into letting me get an apartment in the city. A bass player from White Plains named Harlow Atwood, whom I had known for some years, found a place for me in the building where he lived. He came out to see my parents and assured them that he would keep an eye on me. He was an older man, very business-like, and because they liked him they felt at ease with the proposition. In this way I acquired my first apartment in the city, a tiny little cubicle in a horrible old building dating from the turn of the century and situated at 112th Street and Broadway. I shared it with Dick Wellstood and Denny Strong. It wasn't much of a place, but we loved it, right there on the scene.

Up to now I had been playing anywhere and everywhere around Westchester with our group of jazz-crazy kids. Some of our gigs were USO dances – servicemen were farmed out to local families for Sunday dinner and then taken to nearby country clubs for late-afternoon dances. We got the gigs because the USO couldn't afford to pay any money. We did a lot of up-tempo jamming, which made it somewhat difficult for the poor souls to dance.

Towards the end of 1945 a permanent band began to take shape. While still in high school, our gang used to jam every weekend at each other's homes, and also at the home of Amy Lee, who lived in Larchmont. Amy played piano in the style of Jess Stacy and was a writer for the *Christian Science Monitor*. She was very aware of the keen interest in jazz in the Westchester area, and one day she went up to Greenwich to hear a dixieland band she'd heard about organized by Dick Wellstood and Charlie Traeger. She invited them to a battle with the Scarsdale band, the outcome of which was that Dick and Charlie joined forces with us. When Charlie found out that there were already two trombone players in our outfit, he decided to change to bass. His father, a doctor, played classical bass and taught his son the fingering, so Charlie became our regular bass player. In Larchmont Amy came across Eddie Phyfe, leading his little group called Eddie Phyfe's Four Hungry Cannibals, and, in similar fashion, Eddie teamed up with us. Meanwhile, the high-school gang had added Johnny Glasel on cornet, and a new arrival from California on trombone, Eddie Hubble.

The Wildcats were born, and we immediately began to achieve a measure of success, helped greatly by an article written about us by Amy and published in Art Hodes's magazine the *Jazz Record*. This gained us much favorable publicity as the first band to be doing in the East what Lu Watters and Turk Murphy were doing on the West Coast – that is playing the music of Morton, Armstrong and Oliver. Whereas the West Coast outfits didn't deviate much from the old style, we didn't want slavishly to copy the old records but rather to improvise freely in the context of the New Orleans idiom. Jim Moynihan, the publicity director of the historical film series "The March of Time," was another source of encouragement for us. Moynihan was a clarinetist, the greatest living disciple of Larry Shields of the Original Dixieland Jazz Band. He could copy all of Shields's recorded solos note for note. Jim was a tall man, six foot six inches in height, and thin as a rail. When he played he sat upright on the chair with his clarinet straight out in front of him, moving his bony knees open and shut to the music. He was about 60 years old, but he had a very youthful spirit. Jim introduced me to many things: "Hey, just listen to Johnny Dodds's break on *Snake Rag*," he'd exclaim. He also drew my attention to Bechet's fantastic clarinet chorus on *I'm just wild about Harry*, an obscure recording by Noble Sissle from the 1930s. There was no generation gap with Jim. He was a good friend who wanted us to hear the right things. It knocked him out to see these youngsters wanting to play the old jazz. His daughter, incidentally, was a very beautiful girl. Dick Wellstood and I both fancied her, but being the shy kind of person I was, Dick emerged as the successful suitor.

Another fan was Bill Grauer, who later had Riverside Records. He was attending Columbia University. Bill hired a studio and recorded the Wildcats. We cut eight numbers, of which only two were ever issued, and that was many years later in 1960. This was my third recording session. The first was a private recording in Schirmer's Music Store in 1943. At home we had musicales with Dad playing piano, me on clarinet, my mother singing and my sister on cello. One Saturday Dad took us into New York to Schirmer's, where they had a studio in which you could make your own recording. Dad and I worked out a classical piano and clarinet duet and then decided to try some jazz. Our choice was *Rose Room*, which I had learned from the Bechet record and which was also one of Dad's favorite tunes. He remembered hearing it when it was introduced by Art Hickman's band in San Francisco in 1919. I stole some licks from the Bechet record, but they weren't Sidney's licks – they were Charlie Shavers's. I was fascinated as much by Shavers's playing as by Bechet's. My second recording effort had been in Arthur Ecker's living room. One of the guys brought a home recording machine and cut a wax disc of our little group playing *Dear Old Southland* with Willie "the Lion." I don't know what happened to that record – maybe it's lying in a junk shop somewhere, awaiting discovery.

We got to know Milt Gabler from our visits to his Sunday sessions at Ryan's. We used to pester him to let us play, and finally he relented and let us sit in one afternoon. The people liked our band, so Milt started featuring us on a regular basis. His Commodore Record Shop on East 42nd Street was for years the Mecca for the jazz collectors in the New York area. We made the place our favorite daytime hangout, as we waited to see or meet the musicians who came in to stash their instruments, get a check cashed, or borrow some money from

Gabler. Milt provided us with our first real recording opportunity by setting up a date in early 1947 for the Commodore label. We should have had Eddie Hubble on trombone, but the day before, when I phoned the guys to give them directions, Hubble's father told me that Eddie had just left town with Alvino Rey's orchestra. These were war years and the big bands were full of teenage musicians. Eddie, having left school at an early age, already had a great deal of big-band experience under his belt: he had spent time with Buddy Rich and played in the short-lived band of Jess Stacy. We really missed not having him. The session produced four numbers, one of which was that first composition of mine, *Blues For Fowler*. It wasn't an easy session. Treager had borrowed a bass from Pops Foster that was supposed to be only "slightly cracked," but which turned out to be split all the way up the back, and nobody had remembered to bring Denny Strong's drums. We started at 4.30 p.m. and we worked for five hours before Milt was satisfied.

Other opportunities started opening up. We played at Mezzrow's "Really the Blues" concert on New Year's Day 1948. The job of the Wildcats was to open the proceedings, re-creating the sounds of the Original Dixieland Jazz Band. Later on we joined in the jam session at the end. There is a recording available on which you can hear the Wildcats in the finale – *High Society* – with Sidney Bechet, Muggsy Spanier and Baby Dodds. We also played at the Newspaper Guild's "Page One Ball" at the Waldorf, where we were jubilant to find that we were being paid $4 a man more than Eddie Condon's band. On New Year's Eve 1947, the night before Mezzrow's concert, we played for a private party at Miriam Hopkins's east-side town house. The place was full of famous people from the theater, the movies, and the worlds of art and journalism. Musicians kept dropping by after their gigs to jam. Around 4 a.m. Django Reinhardt came in with his manager. (Django was playing at Café Society prior to doing a tour with Duke Ellington). He got out his guitar and we were informed by his manager that he'd like to play *Tea for Two*. Django's only comment was when he turned to Dick Wellstood and growled cryptically, "Play oompah."

Life was getting rather hectic. I had a nine-to-five job during the day and I either played with the Wildcats at night or hung out on the Street. I worked as a stock clerk with the Textron Company, buried away in the basement of their building on Fifth Avenue. We had built up such a reputation with the Wildcats that the *New Yorker* published an article about this bunch of jazz-crazy kids. It mentioned that I was an employee of the Textron Company. On the day the magazine hit the stands I was busy wrapping packages in the basement when my boss came up to me and said, "I've had a call from upstairs, Wilber. Vice-president So-and-so wants to see you in his office immediately."

"My God," I thought, "what have I done? It must be something terrible." Full of trepidation, I took the elevator to the top floor and walked past all the secretaries. The Vice-president came out to meet me and said, "Wilber, I understand you're doing a fine job here. We're real pleased to see that in the *New Yorker* article you mention you're working here at Textron. That's some good PR you're doing, boy, keep it up." He continued, "By the way, I understand you're working every night with your band. I suppose it's kind of hard for you to get up at the crack of dawn in order to get to work by 8.30. Well, son, if you're a little late once in a while, we here at Textron will understand. I'll tell your boss to take it easy on you."

This was the green light for me, and I started coming in at any time up to 11 a.m. They stood it for a couple of weeks and then my supervisor had a little talk with me. We mutually agreed that my future did not lie with Textron, so we parted company. That was the last honest day's work I ever did!

I was enjoying living in New York and was developing warm and rewarding friendships with many musicians, most of whom were of an older generation, and many of whom were black. One such person was Willie "the Lion" Smith. I used to go up to his flat in Harlem (which was in the same building as Pops Foster's), to study with him. The first time I went, he remembered me from those Sunday afternoon sessions at Arthur Ecker's: "Well, kid," he said, "whadya wanna know?"

"Willie, I'm trying to learn how to harmonize songs, so maybe you could help me on harmony. For instance, what's the chords on *A pretty girl is like a melody*?"

Willie sat down at the piano, the ever-present cigar clenched between his teeth, and growled, "This is how it goes, kid." He struck the piano keys. Everybody knows what that first chord sounds like, but Willie's chord was strikingly different. In the key of F, the usual chord would be G7th (G, B natural, D, F), but Willie never did anything obvious. To him it became F Minor 6th (F, A Flat, C, D, with the D at the bottom), which then resolved to the G7th. It was so startling. It made you think that everything was going haywire, but next moment your realized that he had done it on purpose. Instead of playing "oompah" (note, chord, note, chord), Willie would sometimes reverse it: chord, note, chord, note. It would sound as if he had lost the beat, but again it was something he did purposefully. After explaining something Willie would look at me with this fierce expression: "What else you wanna know, kid?"

It was so in keeping with his wonderful personality. I love the story of Leonard Feather recording an interview with him. It was intended to parallel Alan Lomax's Library of Congress recordings with Jelly Roll Morton. Leonard opened by saying, "Willie, tell us where jazz came from."

In a very knowledgeable, matter-of-fact manner, Willie said, "Jazz was first played in the brickyards of Haverstraw, New York." With all due respect to the worthy citizens of Haverstraw, their factory town up the Hudson from New York hardly qualified as a hot-bed of jazz activity, but Willie stated this as an absolute fact and there was no way you could dispute it! The Lion was a fantastic character who had total belief in himself. He had evaded fame and fortune all his life; he would much rather play for a bunch of appreciative musicians in some back room than be a big star. His musical standards were of the highest order and he would not be compromised. Although he had a brilliant mind, he seemed to me to be delightfully crazy and totally out of touch with reality. He was always saying that he had a ten thousand dollar deal happening the next week. With all his wackiness, Willie was a great friend and a marvelous teacher. After we finished a lesson he used to say, "Let's go eat, kid," and he'd take me along to Father Divine's. Father Divine was a man who had started a very successful religious order in Harlem during the Depression. At his headquarters you could get a haircut, clothing, shelter and wonderful soul food. If you sat around the main table and took part in the ritual of holding hands and saying prayers, the food wouldn't cost you anything, but if you didn't want to go through the prayer routine you sat at one of the tables along the side of the hall and paid 15 cents for a marvelous meal of collard greens, ham hocks and chittlins.

I was hanging out at Ryan's, furthering friendships with many musicians. I felt at home with them. Sammy Price, the pianist with Sidney's group at that time, was always encouraging me and complimenting me on my playing. Mamma Price, his mother, was a wonderful cook, as I discovered when I was invited to the Price home for Sunday dinner. For a while she worked at Ryan's as ladies' room attendant, and every now and again she'd come out and sing the blues. One number she'd never sing, however, was *The Saints*, which she said was a religious song and should never be sung in a nightclub. She was adamant about that. Hot Lips Page, who used to sit in at Ryan's, was another friend – so warm, so friendly, so encouraging. I also hung around Condon's and got to know Eddie. He was the symbol of all the music I had loved since those days in Scarsdale. He was so clever, sharp and witty, that I was scared to talk to him for fear I'd say something corny or gauche. I remember being on the bandstand with him one night, trying for all I was worth to play every note perfectly. Eddie looked up at me from his guitar, head on one side, eyebrows raised, and said, "Make some mistakes, kid." It was his way of trying to tell me that jazz was fun, and not to be so serious. I was in absolute awe of him and didn't know what to say.

All my feelings about the musicians of that generation are, without exception, good ones. I can't remember a single instance where any musician put me down or sloughed me off. It's amazing, in retrospect, to remember the warmth and friendliness that seemed universal among musicians. It was a part of a long era that was, sadly, coming to an end. In the 1930s and 1940s there was plenty of work for a good musician; nobody felt threatened economically, although no one was making a lot of money. They were all doing what they wanted to do, and there was a camaraderie about it all. The hostility and competitiveness that one felt in the 1950s and right through to the present day was just not there then. I felt surrounded by friends and good vibes, and it made me feel great. The musicians took me seriously because I took their music seriously. They didn't feel threatened because there was work for everybody. I never felt any racial antagonism from that generation of black musicians. Maybe I was seeing the world through rose-colored spectacles, but I never had any feeling of, "Hey, white boy, what are you doing here?" We used to hang out in Harlem all the time, particularly when Bechet started working at Ryan's in 1947. I would end up playing the whole of the last half of the evening with Sidney, and many a night, being hungry after work, he used to take me uptown to Creole Pete's to get some gumbo, or to friends of his up on Sugar Hill. Very often they would be asleep, but when Bechet said, "It's me, Sidney," we would be ushered in with exclamations of, "Sidney, where you been, papa?" and, "Bashay, you no-good so-and-so, you're a sight for sore eyes!" We'd have some drinks and listen to records. If there was a piano, Sidney would sit down and play. After all this was over we'd finish up at Pod's and Jerry's, where "the Lion" might be playing, and then we'd drink, eat and jam until dawn, when we'd take the subway home to Brooklyn, sleepy and broke, but sublimely happy.

If you talk to Dick Wellstood or any of the other guys, you'll find they all felt the same way. Charlie Traeger, Dick, and I used to go every Monday night to a bar in Harlem called the Hollywood. Monday night was piano night, and they used to have cutting sessions when all the stride cats came by. There would be Willie "the Lion," Gimpy Irvis, Marlowe Morris, Willie "the Tiger" Gant, Cliff Jackson, James P. and others. On occasions Tatum would drop in, and nobody else would play when he was there. The three of us would be the only white people in the place. Sometimes they invited us to play, and we were accepted and applauded.

THREE

Studying with Bechet

In the spring of 1946 I started studying with Bechet. I had got to know Mezzrow quite well by this time. One day, when I was hanging out in the office of the King Jazz record company on 42nd Street, he told me that Bechet was opening a school of music and was looking for pupils. Naturally, I was very interested. I had met Sidney at the Pied Piper (which later became the Café Bohemia) in Greenwich Village in the fall of 1945. Weekly jam sessions, known as "Swing Soirées", were held there, hosted by Wilbur De Paris. That particular week featured, besides Bechet, Bill Coleman on trumpet, Wilbur on trombone and Mary Lou Williams on piano. Sidney was there with his Great Dane puppy, Butch. Between sets I shyly asked him what to do about my lip getting sore from the pressure of my teeth while playing. He said he had the same problem, and you had to build up a "callus."

After arranging an appointment for me with Sidney, Mezz gave me directions and I took the subway out to Brooklyn. After changing trains four times I eventually arrived at Sidney's place on Quincy Street. It was an old, ramshackle, three-story wooden house with french windows that Sidney said reminded him of New Orleans. He owned the property and rented out the top two floors, while he occupied the ground floor and the basement. Hanging beside the front door was a modest sign that read "Sidney Bechet School of Music." We arranged for lessons by the hour. I was his first and, for a while, his only pupil. He was very interested in teaching and wanted to write a book on jazz improvisation because he felt that so many young musicians didn't understand what it was all about.

I seemed to be achieving everything I had wanted when I put Scarsdale behind me. I was enjoying this wonderful freedom to live the kind of life I wanted, there was the color and excitement of the New York jazz scene, and there were all the wonderful and talented musicians who had so generously welcomed me to their midst. My playing was beginning to sound like that of a professional. Unfortunately there was one area that was still a problem: I was still painfully shy and insecure with the opposite sex. While I wanted to be a flamboyant, extrovert jazzman, I was too unsure of myself to dress the part, so I hid myself away behind my glasses and my upper-middle-class uniform of button-down shirt, conservative tie and dark suit. I wanted to attract attention to myself as a musician, but I was too timid to attract attention to myself as a human being. I wanted people to like me, but I was always too scared to make the overtures. I began to believe that perhaps my fate was to remain celibate for the whole of my days.

My studies with Bechet were everything I had hoped for. He was a marvelous teacher and a wonderful man. Having by this time resigned from my job with the Textron Company, I was short of money, so Sidney suggested that I move in with him at the house on Quincy Street. My parents came down from Scarsdale to see Sidney at Ryan's to satisfy themselves that I was in good hands, and, quite unknown to me, they came to a financial arrangement with him. Such was my rebellious nature at that time, they were probably afraid that I would find out and fling the money back in their faces. Mother and Dad were very taken with Sidney. He could be very lovable and charming when he wanted, with a voice that was like honey – soothing and gentle. He had a way of making meaningful contact and being at ease with all sorts of people from all walks of life and all stratas of society, many of whom might never have had much contact with a black man or a jazz musician. To give the reader a feel for the gentle, kindly side to Sidney's nature we have reproduced a letter he wrote to my father. Although his lack of formal education is evident from spelling mistakes, his charm and dignity shine forth from the page (see first plate section). Dad always insisted he'd had a subsequent letter from Bechet in which Sidney said, "I've taught Bobie everything I know and now he's teaching me," but we've never been able to find it.

One incident that springs to mind and illustrates Sidney's way with people concerns Tallulah Bankhead. Tallulah came from a wealthy southern family; her father was a senator. She and Sidney had become good friends, and when she was invited to a dinner in Philadelphia at which the guests represented the cream of Philadelphia society, Tallulah took Sidney with her. He was introduced as an atomic scientist working on a top-secret government project. Sidney carried off his part to perfection and nobody suspected him of being anything else until, just before the dessert, Tallulah gave him the nod. Sidney left the table, came back into the room playing his soprano, and entertained the startled guests for the remainder of the evening.

Sidney very quickly persuaded my parents that the proposed arrangement would be a good thing for me. Being Christian and very liberal in their outlook, they saw nothing wrong with my being taken under the wing of this black man. In fact, there has been a history of this kind of understanding attitude running back through the family. One particular incident that is recorded concerns my great-grandmother, who lived in Cincinnati. The Ladies' Guild had invited as guest speaker Mr Booker T. Washington, the famous negro author, and this being the post-Civil War period, it can be appreciated that it was a rather daring and out-of-the-ordinary thing for them to have done. When Mr Washington arrived, the ladies realized, to their dismay, that they had not made any arrangements for his accommodation. A hotel, of course, was out of the question, so my great-grandmother announced that Mr Washington would stay with her family. During his four-day stay he asked for some writing facilities, as he had a deadline drawing near. He was provided with a writing desk in the comfort and privacy of the drawing room. It was not very long after this event that Washington's famous book *Up from Slavery* was published. The family always liked to think that some of its pages might have been written there in great-grandmother's drawing room. It was no different from the courteous way in which my own parents were now dealing with Sidney.

So it was that I moved into Quincy Street to join Sidney, his mistress Laura and Butch, the Great Dane I had seen at the Pied Piper, who by now had grown to a gigantic size. Bechet was a great teacher. I have always felt it was a pity that he and other great jazzmen of his era didn't have the opportunity to do more teaching; they had so much to give and to pass on. I firmly believe that there is no better way of learning than apprenticeship to a master. His piano, a venerable old upright, sat in the corner of the front room, and when Sidney gave the lesson he sat on the piano stool with his Brush Soundmirror tape recorder alongside. I sat by the other side of the piano, and he could swing around and switch the tape machine on to play back what we had been doing. He had everything well organized. Like the piano, the furniture was all very modest and makeshift, hand-me-down stuff that had been there for years. The carpets on the floor were worn and had seen better days. It all had the air of a cheap boarding house, but what really appealed to Sidney were those french windows. He used to sit in front of them, looking out at the Brooklyn Street and daydream of New Orleans.

He started out by teaching me *Raggin' the Scale*. It was a way of practicing the scales and yet having fun with them. Bechet's idea of practicing concentrated on making logical variations and swinging. Always, he used to tell me, I should have the rhythm in my head and swing against it. He would sit there on the piano stool, tapping his foot in 4/4 time and making the "ting-tink-te-ting" of the cymbal on his knee with his hand. Then he went on to explain his concept of interpreting a song. He showed me how to start out by stating the melody and bringing out its beauty. Using that as a foundation, the next step was to start the variations, but always initially relating them closely to the melody. As they progressed the variations gradually moved further away from the melody – in fact became new melodies based on the harmony – before the piece concluded with a return to the melody and, often, a coda. It was Sidney's way of telling a story. To tell a story, to grab the listener's attention, to carry him away on a continuously rising curve of excitement to the inevitable triumphant conclusion, this was Bechet's musical credo; it was a principle he fervently believed in and practiced every time he lifted his horn to play. If ever a jazzman's music was meant not to be background, but to be listened to with rapt attention, it was Sidney's. The sheer intensity of his vibrato served as an imperative command to "pay attention!" Many was the time I saw him face a noisy nightclub audience and reduce them to a respectful silence in a few seconds with his commanding presence. Incidentally, Sidney was much more harmonically oriented in his musical thought than most players of his generation; his contemporaries Johnny Dodds and Jimmie Noone never advanced beyond the use of dominant seventh chords. Sidney, however, had perfect understanding of augmented, diminished and ninth chords, and was perfectly at ease with the sophisticated harmonies of

Gershwin, Kern, Porter and Ellington.

Sidney loved to compose. He was constantly dreaming up new melodies and working them out at the piano. His tape recorder was always running so that he could play them back and study his efforts. The one piece of music that was most important to him at that time was something he had been working on for many years, his "Great Creation," as it were: he called it *Voice of the Slaves*. Later on much of the material was used in his ballet score *La nuit est une sorcière*. It was his attempt to combine spirituals, blues, and ragtime with his own conception of classical music, which was mostly derived from 19th-century Romanticism. I suspect his first trip to Europe in 1919, when he appeared as a soloist with Will Marion Cook's Southern Syncopated Orchestra, had had a profound and lasting influence on him, and had, in fact, been the principal motivation for him to compose "classical" music. Every day, after my lesson was over, he would set up the tape recorder, sit down at the piano with me by his side, and work away on his "big work," all the while explaining to me what he was trying to achieve. Sometimes, in order to approximate all the orchestral parts, we would play piano four hands, with Sidney assigning me french horns, oboes, violins, or whatever. Nothing brings back to me more vividly recollections of my teacher than listening to those tapes we made all those years ago.

Sidney was indefatigable, always working on various projects simultaneously. He was intrigued with *Intermezzo*, the tune from the Ingrid Bergman–Leslie Howard movie, and was working out an involved set of variations on the melody, which had a lot of notes that Sidney harmonized with passing chords. The variations were to be played in double time against the melody in long meter, and Sidney had the verse in there as well. Funny thing was, he never got round to playing it in public; it would really have been something if he'd ever finished it. To Sidney, his featured showpieces were an extremely important part of his repertoire, and he never tired of playing them. Pieces like *Summertime* (with his quotes from Massenet's *Elégie* and the sextet from Donizetti's *Lucia di Lammermoor*) or *Dear Old Southland* (in which he interpolated the famous "Clown" aria from *I Pagliacci*) were magnificent interpretations conceived on a grand scale. Generally speaking, although Sidney improvised freely when playing the blues, he would nevertheless follow the theme and variation form and make a definite development from chorus to chorus. The result would be an interpretation which, in its effect, was a composition. The best example of this is probably *Blue Horizon*, in which Bechet lends a unity to his performance by repeating the same moving blues phrase in the last four bars of each chorus.

The ingenious way in which Sidney used to work out composed choruses on tunes was particularly interesting to me. Over the years he used these choruses as the finale or climax to his interpretations. I suspect that the variations that he always played on *China Boy*, along with choruses on *The Sheik of Araby*, *I know that you know*, and others, had been in his repertoire since the 1930s or before. They were set things that he would lead up to with improvised choruses. He always had them ready when he was flying and needed something to top what he had already done. So many musicians get to their climax, only to lose themselves because they have nowhere to go, nothing to top what they've already played. Sidney made a point of teaching me all his set choruses. When I first started studying with him I hadn't realized that Johnny Hodges had been an earlier pupil, but when I heard Hodges's solo on Duke Ellington's recording of *The Sheik of Araby*, I realized that Johnny was playing the same chorus that Bechet had taught me. You can hear Sidney playing it (curiously, on tenor saxophone) on the last chorus of the celebrated one-man-band recording on Victor.

Sidney felt very strongly that there was a right way to play jazz – one which embraced this concept of theme and variation, and which had respect for the melody and the parts that all the different instruments should play. Like Jelly Roll Morton, he wanted discipline in his music, and never went for complete freedom of expression without regard to how each part fitted in with the others. He liked to play the lead on soprano, and often did so, even when there was a trumpet in the band. He often played without a trumpet because he had difficulty in finding players who didn't get in his way. Not even Louis Armstrong was exempt from Sidney's criticism. He wasn't happy with the way that Armstrong played at their 1945 Esquire All-Star Concert; he said it was different from the way Louis used to sound in the old New Orleans days. When Louis said, "I ain't gonna have no two leads in my band," they had quite a row. A couple of years later, in April 1947, Bechet was supposed to play at the Town Hall concert which was advertised as the great reunion of Louis and Sidney. Sidney never showed up. The promoter, Ernie Anderson, invited me to take his place, but I didn't think I could play well enough at that time, so I declined. When I got home to Quincy Street that night Sidney told me he'd had an attack on the subway and had ridden back and forth unconscious for hours. I accepted his story, but have often wondered if he made it up because he didn't want to share the spotlight with Louis.

Bechet was masterful at playing counterpoint to a lead, and he had a tremendous ear, when playing in an ensemble, for finding the note that nobody else was playing or that little space that gave him the opportunity of putting in something that was meaningful. To say that Sidney was only interested in self-expression without regard for what was happening around him is far from the truth. He was all too conscious of what the other players were doing and wanted his part to fit in like everybody else's. He saw jazz as an art form, and within that form there could be new players developing and expressing new ideas, but always staying within the form. He saw no reason for trying to keep jazz the same as it was played in New Orleans in the early days.

Some of his best recordings were made for Victor when his career was at a low point, in the late 1930s and early 1940s. *Shake it and break it*, with its electrifying breaks, is a masterpiece, as is *Indian Summer*, in which Bechet interprets Victor Herbert's beautiful melody with sweeping lyrical grandeur. It was the period when his playing matured. There was still the youthful exuberance that may be heard on the 1932 Feetwarmers recordings, but he now knew precisely the limitations of his horn, how to control the intonation and vibrato. It was a wide vibrato; it didn't (and still doesn't) appeal to a lot of musicians, but it expressed the intensity with which Sidney approached music. The vibrato and the unique instrument he chose to play were the trademarks that set him apart from all other jazz musicians.

A soprano is very difficult to play in tune, but it is also a very flexible instrument: you can alter the pitch of a note by using your embouchure. Providing you can hear the correct pitch in your head, you can play it in tune, but even so it can be difficult, particularly in the upper register. If the tip of the mouthpiece is very open you get more power, but you also get serious intonation problems, and the instrument is much more difficult to control. Making a mouthpiece facing is a very precise operation, done on a machine and calculated to the thousandth of an inch. Sidney never bothered with such refinements, however. He used to open the tip of his mouthpiece himself by using a file – a very crude method – but he got the results he wanted. Sidney's tone changed over the years. When I was studying with him it had a different texture compared with that of the Feetwarmers recordings. It was heaver and coarser, with a dark, rough-edged quality that hadn't been there a few years earlier: then it was characterized by its purity and brilliance. You can detect this quite easily when you compare the Feetwarmers recordings of 1940–41 with those made with Mezzrow in 1945 for King Jazz. The change in tone may have resulted from the switch he made from a Conn to the Buescher he bought around 1943; extensive dental work, necessitated by years of neglect, may also have been a factor. Whatever it was, when I was with him, Sidney's playing seemed to be that of an older man expressing an older man's thoughts.

Sidney first had me concentrating on the clarinet, which is the more difficult instrument. He firmly believed that once the clarinet had been mastered the soprano saxophone would be no problem. His clarinet was the old Albert system instrument, while mine was a Boehm. I used to knock myself out trying to play on the Boehm things that he did on the Albert. Almost all the New Orleans clarinetists played the Albert, which was the only instrument available in the early days. In comparison with the Boehm it presents formidable technical problems; it is a harder instrument to move around on and there are fewer keys – and therefore fewer alternative fingerings for each note. But it gave Sidney the sound he wanted. Generally speaking, he had to fight the clarinet, whereas he could fly on the soprano. He had the fastest articulation of any musician I have ever heard; his tongue was like lightning, and each note was attacked percussively and with great definition.

I was a scraggy kid, as thin as a rake, and most of the things that Sidney had me playing were pretty demanding – I never seemed to have enough breath in my body. So one day Sidney decided to put the problem under the microscope. Out came his tape recorder to give an air of authenticity to the occasion, and off we went. First of all, Laura spoke her piece: "You're drivin' the boy too hard. He's only young, and he ain't gonna come back."

"No," said Sidney, "he's a good musicianer. He want to play. He come back. What he need is more strength. We build it up wid' sherry. We got any sherry in the cupboard, Laura?"

"Hold on, man," said Laura. "Take it easy. He's only a young boy and you shouldn't be givin' him all that stuff. You pushin' him too hard. We don't want him to be a drunk, like you."

"Aw, shut up. I ain' no drunk. If I don't build 'em up, he never blow that clarinet. He got to realize that it don't blow isself. I'll start him off gentle-like, and when he get used to it, I'll give him more."

Sidney was obsessed with his tape recorder and, indeed, with all gadgetry. There was nothing he loved more than browsing around pawn shops looking at camera equipment. He wasn't so much interested in taking photographs as in owning the stuff, and he used to spend a fortune buying the finest cameras and lenses available. He also loved expensive rings, which you would see flashing every time he played. The pawnbrokers regarded him as their greatest friend – he went through money like wildfire, and was always pawning something in order to raise more. Gambling was not one of his vices, but from time to time he felt the urge to go on a spree. He would start drinking before work, and then drink through the whole evening at Ryan's. Then, when we packed up, he would say, "We goin' up town now, Bobbie, and have us some fun." The next morning his pockets would be empty. He shouldn't always have been broke because he used to earn a lot. His fee for concerts was twice that of the other musicians, which simply reflected the fact that he was a musician at the top of his form, always able to be the most exciting performer at any jazz event he took part in. Sidney topped everything and everyone, but with money it was easy come, easy go.

I was totally absorbed in the man and in his music. Every single day with him taught me more about music than a full year at Eastman could ever have done. The emphasis was always on the importance of communication, the telling of a story. Watching him, listening to him and playing alongside him was a constant revelation. Although I was immature in many ways, I realized at the time how privileged I was.

Our duets at Ryan's became quite a feature and went down well with the audience, but on one occasion they led us into a bizarre situation. Tallulah Bankhead was playing on Broadway in *Private Lives*, and after the show she used to come into Ryan's to see Sidney. One week-night at the club, around 3.00 a.m., the place was empty. All you could hear was the bartender totting up the night's receipts on the cash register, when the phone rang. I answered and a deep-throated voice at the other end demanded imperiously, "Get me Sidney." I told her that he'd just stepped outside for a breath of fresh air, to which she replied, "This is Tallulah. Just tell him to get the hell up here." I gave the message to Sidney, and at 4.00 a.m., when we finished, he said, "You wanna have some laughs? Pick up your horn and come along with me." We took a cab to her hotel, went up to her room and knocked. Tallulah opened the door to greet us, stark naked!

"Come on in, dahlings," she said. "Get out your horns. I want to hear some music." She sashayed across the room and climbed back into bed to rejoin her gentleman friend. We took out our sopranos, and, seating ourselves at the foot of the bed, we started to play the blues. Whenever her friend left the room, apparently to pursue a large parrot that had escaped from its cage, Tallulah beckoned to me, and, pointing towards the kitchen (where I could see a bottle of bourbon on the table), she whispered hoarsely, "Quick, get me a drink." I soon realized that my main job was to sneak her drinks while her companion, who I gathered was her leading man, was chasing his recalcitrant feathered friend around the apartment. Apparently the producers had given the fellow the specific job of keeping Tallulah sober between performances, but I think I probably jeopardized his position that night! So Sidney and I played the blues while Tallulah carried on a non-stop monologue, mostly about how absolutely horrible everybody else was in the play. After I had made several trips to the kitchen to replenish her drink she announced stentoriously, "OK, OK, that's enough," and, still naked, led us to the door. She bid us goodnight and we left.

Sidney's other great passion, besides music and gadgets, was motor-boats. While I was living with him, he bought one. He'd gotten to know a Russian taxi driver who had a boat for sale in a boatyard at Sheepshead Bay, in Brooklyn. Sidney invited the Russian round to Quincy Street to negotiate a deal. So that there could be no possible dispute about what had or had not been agreed, the tape recorder was set up. There was a tremendous gap between the Russian's asking price and Sidney's opening offer, but gradually, and aided by a never-ending flow of vodka, they arrived at a meeting point and a bargain was struck. It was signed, sealed and delivered by a series of toasts and celebrated by a succession of songs. The more drunk they became, the more they fell back on their ethnic origins. Sidney sang in his Creole patois, while the Russian warbled Caucasian folk songs. Eventually, in the middle of one particularly maudlin number, and with their arms round each other's necks, they subsided to the floor and passed out. Butch, the Great Dane, loped into the room and flopped down between them.

Having bought the boat, Sidney naturally had to have a launching ceremony. He had Fred Robbins announce it on his radio show, and champagne and food was ordered. The boat was poised on the slipway with Sidney standing at the wheel and all the guests lined up on either side. As the boat slid down into the water, everybody raised their glasses for Fred Robbins's toast – "To Captain Sidney Bechet and the *Laura!*" As *Laura* slowly slid into the water, Sidney, with a huge smile on his face, pressed the starter button. He pulled the throttle out, fiddled with the choke, and pressed the button again. Still nothing happened. After numerous abortive attempts, Sidney's smile gradually changed into a puzzled scowl, and, as the boat drifted away from its moorings, the guests started heading for their cars. Sidney threw me a rope so that I could secure the boat. His main preoccupation for weeks after that humiliating occasion was a search for the Russian, but unfortunately, or perhaps fortunately, he had vanished without a trace. Every Sunday at noon Laura would cook dinner, and over our meal Sidney would wax lyrical about his plans to go to New Orleans by sea. He made it all sound like a luxury cruise on some fabulous yacht. After dinner we would go down to the boat and work on the engine. Sidney never did get it to start, and eventually had to admit defeat. Once he came to terms with the fact that *Laura* wasn't going anywhere, our Sunday afternoons settled into a routine of rowing out to the boat with a bag of shrimps and some six-packs of beer. We'd stretch out on the deck and enjoy our little feast. Then, in a pleasant and relaxed frame of mind, we'd row across the bay to the seedy little yacht club, where Sidney would sit down at the upright piano and in no time at all the joint would be jumpin', the whiskey flowing and Sidney's fellow yachtsmen and their ladies dancing happily around.

In July 1947 George Avakian set up a recording date for Sidney with Columbia Records. Instead of doing the whole session with the quartet that he led at Ryan's, Sidney suggested that half should be with the Wildcats. It was a generous gesture on his part to help get the band established, and George, being a fan of the Wildcats, agreed. We had the usual gang, with Johnny Glasel, Dick Wellstood, Denny Strong, Charlie Traeger and myself. We also had a new trombonist, by the name of Bob Mielke, who had just come East from San Francisco. This presented us with a problem, because to record in New York you had to have a Local 802 union card. Bob didn't have a card and it normally took six months to get one. Charlie Traeger's father was a doctor who had paid his way through college and medical school in the 1920s by playing bass, tuba and sax with dance bands. In later years he turned to classical music and was first bassist with the Doctors' Orchestral Society of New York, popularly known as "The Doctors' Symphony." More importantly, he was doctor for the top union officials. Somehow Mielke became a fully fledged member of Local 802 in less than 24 hours! We were very excited, but nervous about the prospect of recording with the master, and we rehearsed endlessly in the front parlor at Quincy Street. Musically we weren't in the same league as Bechet; he couldn't really fly in his customary fashion with our stiff rhythm section. Nevertheless, he enjoyed having these young admirers around him, and, instead of dominating us all, he played a true ensemble role. The musical ideals that he had stood for all his life were under attack and being ignored by young musicians of his race. Bop was all the rage, and Ryan's was the only traditional-jazz spot left on 52nd Street. Sidney felt all this very acutely, and I think he believed that through this group of young, willing pupils he could perpetuate his musical message.

That fall Milt Gabler asked us to cut some sides for Commodore. By now we had added Jerry Blumberg on second cornet and we were very much into the sound and repertoire of the King Oliver Creole Jazz Band. We rehearsed in a studio on Broadway called Nola's, where all the big bands rehearsed. One afternoon we were wailing away on *Snake Rag* when the door opened and Dizzy Gillespie, who was rehearsing his new big band down the hall, looked in. Eyeing us quizzically, he asked, "What kinda stuff you guys playin'? Man, that's some crazy shit. You cats are so far in, you're far out!" Finally, feeling we were ready for the challenge, I phoned Milt to get details of the date. He was full of apologies and explained that he had got caught up in the approaching recording ban. Milt had gone to work for Decca, who wanted to stockpile recordings in order to have some product to sell during the ban. Consequently, he was having to work round the clock, and couldn't spare the time for our session. One of our fans, who worked at the Commodore Music Shop, was Harry Crawford. He felt sorry for us when he learned of our disappointment and phoned George Avakian to see what could be done. The outcome was that George put up the money, and he and Harry Crawford went into the record business to form Rampart Records. We made a dozen titles for the label, just managing to complete the session before the ban became operative on New Year's Day 1948. We were lucky to have the support of George, who only the year before had reviewed our first recordings in *Jazz Record* magazine: "The records are sensational. The ensembles will remind you of those marvelous Ladnier–Bechet records of years ago, and that's a pretty marvelous sound. The total effect is the biggest shot in the arm yet recorded for the future of jazz."

The time was right for our success. We had absorbed the music of the innovators – Oliver, Armstrong, Bechet and Morton – and we had also been influenced by the Chicagoans – Bud Freeman, Jimmy McPartland, Dave Tough, Gene Krupa, Pee Wee Russell, and Benny Goodman – who themselves had been inspired by the New Orleans pioneers. When Bunk Johnson arrived in New York from New Orleans in 1945, with George Lewis, Jim Robinson, Alton Purnell, Lawrence Marrero, Slow Drag Pavageau and Baby Dodds, he generated great interest in the kind of music we were playing. He brought the melodic beauty, rhythmic drive, lyricism and counterpoint of New Orleans music to a receptive audience that could not relate to the complexities of the bop idiom. I'll never forget that first night at the Stuyvesant Casino after I returned from the cold atmosphere of Rochester and the Eastman School of Music, walking through the door and hearing the sound of Bunk's band floating down the stairs from the ballroom. It was the first time I had heard authentic New Orleans jazz in person, and it thrilled me to the core.

Human relationships outside of music were still a mystery to me. One afternoon Sidney went into town on business, and I was left in the house with Laura. Laura was an Indian lady from Canada who had a propensity for the bottle. (Her complaint about Sidney's drinking during the discussion about giving me sherry was truly the pot calling the kettle black!) She drank steadily, dancing around, while I practiced, and then, in a state of intoxication, she enticed me into bed with her. Laura was so obviously drunk and out of control, that I just don't know why I didn't refuse her advances. I was ashamed of the whole episode, but in a state of mind where any lady, even this drunken lady, who offered her favors to me seemed to be paying me a compliment that I was powerless to reject. Why, oh why, was it so difficult for me to deal with normal youthful lust?

Sidney never did find out about this. In truth I was terrified that he might. For weeks afterwards I used to break out in a cold sweat at the thought of Laura trying to make Sidney jealous by describing to him in detail the whole sorry incident. He had this switchblade that he always carried in his pocket, and, although I never saw him use it, it was always there, ready to be whipped out at any provocation. He was well known for his temper and wild behavior when drinking. In the early 1920s he was deported from England for roughing up a prostitute. Later there was the famous duel in Paris that landed him in jail. He and a fellow musician were on rue Pigalle at seven o'clock in the morning after a night of heavy drinking, arguing about the merits of Mike McKendrick, the banjo player from Chicago. The argument got more and more heated, with aspersions being cast on each another's credibility and origins, until eventually they decided that the only way to settle the dispute was by way of a duel. Both of them carried pistols, a practice that was quite common among black musicians in that period. There, on "Pig Alley," they stood back to back in classic fashion, took 20 paces, turned and fired. Sidney's shot went wide, ricocheted off a wall and struck a woman who was passing by. She screamed, the police arrived, and Sidney was arrested; he ended up in jail for 12 months, after which he was deported from France. In later years his pistol was replaced by the switchblade, just as lethal and totally illegal, but always at the ready.

Sidney was a man who lived in a world of his own creation. His fantastic flights of imagination were the result of a very romantic nature, but, in common with Jelly Roll Morton, he sometimes seemed incapable of dealing with reality. He was the world's worst businessman. When all the great New Orleans players were in Chicago, recording and making reputations that would establish them as the great figures of that period, what was Sidney doing? He was wandering around Europe, going from band to band. In 1925 he left New York for Paris with the *Revue nègre*, the show which made Josephine Baker a star, and he didn't return until 1931. There isn't a single recording by Bechet between 1925 and the first Feetwarmers records in 1931. In the meantime the world had changed and Bechet was the forgotten man of jazz. He was thought of as an old man, his hair having turned prematurely gray from his prison experiences. In the 1930s, at the height of the swing era, when he should have been reaping the rewards of his tremendous talent, he was reduced to running a tailor's shop in Harlem. It was the same tragic story as that of Morton; Sidney existed in a shadow world of near anonimity, hearing the music he'd helped create make younger musicians wealthy.

Jelly was unlucky in that he died in 1941. If he'd lived a few years longer he'd have reaped the same rewards that Sidney did from the revival of interest in the music of New Orleans. Sidney was able to take advantage of the postwar revival in his last ten years, when he lived in France; but then he was a big record seller and an international celebrity. It was an upbeat and triumphant ending to his life – unusual when you consider how his contemporaries Morton, King Oliver and Johnny Dodds slid into near total obscurity. One thing is for sure – Sidney went out with flying colors!

Sidney could be utterly unreasonable at times, but with me he was all gentleness and kindness, like a loving father. He was very flattered by my interest in him and my desire to play the clarinet and soprano in his style. I was his protégé and he was proud of me, but of course he never felt threatened by me musically, nor indeed should he have been; he was still at the height of his powers and I was just beginning. My apprenticeship with Bechet, however, was now drawing to an end. In the fall of 1947 Sidney left Ryan's and took a job as featured soloist at the Jazz Ltd club in Chicago. (I had left Quincy Street and moved to Greenwich Village that previous spring.) One afternoon in January 1948 I was at Condon's rehearsing the Wildcats, when the phone rang. It was Mezzrow, and he was very excited: "Hey man, it's Poppa Mezz. How'd you dig going to France? Panassié is putting on this festival at Nice. Bashay is tied up with his contract at Jazz Ltd and they won't let him off. He said I should take you in his place. We're goin' to have Baby, Pops, Sammy, Henry Goodwin and Little Jimmy Archey, and Louis will be there with Tea, Barney, Big Sid and Earl, plus a lot of other bands from all over the world. What'ya say, man? You interested?"

Was I interested? What a fantastic break! My first thought as I put the phone down was that I would be letting down the other guys. There I was, questioning my own right to feel elation! That call signaled the end of the Wildcats episode and the start of a new chapter in my career. The guys went their individual ways. John Glasel went to study music at Yale and became a freelance musician in and around New York; along the line he got interested in union politics and ended up as president of Local 802. Bob Mielke returned to his home in San Francisco and still pursues a career in jazz there with his group the Bearcats. Denny Strong also went home, to his parents in Greensboro, North Carolina, where he worked with his brother in their father's tire business; he developed an interest in racing cars and came to a tragic end when the Jaguar he and his brother were driving in a race crashed, killing him instantly. Dick Wellstood went on to have a long and successful career in jazz; he is known all over the world as a master of stride piano. Jerry Blumberg returned to Baltimore and went into academia. Charlie Traeger continued to work as a freelance bass player in New York. Eventually his interest in the bass led him to open a shop in Greenwich Village, where he bought, sold and repaired basses.

On February 14th Mezzrow's band, along with Louis Armstrong's All Stars and the saxophonist Lucky Thompson, who was going over as a single, boarded the plane for France. I remember vividly that flight, my first across the Atlantic. All the guys were excited, discussing all the things they were going to do, all the places they would see, and all the French chicks who would be welcoming them with open arms. I shared in their excitement as France got closer and closer. The French government radio service arranged for a broadcast from the plane during the flight. Midway across the ocean we all got our horns out and Louis led us through *The Marseillaise*.

I was on my way!

FOUR

The Nice Jazz Festival

The festival, held in late February 1948, lasted a full week. The atmosphere was electric. It was the first major jazz festival ever held, and it was taking place in a country that had been ravaged by war and starved of jazz for six long years. The event was sponsored by the Hot Clubs of France under the chairmanship of Hugues Panassié, and its focal point was the triumphant return to Europe of the great Louis Armstrong, the most celebrated and beloved artist in jazz history. Supporting Louis were his newly formed All Stars, comprising Earl Hines, Jack Teagarden, Sid Catlett, Barney Bigard and Arvell Shaw, with Velma Middleton on vocals. Also from the States came Mezz Mezzrow's band, together with a six-piece outfit, led by Rex Stewart with Sandy Williams on trombone, which had been touring Europe. Django Reinhardt and the Quintet represented France in the swing era, while Claude Luter's band symbolized the New Orleans revival.

The English band was something of a mixed bag, all the musicians having been chosen individually by way of a *Melody Maker* readers' poll. They came to Nice with little or no rehearsal, all players of different styles and backgrounds trying to find some common ground on which to play, and consequently somewhat ragged. In a way I felt sorry for them. While we were living in absolute luxury at the Negresco, the finest hotel in Nice, the poor British musicians, who were underpaid and who were severely limited by currency restrictions as to the amount of money they could take out of England, had to stay in some pretty primitive digs. Nevertheless, it was my first opportunity of meeting some of the British lads, including Humphrey Lyttelton and Dill Jones, and the jazz writers Max Jones and Sinclair Traill.

I sat behind Louis and Jack Teagarden on the plane. They never stopped talking to each other from the moment we took off till the moment we landed; they were like brothers with much mutual love and respect. All the time they were talking, Jack was working away on a mouthpiece that he was fixing for Louis. In fact, Jack took a lathe and a generator on the road with him so that he could work on such projects. Getting all this machinery in and out of trains, planes and buses was always a major headache for the group's manager, Joe Glaser. Louis didn't make it any easier for him, either. He had a lifelong obsession with the necessity to clear his bowels each day, and, to help in this direction (this was before he discovered Swiss Kriss), he had brought with him a huge number of gallon jugs containing "Pluto Water," a very effective laxative.

Together the two brass players represented a tremendous logistical problem for Joe.

It was just after dawn when our plane came down at Orly Airport. We could see that, although the runway area had been kept clear, there were thousands of people milling about the airfield with cameras and flash bulbs. Joe Glaser was responsible for the American package; he was particularly excited because this was going to be his great moment when he triumphantly brought Louis back to Europe – his first visit since 1933. As the plane slowly taxied towards the disembarkation point, Joe was busy organizing the order in which we left the plane: "OK, now. Louis, you get to the front so they see you first. Take your trumpet out. Wave your handkerchief. And then you next, Earl. Don't forget your cigar, and smile, dammit, smile. Then you, Jack, followed by Mezz." And so on right the way down the pecking order. Joe was so engrossed in what he was doing that he didn't notice Lucky Thompson, with his tenor slung over his shoulder, standing quietly at the front of the plane, waiting for the door to open.

Joe suddenly spotted him. "Goddamit, Thompson, get back here in line. Louis gets off first, then Earl. You're back here."

Lucky replied, cool as a cucumber, "I'm not working for you, Glaser. I'm getting off soon as that door opens. Gonna grab my bags, catch a taxi to the hotel to get some rest. Don't tell me what to do, man."

"Goddamit, Goddamit," yelled Joe. "You'll never work again in the States, Thompson. You'll never work again – I'll see to that!" Poor Lucky. His career never lived up to his nickname from that time on.

Joe was the great organizer, but somehow things always had a habit of going wrong. On the train from Paris to Nice, Joe had arranged for the "Royal Party," comprising Louis, Jack, Earl and himself, to travel in a luxurious first-class carriage all to themselves, while the peons were back in second class. As the train pulled into Nice, another huge crowd was waiting for us, led by the mayor. Unfortunately for Joe it was our second-class coach that stopped right in front of the mayor and his party, and we all stepped out onto the red carpet to a tumultuous reception. As the mayor embraced me I turned my head to receive his kiss on my cheek and caught sight of Joe way up at the far end of the platform running towards us with his stars in tow, looking as if he was about to burst a blood vessel as he yelled, "Wait for us, wait for us."

The first concert at the Opera House opened with the Armstrong All Stars. Behind the curtain Louis led the band into the majestic opening strains of *Sleepy Time Down South*. As the curtain went up, a wave of emotion swept across the audience, with people unashamedly crying, overcome by the atmosphere of the event. Immediately things started to go wrong. Earl had just joined the band, replacing Dick Cary, and there had been no time for rehearsal. This was 1948, when the whole big-band scene was taking its worst nose-dive ever, and leaders were quitting left, right and center. In that year alone, Woody Herman, Count Basie and Benny Goodman had given up, and everybody else was cutting down to small groups. Earl had left his own big band to join the All Stars. That opening night at Nice, Louis would say, "We gonna lay a little *Monday Date* on you cats.

Four bars. You got it, Pops!" Earl would hit a rousing intro in his breezy style – perfect, except that he was in the wrong key. Louis would come in, scuffling, while Earl was whispering to Arvell Shaw, "What the fuck key we in?" They had a hell of a time getting things together.

And then there was a lot of grumbling by the French fans who wanted to hear *Cornet Chop Suey*, *West End Blues* and all the early classics; they were getting too much of *That's my Desire* and *La vie en rose*, and they felt cheated. They somehow expected the All Stars would be a re-creation of the Hot Five, which of course it wasn't. In fact it was never what I would call a cohesive New Orleans type band. Jack Teagarden, for instance, was not a tailgate trombone player – he had no desire to play in that style and he just didn't think that way. He really played trumpet style on the trombone, brilliantly, better than anybody, but he was no Kid Ory. Barney Bigard had his New Orleans roots, but in all those years with Duke Ellington his playing had developed a fritteryness about it, embroidering the ensembles with a million notes. It didn't mean anything, however, in terms of a New Orleans ensemble. It all sounded very unorganized, not at all like the Hot Five. And of course Louis, having fronted a big band for so many years, wasn't playing down in the middle register which is so right for the balance of a three-horn front line. He was up on top, like when he used to soar over five brass and four saxes; although now fronting a small group, he played like he had with the big band. As a result the All Stars never achieved a cohesive, balanced ensemble.

As the years went by the All Stars became increasingly a backdrop for Louis – more and more of a vaudeville show and less and less of a jazz presentation. As the program became increasingly solidified, it settled down into constant repetition; for instance, it always opened with *Indiana*. Ironically, Louis became better known by the public for all this than for his really great, important contributions from the earlier years. It has been difficult for younger generations of jazz musicians to appreciate Armstrong, to really dig him, because they have in their minds the image of the All Stars with Louis's toothy grin, the handkerchief and all the mugging – they can't think of him as a dedicated jazz player.

There were two little incidents concerning Louis that left a lasting impression on my mind. We were waiting in the bus outside the hotel in Paris, ready to go to the train for Nice, everybody there but Louis. He got on the bus, realized he had been holding things up and was embarrassed about it. "What's all this shit here?" he asked, which was his way of covering up his nervousness about holding up the departure. He still felt like a sideman who was late, not the great Louis Armstrong without whom the bus couldn't leave. He was a very humble man really, very humble about himself. The other incident was when I went over to the Opera House one night before the concert, wanting to find a good reed. I went backstage; the place was absolutely deserted except for Louis in his dressing room. He had his horn out, doing warm-up stuff, getting ready. All the other guys were either sleeping off the effects of the party the night before, or they were out drinking or romancing, but not Louis. He was back there getting ready to go on. I was impressed: here was a man to whom, despite all the adulation, the only thing that mattered was to be ready when that curtain went up. Everything else came second to that. His dedication to his horn was total. He never put on airs, never tried to be somebody he wasn't. He was just a down-home cat trying to do his job. He used to say that he just wanted to play that lead, to play it the way Papa Joe had taught him.

From time to time, Louis was accused of being an Uncle Tom, which was grossly unfair. It really hurt him. He would say, "What are you supposed to do, man? You got people out there who want to be entertained. If you don't entertain 'em, they ain't going to come back. You got an obligation to your audience."

Louis made some really strong statements about the whole racial business in the 1960s, when he was upset by Governor Faubus attempting to block integration at the schools in Little Rock. Anybody who accuses Louis of being an Uncle Tom is way off beam, for he felt very strongly about black rights. No, Louis was never an Uncle Tom, he was just kidding around. He was a showman and he loved it. He loved to make people laugh and enjoy themselves. When that horn went up to his lips, however, the clowning stopped. The horn was serious business; he just played that serious lead. And he had this natural sense of humor. He always saw the funny side of things and loved to laugh, but he could be very serious at times. The last time I saw him was on Cape Cod, right at the height of his success with *Hello Dolly*. He finished the concert with that number, but the crowd just kept yelling for more. He'd just stomp off the band and start playing it again. He ended up playing six encores of the tune. I went backstage after the show and he was really beat, not at all the smiling, fun-loving Satchmo the audience had seen a few moments before.

"Hey, Pops, how ya doin'?"

"I'm gettin' a little tired. Seems like we been doin' nothin' but one-nighters for months. But the people out there love the band and they sure dig that *Hello Dolly*. They keep shoutin' for more and I just keep layin' it on 'em."

It was a tremendous obligation that he felt to his audience. I heard a story about when he and Cozy Cole got into a big scuffle. The band was on stage waiting for the curtain to go up and angry words were exchanged. Cozy said, "I ain't going to take that shit," and he jumped down from the drums and they started fighting. Next thing they were down on the floor, wrestling, fists flying. At that moment the stage manager shouted, "Curtain going up," and in a flash they were both up on their feet, Cozy smiling from behind his drum kit and Louis playing the opening bars of *Sleepy Time Down South*. The moment the curtain came down at intermission, Cozy jumped down from his drums again and they were ready to go at it again!

Then there was the occasion when Louis got mad at Trummy Young for something or other and really ripped into him. Trummy was crestfallen, shattered. He worshiped Louis, and his idol had just called him a motherfucker and every other name under the sun. While Trummy was sitting there in the dressing room, practically in tears, Louis stuck his head round the door and, with a twinkle in his eye, said, "Well, you can forget about the motherfucker." That was Louis's way of apologizing, of saying he'd lost his head, although he wasn't going so far as to take back everything he'd said. There was so much humanity in the man. I was very privileged to have known him.

Mezzrow's band was a success at the festival; it was rough and ready, but it swung and generated a lot of excitement. The most marvelous part for me was working with Baby Dodds. He was, to my way of thinking, possibly the greatest jazz drummer. He was not merely a timekeeper as so many drummers are – he was a percussionist. He thought of drums in terms of colors and how to mix them. He was fanatical about tuning his drums, and he would be on the stand a half hour before showtime, tightening and tapping, getting the pitch of each drum just right. His timing was superb and his whole playing was heavy and low. He played a heavy beat on bass drum in two or four, and beautifully executed press rolls on his snare. He didn't have a hi-hat but he had a ride cymbal which he played four beats to the bar – "ting, ting, ting, ting" – his head down low and his right arm crooked over his head like a dancer, with the cymbal and his whole body shimmying and shaking in time to the music. It was an unbelievable lift to have Baby behind you. It was not so great working with Mezz, though. I had received a great amount of publicity as the protégé of the great Sidney Bechet, so Mezz and I played the duets that he had recorded with Sidney. It would not be boastful to say that Mezz didn't have the control over his instrument that either Sidney or I had. When he squeaked, as he often did, he would look over at me with a pained expression to give the audience the impression that I had been the culprit! Henry Goodwin and Jimmy Archey were splendid guys to work with. Henry's playing had a wild, frenetic quality. His greatest talent was with the wah-wah mute; he did the Cootie Williams and Bubber Miley things very well, but he had his own way of doing them. Duke always liked his playing very much and asked Henry on various occasions to join the band, but it never worked out. He was a good friend and a lovely man. Henry was six feet tall and as thin as a rake, while Jimmy Archey was about five foot four and well filled out. They made a real contrast on the stand, little Jimmy and big Henry. Jimmy was not well known, but he had broad experience. He was 46 years of age at that time and had played with King Oliver, Luis Russell, Louis Armstrong, Benny Carter, Earl Hines and many others. He, too, had impressed Ellington, and on occasions had deputized for Tricky Sam Nanton and Juan Tizol. Pops Foster and Sammy Price, along with Baby Dodds, made a superb rhythm team. They were both foundation players: Pops would stick to the important notes, the roots and the fifths of the chord, playing with a big powerful tone, while Sammy had an impeccable harmonic sense. He didn't do anything that was particularly fancy or subtle, but everything was right. That rhythm section was really cooking right from the start, in contrast to the All Stars with all their problems.

I may be biased, but I think our band made more of an impact with the real jazz fans than the All Stars did. Humphrey Lyttelton described our performance in the following manner: "Mezz leads the group by sheer force of personality. Technically, he sounds very amateur beside the rest of his musicians, although he often plays with great sensitivity and beauty, especially in slow blues. In fact, blues playing was the strongest point of the whole band and we heard some fine work in that idiom from Henry Goodwin and pianist Sammy Price. With Jimmy Archey on trombone and Pops Foster on bass, this was indeed a band of veterans. But they played with a vigor and freshness that put many of the younger musicians to shame, and which also gave added certainty to what was already clear from their high spirits off duty – that they were having the time of their lives at Nice."

The financial deal for me at Nice was all expenses paid, but no salary. I believe, in retrospect, and I hate to say so, that Panassié had probably allocated a certain salary for me which Mezz neatly stuck into his own back pocket. Mezz would not have been above such a practice. There was a curious ambivalence in his whole attitude. He loved to be thought of as a black man and affected a real black accent; it was ridiculous to hear this Jewish guy from Chicago coming out with a rich southern drawl. On the other hand, there was also a paternalistic streak in him: the Great White Father looking after his slaves. The black musicians were very conscious of this patronizing attitude, and they resented it. If anything went slightly wrong, they would take their dissatisfaction and frustration out on Mezz. I remember an incident after the festival, when we were doing a string of one-nighters and everybody was tired and short of rest. Baby Dodds so resented Mezzrow's attitude over some trifling incident that he picked up a leather briefcase in the lobby of our hotel and hurled it with all his might at Mezz, cursing and swearing at him as he did so. There was a pent-up resentment in the usually easy-going drummer that finally had to explode.

On the last night of the festival the organizers had all the bands in the circular ballroom at the Hotel Negresco with separate bandstands all the way round the room. The event went on all evening with dancing and champagne. Each band would play in turn, followed by its neighbor, and so on, round the room. On the stand next to ours was Django and the Quintet, then the English band, and then Rex Stewart's group. On the other side of the circle were the Armstrong All Stars. The big event of the evening, which was broadcast on national radio, was the presentation of the Severase Vase. This was an honor bestowed by the French government on visiting dignitaries who had made their mark in art, culture, science, medicine, etc. That night it was being presented to Louis, together with a message from the president of France, in recognition of his great contributions to music. As the big moment drew near, the tension and excitement built up. The bands were all in place, the French government representatives were grouped around the microphone, and the audience had risen to their feet, everybody with champagne glasses ready for the toast. Everything was set to go on the air, except that Louis was missing. Joe Glaser was running round and round like crazy, yelling, "Goddamit, Goddamit, where's Louis, where's Louis?" Someone suggested that perhaps Louis was in his room, whereupon Joe shot out of the ballroom, up the stairs, banged on Louis's door and burst in. There was Louis, lying on the bed in his underpants, his glasses perched on the end of his nose, reading a comic book. "Goddamit, Louis. You're supposed to be downstairs accepting this honor from the president. Come on, get dressed and get your ass down there."

"Oh, is it time for that?" asked Louis.

It was great fun riding the trains through France on all the one-night stands after the festival had finished. There was plenty of time to sit and talk with the musicians. I particularly enjoyed the many conversations I had with Baby Dodds, a marvelous, lovable and personable guy, a real fun-loving little roly-poly. He loved to talk about the Creole Band, of how he couldn't wait to go to work each night, and what a thrill it had been to play that music. He told me about the excitement when Louis joined the band and what a lift he gave to all the other musicians. He was full of funny anecdotes, and we all roared with laughter when he told us about Louis "poppin' his dickie": "Man, Louis would go for one of them high notes and pop his dickie every time."

"What do you mean, pop his dickie?"

"We're playin' the Lincoln Gardens, summer of '23. Two thousand people packed in there. Place is hotter'n hell. We ain't wearin' no dress shirt under our tuxedos. We just gotta starched front called a "dickie" held in place by a ribbon that come down the back and tie round the front. When Pops went for a high note his chest would expand, the ribbon would break and that ole dickie would pop out and shoot up, hittin' 'em under the chin. Wouldn't stop him playin', though, that dickie scrapin' his horn and the sweat rollin' onto his fat ole belly. Jus' seemed to make the people applaud that much harder."

Part II. Despair

FIVE

In Bechet's shadow

After my return to New York I reflected on the Nice Festival. Life had consisted of one endless round of parties, with all the nightclubs open late and jam sessions going on all over the place. My feelings about Mezz were ambivalent. I was certainly grateful to him for the chance to have been part of a great celebration of jazz, but I couldn't forget those duets on the stage of the Salle Pleyel and Mezz pretending that his squeaks were mine – dirty pool. I thought, too, of valued friendships that I had developed with some of the European musicians. Claude Luter was one: while neither of us could speak the other's language, we spoke the same language musically. There were also Dill Jones and Humphrey Lyttelton, two British musicians who became particularly good friends in later years.

Back in the States, a civil war was raging between the two factions of music, the New Orleans style, or dixieland jazz, on the one hand and modern jazz, or bebop, on the other. The whole emphasis at Nice was on the New Orleans music, with bop represented only in a mild form by the Belgian band of Jean Leclere. The festival had been a great success both from the promotional point of view and for me personally. I returned to America with an enhanced reputation and found myself referred to in some quarters as "the great white hope of jazz." It was all very flattering, but I didn't approve of the description. It was difficult enough to have the jazz world dividing into two camps, but to divide jazz into black versus white was the last thing I wanted to see happen. The idea was being sown by some jazz critics that the white man was merely an imitator of the black man, that jazz was the black man's music, and that any white man who tried to play it was naturally inferior because he was white. I'd never heard this idea expressed before, but I recognized it at the time as racial bullshit, just as it is racial bullshit today.

When I heard these ideas expressed I asked myself some questions. Who did Jack Teagarden imitate? He sure didn't sound like Kid Ory or J. C. Higginbotham or Lawrence Brown. He was, to me, the most original jazz trombonist who ever lived. Where did Pee Wee Russell come from? Who did he imitate? He didn't sound like Johnny Dodds, Jimmie Noone or Bechet to me. Every trumpet player in the late 1920s, black and white, wanted to sound like Louis, but Bix Beiderbecke just went his own way; if he hadn't drunk himself to death he would have been one of the great players of the swing era. Lester

Young's favorite saxophone player was Frankie Trumbauer. Charlie Christian worshiped Django Reinhardt. So who was imitating whom? I didn't buy the racial angle then and I don't buy it now. Jazz is American music, only nowadays we have musicians from all over the world, of every nationality and color, who can play it.

So it was that I returned to New York and to the polarized jazz scene of old versus new, black versus white. It was all so very different from the happy, carefree scene of only a couple of years earlier, and it wasn't made any easier by the postwar economic slump. In the spring of 1948 I renewed my acquaintance with Willie "the Lion" Smith. Tennessee Williams was bringing his play *A Streetcar Named Desire* to Broadway and it was going to star the then unknown Marlon Brando, with Karl Malden and Jessica Tandy in support. Eli Kazan was the director and Irene Selznick the producer. Although the play contains music, it wasn't to be played on stage. Williams's idea was to have a jazz band playing backstage to provide atmosphere and underscore the dramatic action. George Avakian was the musical adviser. He recommended Willie as the leader, with Sidney De Paris on trumpet, Arthur Trappier on drums and myself on clarinet. We started to rehearse, with the producer and director explaining what they wanted. Irene would say to "the Lion": "Willie, the setting is a summer night in New Orleans – it's that hot, sultry, southern atmosphere. We want you to play some old-time blues."

Willie: "Ya got it, ya got it," and clenching his cigar between his teeth he'd start playing. Well, Willie couldn't play the blues. He could do everything else, but he didn't have a blue bone in his body. It was against his nature to play anything that suggested he felt sad or resigned about life or had the slightest bit of self-pity. He just didn't feel the blues – it was as simple as that.

Irene kept saying: "No, Willie, that's not quite what we had in mind. We want those old southern blues."

"Ya got it, ya got it. Listen to this. Jelly Roll wouldn't have thought of these licks if he'd lived to be a hundred. In fact, my boy Duke stole this one and he's welcome to it – no charge." Willie always had to embellish everything with those delicate Chopinesque harmonies and marvelous lacy patterns. It was beautiful, but it wasn't the blues. Some acceptable formula eventually emerged and everything went along fine, until Willie discovered we weren't going to be on stage. The dialogue between Willie and Irene continued: "Irene, I gotta have a feature spot in the show."

"Willie, you don't understand. This music is to provide the atmosphere, a backdrop for the dramatic unfolding of the story."

Totally oblivious of her comments, Willie continued: "I'm gonna open the second act. I think I'll do *Shimmy like my sister Kate*. I sing the second verse in Yiddish, ya know – brings the house down every time."

Willie, incidentally, was Jewish, and a cantor to boot. This dialogue went on and on, until eventually it reached the point where Willie gave an ultimatum; if there was to be no spot in the show for him, then that was it as far as he was concerned!

I had left the show by this time because I could see that, with Willie's ideas, it wasn't going to work out. In any case I had received an offer to take a trio up to Boston, which seemed like a good opportunity for me. It came about through a fan of mine, Dick Schmidt, a banker in Milton who had been an amateur promoter of jazz for many years. He was a friend of Steve Connally, manager of the Savoy Cafe in Boston, and had persuaded him to hire Bechet in 1945 when Sidney brought Bunk Johnson up from New Orleans. That venture hadn't worked out because Bunk had an alcoholic problem. He couldn't resist the offer of a drink and was ending up drunk every night. Despite the problems with Bunk, the band achieved a good deal of success and gained a big following in Boston. In the spring of 1948 Dick Schmidt suggested to Steve that there was this young musician, a protégé of Bechet, who was coming along nicely and that it might be a good idea to give him a try, perhaps with a trio. Through Dick's good offices I got the job, my first experience of leading a group on the big-time circuit. The Savoy Cafe was in a black neighborhood of Boston and catered almost exclusively for Blacks. The kind of bands they were booking played in a pre-bop riff style made popular by Lionel Hampton, Louis Jordan, Arnett Cobb and others. I went in as the intermission group, opposite altoist Tab Smith's band. Tab led an eight-piece group playing riff numbers like *Red Top* and *Flying Home*. *Flying Home* was to that idiom what *The Saints* was to the dixieland movement: it was always the high spot of the evening. I was playing basically New Orleans music, which meant nothing to those fans coming to hear Tab. At the same time there was a growing group of young students from the various schools around that area who were discovering New Orleans music, and they started coming in to the Savoy to hear me. Consequently I started to build up a following; from night to night you could literally see the complexion of the audience in the club start to change. From being predominantly black, it became evenly divided, with one half supporting Tab and the other half supporting me. Eventually Tab left and was replaced by Joe Morris and the Hucklebuckers. *Doin' the Hucklebuck* was their big hit, but they also played *Flying Home*, with the tenor man playing Arnett Cobb's chorus from Hampton's record, and the crowd singing along. The tenor man was a young 17-year-old by the name of Johnny Griffin. My original trio had Baby Dodds on drums and Norman Lester on piano. When Baby left to go home to Chicago, Pops Foster came in on bass and Dick Wellstood replaced Norman, whom I had to fire when he fell asleep during the piano solo on *Basin Street Blues* one Sunday afternoon, leaving just Baby thumping away. Dick had been playing with Bechet at Jazz Ltd in Chicago. With all these changes going on I was glad to have my old buddy from the Wildcat days with me. Later still, Pops Foster left and Kaiser Marshall came in on drums.

The trio developed a large following and eventually Connally told me that he'd like me to add three more players and become the main attraction. I left the Savoy for a short while to re-form and decide who to use. I'd gotten on well with the guys in Mezzrow's band at Nice, so I completed the front line with Jimmy Archey and Harry Goodwin, with Wellstood and Pops Foster returning on piano and bass. After the trio closed at the Savoy, Kaiser had gone to Chicago to record with Bechet for King Jazz. He contracted pneumonia and died very suddenly, so I got Tommy Benford on drums. I had admired Tommy's work on Morton's Red Hot Pepper recordings. He was around in New York, not doing much, and he was pleased to join us. We opened in the fall of 1948 playing the music of Ellington, Oliver, Morton, Bechet and Willie "the Lion" Smith. We were, in fact, the first and only band on the East Coast with this kind of repertoire.

I'd gotten to know Rudi Blesh, the jazz critic and author, when I was living with Sidney. He'd had a Saturday afternoon jazz show on radio called "This is Jazz," and I'd guested a couple of times with Sidney, doing the duets we'd worked out at Ryan's. Rudi had kept abreast of my activities, and he came up to Boston; he liked the band and offered us a recording date. We went into the studio in April 1949 and recorded six tunes for Circle Records, playing our best numbers from the Savoy, with the exception of *The Pearls*, which was our biggest hit. The college kids loved Morton's unique composition, and why I didn't include it on the album is, in retrospect, inexplicable to me.

A short while later Rudi and I had the idea of asking Bechet to join the band as a guest for another album, consisting of Sidney's compositions. Bechet liked the idea, so we cut another six titles. Unfortunately, Blesh, with an eye to economy, used a cheap studio and the recording quality was very poor. There were some displays of temper by Sidney because things in the studio didn't go the way he wanted. He was always a perfectionist, very easily upset if things were not right. We were playing new material, all Bechet originals. Wellstood was having to read all these new arrangements written in my primitive scrawl, and, not wanting to make any mistakes, had been somewhat tentative. At the end of the session we packed up, and as Sidney and I were going out of the door we heard Dick tearing the hell out of one of James P. Johnson's stride pieces. Sidney stopped dead, listened for a moment, then roared back into the studio. "Goddamit, man," he yelled at Dick, "you spose to play that way on my record." With all the tension of trying to read unfamiliar music gone, poor Dick was just relaxing. As he explained later, "Bechet just turned my fingers into frozen sausages."

Sidney, however, had taken it as a personal affront, convinced that Wellstood didn't want to play "his best stuff" on his, Sidney's, record. It was typical of the paranoia I've observed among New Orleans musicians. They weren't always a loving brotherhood as one would like to imagine. (King Oliver's Creole Band, perhaps the greatest of all New Orleans groups, broke up when the sidemen discovered that their leader had gotten a raise and wasn't sharing the extra money with them.) Sidney could be utterly unreasonable at times; you just couldn't win with him when he was in an irascible mood. If a sideman wasn't playing well, at least by Sidney's standards, he saw it as a deliberate act of sabotage. On the other hand, if the sideman was brilliant, eliciting applause from the audience, Sidney was convinced that he was trying to steal the show. A lot of this had to do with money. Bechet invariably took the full fee for the whole band and deducted a large chunk off the top for himself, not leaving much to distribute among the sidemen. As a result he couldn't afford to get the really good players who were on his level. He used his favorite drummer, Big Sid Catlett, on recordings but wouldn't pay him enough to work at Ryan's. As a result the drummers were always catching hell because they didn't have "no damn beat like that guy 'cross the street with Hawkins" (Big Sid).

These flashes of temper from Bechet could often be seen. Yank Lawson recalls the first time he played with Sidney at Stuyvesant Casino. Yank stomped off *Jazz me Blues*, only to have his efforts summarily dismissed at the conclusion by Sidney's acid comment, "Young man, you played that song too fucking fast." Dick Wellstood remembers the engagement at Jazz Ltd. Dick and the drummer Bob Saltmarsh were playing hockey in the kitchen between sets, using two broomsticks and a block of ice. When Sidney came in and saw them he blew his top: "What are you guys doin' playin' that silly game? You should be sittin' here thinkin' about all them mistakes you made last set."

Sidney's paranoia came out in many ways. His version of the happenings at the Savoy Cafe with Bunk Johnson is an example. You only have to listen to the airshots to tell that Bunk wasn't in Sidney's class musically and just couldn't keep up with him. Everybody knew Bunk had a weakness for drink but, as Sidney saw it, under his protective wing he was going to be no problem at all. One day we were sitting in the front room at Quincy Street, fooling around with the tape recorder, when Sidney started to tell me his version of what happened: "We was doin' jes' fine, but that damn ol' Gene Williams wanted to make Bunk into a bandleader and steal him away from me. He used to hang around the Savoy and get Bunk drunk between sets so that he couldn't rightly play. I had to fire Bunk because of Gene Williams. Well, what happen as soon as I fire Bunk? Gene Williams take him to New York, get him a band, and make some records for Victor."

After Sidney fired Bunk he hired young Johnny Windhurst on trumpet. When you listen to airshots from the Savoy you cannot help but be impressed by Johnny's playing; his was a fantastic, natural talent. He couldn't read music and rejected every attempt to persuade him to learn, believing it would inhibit his ability to improvise. Many of the top bandleaders of the day, including Les Brown and Benny Goodman, offered him jobs. Woody Herman, for instance, told him that all he had to do was to sit at the end of the trumpet section and play the solos while the other guys would gradually teach him to read. This offer, like all the others, was turned down by Johnny. His greatness was achieved at a very young age. He was 16 when I first heard him sitting in on a Sunday afternoon at Nick's with Bobby Hackett, and 19 when he played with Bechet at the Savoy. He gradually developed a drinking problem and his playing became erratic. He worshiped Eddie Condon, whom he admired for his tough-guy stance, his Irish wit, and, unfortunately (for Johnny), his ability to consume immense amounts of alcohol. Johnny ended up playing weekends at the Last Chance Saloon in Poughkeepsie and on his way home one night, rather the worse for drink, he was beaten up and suffered brain damage. He never recovered and died a short while later.

Johnson returned to New Orleans, where he formed his own band, but it wasn't all because of a plot by Gene Williams as Sidney would have you believe. In fact, Gene was one of the most idealistic, jazz loving critics you could wish to meet. He believed in New Orleans music and would do anything to help its players get recognition. Gene took Kid Ory's band out on a nationwide tour and lost his shirt because he didn't know how to promote things. He had this fantastic vision of Ory's band from the West Coast and Bunk's band from the East Coast criss-crossing the United States, transforming American popular music, with everybody listening, dancing and singing to the New Orleans sound. Sidney's version was typical Bechet paranoid fantasy. So many of the black musicians used fantasy as a crutch. They didn't want to face the reality of the white-dominated power structure. They knew they would never get the big money and the recognition of a Goodman or a Dorsey, but they didn't want to face this disillusioning fact, so they invented a fantasy world where things were always about to happen – tomorrow, next week, next month. Pops Foster, for instance, got tired of traveling on the road with Louis's band and came home to New York and a job on the subway as a guard because there was no work as a musician. That was in 1940 – what we like to regard as the Golden Era. This was reality for black musicians. The other bitter pill for them to swallow was the fact that they knew their bands were just as good as, and in many instances better than, a lot of the white bands, but yet the white bands were making so much more money. The men in Bob Crosby's band, for example, made four or five times as much as those in Count Basie's. Moreover, when the white guys came off the road there would be studio or staff jobs in films, radio and television, but for the black musicians those were closed doors. It destroyed so many good people. It certainly destroyed Lester Young and in the end it destroyed Coleman Hawkins. Hawkins finally realized that, with all his ability and talent, nothing was going to happen – he was just another black saxophone player. He was the best, he knew he was the best, and he wanted to be treated as a great concert artist – a Heifetz or a Horowitz. In the end he just gave up and started drinking himself to death.

Funnily enough, Sidney never thought of himself as a black man. He was a Creole, the product of the fusion, generations before, of French and negro blood. Creoles like Bechet and Jelly Roll did not see themselves as black, yet they were not accepted as white men. This sometimes resulted in strange statements from Sidney, like, "Them Goddam niggers, doin' this and doin' that, and givin' us all a bad name." We once sat down in front of the tape recorder while he expounded on this subject, extolling the virtues of the infamous southern racist senator, the notorious Senator Bilbo, who had connections with the Klu Klux Klan and all the worst aspects of that business. Sidney said, "Bilbo's doin' a good job. He's for law and order. He keepin' all them people in their places."

"Good God, Sidney," I said, "the man's a racist. He's a hate-monger."

"Naw, naw. He's a good man, ol' Bilbo. He doin' a fine job."

A most complex character, was Sidney. If you were his friend you knew it. If you were his enemy you knew it. A man of kindness and meanness, of hostility and gentleness, of arrogance and charm. I saw it all, on Quincy Street. I'll never forget, for instance, when a wedding party was held there for some friends he'd met at the boatyard. Sidney put on his radio interviewer hat, got out his recorder, and spoke to the bride and bridegroom. He was so gentle with the girl, so solicitous for her future happiness, but mischievously intent on persuading her to tell what she might be doing when the party ended. Sidney's questions were punctuated with exaggerated yawns, until in the end the poor girl could scarcely keep her eyes open.

My band at the Savoy wasn't a heavy drinking band, which was one of the good things about it. The great problem when you have heavy drinkers in a band is that they can be brilliant one night and hopeless the next, but the Savoy band achieved a very consistent sound from night to night. So consistent was it that I began to feel bored. There was no feeling of excitement, of something new happening, and I used to get annoyed because everybody got set in their solos. Dick Wellstood and I were jazz romantics in those days – we believed in improvisation and the idea that every solo should be different. We were the kids in the band, exploring, developing and looking into new things, but the older guys were very security-conscious and wanted everything to sound perfect. Jimmy Archey used to say, "No, man. You get your thing set and you play it that way. You don't change it."

Buddy DeFranco once fell foul of Tommy Dorsey on this same point. Tommy used to insist that Buddy play his solo on *Opus I* exactly as on the record, and when Buddy tried to tell Tommy that he was a jazz man and that he had to improvise, Tommy replied, "You're not a jazz man on my time, kid. You're fired!"

In money terms, the Savoy job was a very well-paid one. The guys used to make $125 per week, while, as leader, I got $250. This was good pay for the time, bearing in mind that the average pay on 52nd Street in the late 1940s was between $75 and $100. Earlier in the decade it had been as low as $35. Despite our success, however, the band had become stereotyped, and I started to lose interest in it. There were also the beginnings of some feelings of uneasiness about myself as a musician and, in a very gradual and almost imperceptible way, I began to lose my direction, my belief in myself, and my belief that I could conquer the world. I started to listen to other kinds of music. We used to work for 40 minutes with a 20-minute intermission, seven nights a week with a Sunday afternoon matinée. We really did work hard in those days. During intermission, Dick Wellstood and I would rush out of the Savoy and down the street to another club on the corner called the Hi-Hat to catch a couple of numbers by Charlie Parker, Howard McGhee, Stan Getz, or whoever else might be appearing there, and then we would rush back to the Savoy for our next set. If there was nobody at the Hi-Hat we wanted to hear, we would rush in the other direction to Jack's Record Store to see what new records were in. We listened to Lee Konitz and Lennie Tristano, to Bird and Dizzy, to Bud Powell, Fats Navarro, and Thelonious Monk. This was not because I had lost interest in the older music, but I knew all the older things and I wanted to see what these new sounds were, I was intrigued with what I heard. There were quite a few jazz sessions held around the town, and I remember jamming with Howard McGhee and Stan Getz on occasions. Although the fans at that time were totally divided, the musicians were not. Looking back, I can remember only one occasion when this kind of mutual tolerance was lacking. It was when Bunk Johnson was in New York. After he finished work at the Stuyvesant he used to go up to 52nd Street with his horn and sit in. On this particular occasion he asked Miles Davis if he could join him. Miles agreed but was very cruel to Bunk. He called out *Cherokee* at the fastest possible tempo and poor Bunk just couldn't handle it. Yet I remember Bunk at jam sessions at Ryan's making beautiful music with Pete Brown and the others. It's an interesting fact that, when Bunk came to New York, all the record collectors, who were very intense and serious students of jazz, wanted Bunk to play all those old jazz numbers, whereas Bunk regarded the band as a dance band. He would listen to the hit parade on radio each week and go and buy sheet music for the latest hits so he'd be up on the new tunes. This was what he had been used to doing in New Orleans, where the people wanted to hear the songs that were on the jukeboxes. Those New York fans couldn't understand why Bunk wanted to play such things as *White Christmas* and *Bell-bottom Trousers*, and Bunk couldn't understand why the jazz fans wanted him to play all those old New Orleans tunes from 40 years ago!

Another thing had begun to trouble me, and that was my identification with Sidney Bechet. I was starting to feel uneasy and dissatisfied about living in Sidney's shadow and always being known as his protégé. I had now been playing professionally for five years and I was totally identified in the public mind as Bechet's pupil. Large numbers of fans were coming, not to hear Bob Wilber, but to hear someone who sounded like Bechet. I had lived, studied and played with Sidney for some eight months and knew every record he'd made, so it was inevitable that I would sound like him, particularly on soprano with that distinctive vibrato. Georg Brunis, the trombonist, referred to us as "Bash and Shay"! I began to feel like some sort of freak show, and there came a time when I just had to break away from it. Sidney understood those feelings. When he returned to the United States in the early 1950s and heard the changes in my playing, all he said was, "That's all right, that's all right. He finding his own way." The problem was in finding something to replace the Bechet style. There was much curiosity on my part in the things that were happening in jazz. The period was a time of great ferment. The fans were becoming more and more divided into the two camps of modern and traditional jazz; they were really two separate factions with two very different types of fan. The atmosphere at Birdland was totally different from that at Nick's or Condon's, and I couldn't figure out why this was. I was interested in the contributions of the new players, but emotionally I didn't identify with them. On the other hand, it was difficult for a young musician to succeed in traditional jazz at that time because so many of the originators of the older music were still around. If you take the clarinet, for example, in 1948, still active in New York alone, were Pee Wee Russell, Buster Bailey, Edmond Hall, Peanuts Hucko, Ernie Caceres, Albert Nicholas and Tony Parenti, all men with big reputations. Younger players like myself had more or less to stand in line and wait their turn. I didn't think about this however – I was concerned only with losing my Bechet image. I didn't realize the difficulties I would encounter without the security of that tag!

My next opportunity came in the fall of 1950. George Wein, just out of college, was a piano player around Boston who used to sub at the Savoy, playing with the intermission quartet opposite my band. As a result I got to know George a little bit. He was a good piano player, a solid musician in the swing idiom. He loved jazz, and when he left college he wanted to become a part of it. He made the wise decision to go into the managerial and entrepreneurial side, and subsequently achieved much success. He found an unused basement in the Copley Square Hotel in Boston, and, having some money, decided to open a club called Storyville. He asked me to put the band together because of my popularity at the Savoy, and I was more or less given a free hand to choose who I wanted. First of all I picked Sidney De Paris on trumpet. My first choice for trombone was Vic Dickenson, but as he wasn't available I turned to Wilbur De Paris, Sidney's brother. My bass player was John Field, an excellent local musician but not known outside of Boston. On piano I had Red Richards, whose work with Tab Smith's band I had greatly admired. When I first contacted Red he was very doubtful and said that he didn't know anything about dixieland jazz. I tried to reassure him by telling him not to worry, that I would teach him the tunes, and that all he had to do was play his own way. I must have sounded convincing, because we got ourselves a fine pianist with a marvelous loose, swinging style. On drums I had the magnificent Big Sid Catlett. He was a very sick man, though, and suffered badly from circulatory problems that made his legs swell up, causing him a great deal of pain; but it didn't affect his playing. George Wein's father was a doctor and he looked after Sid.

Sid had one particularly lovely vignette. The only song that he ever sang was *Sometimes I'm Happy*, and he sang it in a gentle, wistful sort of way. He used to do a drum solo on a feature number, *Stompin' at the Savoy*, which he took at an easy medium tempo, not at all the tempo you would associate with a drum speciality. It lasted for 15 minutes and would end with him walking around the audience, playing on chairs and tables and bald heads. By the time he got back on the stand for us to finish off the number, the audience was screaming with delight. He was an absolute master at building up excitement. We didn't know it at the time but this was the last band in which he would play; he died while backstage at a Jazz at the Philharmonic concert in Chicago a few months later. He was a great drummer, and, as I had with Baby Dodds, I learned so much from him about jazz rhythm, about swing, and about getting the momentum going. He was only 41 when he died.

One night at the club stands out in my memory. The Ellington band was in Boston, playing at a local theater. One evening after they had finished their last show, some of the guys from the band, including Johnny Hodges, came over to Storyville. They sat at a table in front of the bandstand and, spying my straight soprano, urged Johnny to sit in. He demurred, saying that he hadn't played the instrument for a long time. In fact the last time he'd played soprano had been back in 1940, some ten years earlier. Finally, after much persuasion, Johnny was literally pushed onto the bandstand. He picked up my soprano, looked at the mouthpiece and saw that it had a soprano reed on it. He asked me, "Gotta clarinet reed?" I pointed to an open box of reeds sitting on the top of the piano. Without saying a word, he removed the soprano reed, reached into the box and took out one at random. He didn't bother looking at it or wetting it or anything. He simply stuck it on the mouthpiece, tightened the ligature, put the horn to his mouth, and started playing the blues – slow and stately, with that beautiful tone. It didn't have the earthiness of Bechet's blues, but you could hear the influence, the soaring lyricism. I was absolutely amazed, considering that he hadn't played the soprano for so long. What an incredibly natural player! I've always found it fascinating to study the different periods in Hodges's career and note how his playing changed. It evolved as he matured, from the very early days as a hot soloist, when he played a lot of notes all over the horn, through the serenity of his ballads of the late 1930s and the 1940s, to the tough, bluesy, earthy statements of the postwar years. Hodges was a private man of few words; there was an almost oriental inscrutability about him. His real personality, his innermost thoughts and feelings, were only revealed in his music. As Duke said when "the Rabbit" died in May 1970, "God bless Johnny Hodges."

We did a lot of things with the band at Storyville that should have been recorded but never were. It was a hell of a band, but it didn't have the success that the Savoy band had had. I had established a regular audience at the Savoy and they now came to Storyville expecting more of the same kind of traditional music, the Jelly Roll Morton and King Oliver things, all very much in an early vein. The fans were upset by the fact that the band didn't sound like its predecessor; they seemed to think I had deserted the Holy Grail. Little did they know of my desperation to get away from the Bechet imagine or of my desire to master the fundamentals of swing and phrasing. Those things didn't concern the fans, who simply wanted old-style jazz and were upset because that was not what I was giving them. It all helped further to erode my self-confidence. Seemingly the price for turning away from Bechet was to have my fans turn away from me. It would have been difficult for them to appreciate how tired I had become of this total identification with Sidney Bechet. It's a difficult problem that many musicians have to solve. When you are living in the shadow of someone you've tried to emulate, you begin to realize that, no matter what you do, it's going to be compared with what your idol does. No matter how good you might become, the general consensus of opinion is that you will never be as good as the master. Many musicians are content with such a situation, hoping that some day they will sound just like their idol, but I knew that this was an artistic dead-end, and I consciously rebelled against it. I had made my decision to break away. It was the right decision for me, but I lost a lot of my fans because of it.

I was particularly popular with the students from the Ivy League colleges along the East Coast. I was in on the start of the whole dixieland revival in the States. Dixieland bands were springing up on the college campuses, but it was all very razz-ma-tazz and amateurish, getting further and further away from the real authentic thing that had first attracted me. At the same time I recognized the drawbacks of bebop with its clichés and repetitiveness – everybody trying to play like Charlie Parker. I felt that there had to be something better than all this. I became intrigued with what Lennie Tristano, Lee Konitz and Warne Marsh were doing; it seemed to be something different, an effort to escape from the clichés and pitfalls that were trapping everyone else. I knew I wanted to do something different, something more contemporary; I wanted to experiment with new things, not get stuck in a rut.

The Storyville club was in the basement of the Copley Square Hotel. The room, which became known as Mahogany Hall, was very elegant, all wooden paneling, and had at one time been a restaurant. Having fallen on hard times, the hotel management was pleased to accommodate the nightclub. The arrangement was that, in exchange for the use of the room, the hotel took the full profit on all the booze that was sold. After we had been there for three months they began to water the whiskey and sell cheap booze. George fell out with them, so he closed down for three months and then found a new location at the Buckminster Hotel in Kenmore Square. In the meantime Big Sid had died. In February 1951 we opened at the Buckminster with Tyree Glenn on trombone and vibes and my old Westchester sidekick, Eddie Phyfe, on drums, with Sidney De Paris, Red Richards and John Field back from the old Storyville group. In a few months Tyree left, to be replaced by Dick Le Fave. Dick was a disciple of Jack Jenney and was known as "the Barber," since he was studying at the local barbers' college. I used to go there for free haircuts. Next to leave was Sidney De Paris, to be replaced by Johnny Windhurst.

Because of the constantly changing personnel, the band never achieved the cohesiveness of the Mahogany Hall group. In truth, my heart wasn't really in it and I decided to give it up. Perhaps I was turning down success, but I felt I just had to get away and do something different. After I left in May, Jo Jones came in as leader and George Wein replaced Red Richards on piano. On the opening night Jo announced to George that he was fired. Having played with Count Basie all those years, Jo didn't feel that George was up to his standards. Wein, however, countered Jones's imperious edict with a simple statement of irrefutable logic – "You can't fire me, Jo, I hired you."

I was in a musical wilderness. I was losing my Bechet identification, but I had no real idea of what I was going to put in its place. I was becoming disenchanted with dixieland, but I didn't feel comfortable with the beboppers. It seemed that you had to nail your colors to the mast and declare your allegiance to one camp or the other. There was no longer the common middle ground of swing music, which had disappeared, a victim of its own success. Because it had been the basis for popular music for ten years, the new generation of jazz fans, traditional and modern, refused to take swing seriously. Unless you were prepared to go wholeheartedly into the dixieland or the modern camp, it was hard to find ground to exist creatively. Some swing musicians went one way, some went the other, but many players, sidemen in the big bands who could not adapt to the changing scene, found that their careers had come to an end; they were extinct like the dinosaurs. Some people like Roy Eldridge and Charlie Shavers were able to move either way. They had split careers, bopping along with Dizzy in Jazz at the Philharmonic, playing a million notes, then moving over to the Stuyvesant Casino or the Metropole to perform the old traditional warhorses. It was to their credit that they could do both, but in truth neither represented the real Eldridge or Shavers. What they really wanted to do, what they excelled in doing, was passé. Swing was dead, with people like Teddy Wilson and Art Tatum in obscurity. Nobody wanted them.

The process of changing my musical identity meant that my fans were starting to drift away from me. Bebop was not a path that I wanted to follow, and within the traditional field I had become just another clarinetist facing increasing competition for the work that was available. With the Wildcats and the Savoy band I had been doing something different from what everyone else had been doing at that time. I had an inner strength, a confidence stemming from the recognition I got from doing something different, but now it all seemed to be slipping away from me. I didn't feel that I could turn to my parents for help and advice.

I was losing my way musically, and still felt awkward and ill at ease in my social contacts. While working at Storyville I took up with Edie, a waitress in the club. She was considerably older than I, but well experienced in the ways of the world, and she befriended me – took me by the hand, so to speak. I felt good about knowing someone I could talk to and laugh with, and I suppose that I felt flattered by the interest of an older woman. After we finished work we used to go to an after-hours place called the Pioneer Club, where there were jam sessions with a lot of the younger musicians from around Boston. They played mostly in the modern idiom, but I used to take my horn and join in. Afterwards we would go on to a chicken and rib joint and then back to her apartment. I look back on that affair with good feelings. Edie was warm and uncomplicated and made me feel good about myself as a man.

I left Storyville in the spring of 1951 and spent the summer at my parents' home, Oldfields, on Cape Cod, leading a trio at a little club in Yarmouth. A few miles down the road on Route 28 was another roadhouse, where Serge Chaloff was leading a trio. The club owner clearly had an eye for business, for outside the club he had put up a sign which read, in small letters, "Serge Chaloff and his Trio – formerly with" – and then in huge letters – "WOODY HERMAN AND HIS ORCHESTRA." Many people driving past fell for the trick and stopped after seeing Woody's name. We each worked six nights a week with our respective groups, but we had different nights off. On our free night we would go over to Serge's place and I would sit in with his group, playing things like *Four Brothers* kicked off by Serge at a breakneck tempo. On Serge's night off, he and his piano player, Dick Twardzik, would come over to our place and sit in with us, playing numbers like *Ballin' the Jack* and *Beale Street Blues*. It was an interesting contact and I enjoyed the friendship with Serge; he was a marvelous musician, the best baritone player since Harry Carney and Ernie Caceres.

After the summer on the Cape I came back to New York, with nothing in mind or in prospect. I had the feeling that sooner or later things would change for the better. Meanwhile it was a period of confusion, about who I was and where I was going. It was during this period of searching for an identity that I started studying with Lennie Tristano and Lee Konitz. I'd heard Tristano when he first appeared on 52nd Street around 1949, with Billy Bauer on guitar and Arnold Fishkin on bass, and I found the contrapuntal texture of their music intriguing. Later I heard the group with saxophonists Lee Konitz and Warne Marsh at Birdland. Lee and Warne used to come out first and play Bach two-part inventions, with drums playing brushes and the bass walking a line. This was where I got the idea to do it later on at the Henry Hudson Hotel with Dick Hafer and myself. By 1950 the dixieland revival was in full swing. I was sick and tired of *The Saints* and *Muskrat Ramble*, but I didn't really want to play bebop, which seemed as sterile and as full of clichés as dixieland. Tristano and his followers were trying to be fresh and inventive, to really improvise. If at times the music lacked heat, it was better than all the "sound and fury signifying nothing" I was hearing everywhere. I had hoped that Tristano's approach might be the middle ground I was looking for, but I found that it didn't really give me the gut satisfaction the older music did. I found his approach too esoteric, too cultish – he wasn't interested in anything before Lester Young or Roy Eldridge. I talked about the importance of Louis and Sidney, but Lennie didn't want to know, so I gradually lost interest. However, I've enjoyed a friendship with Lee Konitz through the years. I always admired his determination not to emulate Parker but to try and find his own voice, a very difficult and lonely course to take. The Bird imitators fell by the wayside, but there's Lee out there, still doing his own thing.

I started freelancing, but again with no real direction or purpose. The only thing I had clear in my mind was that I didn't want to live in the shadow of Bechet. The overriding problem remained – what could I put in its place? Strangely, the fact that I had a considerable amount of money, bequeathed to me by my grandmother, was something of a handicap to me. Had I had the problem of having to go out to work to put food on the table or pay the weekly rent, there is no doubt I would have had to solve my problems, and quickly too, but the luxury of having this money allowed me to live in such a way that I was never forced to face up to the realities of the day-to-day struggle of making a career, of making a reputation or name that would stand me in good stead in future years. I hid myself away in more and more practice, secure in the knowledge that household bills were the least of my problems, requiring nothing more than a periodic withdrawal from the bank or a phone call to my stockbroker.

In 1952 I was drafted into the army. I was called to take my physical, and, although I'd been rejected in 1945, this time around I was accepted. Immediately following my examination I left for Washington for an engagement with Wild Bill Davison at the Brown Derby Cafe. Wild Bill lived up to his reputation – romancing three girls at a time, often with their boyfriends or husbands present. He was so outrageous he should have ended up in an alley with a black eye, but never did. I think his playing made everybody feel so good that they forgave him anything. I was no Wild Bill, but I was getting better at making contact with the opposite sex, and while playing at the club I met Betty. She helped take my mind off the appalling prospect of donning a uniform, perhaps even ending up in Korea. After long mornings in bed we spent the afternoons viewing the sights of Washington. At the ripe old age of 23 I was making up for lost time! One afternoon I went out to nearby Fort Myers in Virginia to audition for the US Army Band. I didn't do well: my reading was very rusty from years of playing nothing but jazz.

I was also worried about whether I would be able to get into an army band because of playing only clarinet and soprano sax. There was no room in a dance band for a soprano, and clarinet by itself was not enough. This was when I decided to trade in my soprano for a tenor. That was the end of my soprano playing for many years; I didn't resume again until the 1960s, when I came across my present curved instrument. There was also a psychological factor in this decision. Although my voice on the instrument had changed, in that I was trying to play it more like Lester Young than Bechet, it was the final shedding of the identity I had built up as Sidney's protégé. Suddenly I was no longer a soprano player, whether I played it like Bechet or not. For better or worse I was now a clarinet and tenor player, but even on clarinet I had moved away from Sidney: the influence of Buddy DeFranco was now clearly discernible.

I went through the basic training routine and, much to my surprise, succeeded in passing. Actually the training, tough and exhausting as it was, was not a bad thing for me. It was an education mixing with a cross-section of America. Here I was working with men from rural areas, from the ghettos, with different racial and ethnic backgrounds. I was appalled at how many people couldn't get through a sentence without using words like "shit," "fuckin'," "motherfucker," etc. I saw how other people thought and lived, and it jolted me out of that dream world I had been living in. It was a period of physical growth, too, in that I put on quite a bit of weight. I found I could do things physically that I had never thought I could do – long marches, obstacle courses, push-ups, pull-ups, gymnastics and so on. I remember coming back from those long marches with full field equipment feeling exhilarated with my physical well-being and enjoying the sensation of dealing with the physicality of life.

I didn't have much in common with most of the guys, but I had one buddy who was a musician, a tenor player who had spent some time with the Woody Herman band. Whenever we had a little free time at night, we'd go down in the boiler room of the barracks and play clarinet and tenor duets. One night, playing down there, we got an idea. The next morning we went to see the captain and explained that we thought it would be good for the guys' morale if they had a little music when marching out to the rifle range. He said, "Well, what have you got?"

I said, "Just the two of us, sir, clarinet and sax."

"You mean all you guys got is a two-piece band?"

"Yessir."

"Well, OK, but you guys better sound good."

"Yessir, don't worry, we will."

That morning our company marched out to the rifle range to the strains of

The Wilbers skiing at Dover Plains, New York, 1937

A family gathering at Prouts Neck, Maine, 1938: (left to right) Dada, Dad, myself, Auntie Cew, Mary Margaret, Uncle Ralph, Uncle Tom, Auntie Mum, Aunt Sally

Denny and Charlie Strong and me jamming on Ice House Pond, Oldfields, our summer home on Cape Cod, 1941

Left: The first alto sax: my cousin Tommy Alder and me at Oldfields, 1944

The Wildcats at Ryan's, 1946: (left to right) Eddie Phyfe, Johnny Glasel, myself, Dick Wellstood, Charlie Traeger

178 Quincy St
Brooklyn N.Y.
Feb 6/47

Dear Mr Wilbur

I've been wanting to come out to see you concerning Bobie's lessons but been so busy its difficult to get away. Bobie and I been talking around it it. Bobie and I been talking around it it Bobie and I don't the whole situation over, we don't know exactly how many lessons he has had.

The fact is that Bobie is such a good boy and has so much talent that is always for me to trust him all that I don't take I don't know how long it will take.

Now long it will take. I don't know how long it will take. But he is learning very fast now. But he is learning very fast now Bobie two hands Mr Wilbur. I am changing Bobie two hands dollar for that complete course and hope that I will come to your approval. my deep regards to your family and I do hope you will be able to come out and see your son.

Yours very truly,
Sidney Bechet

[note in corner: no. 100 = and 1/40. no. 3 not paid.]

With Sidney at Ryan's, 1946 (*photo William Gottlieb*)

Right: A letter from Sidney to my father, 1947 (note Dad's memorandum)

The Wildcats recording for Columbia with Bechet, 1947: (left to right) Johnny Glasel, Bob Mielke, Denny Strong, Sidney, Charlie Traeger, Dick Wellstood, myself (photo Peter Tanner/ Max Jones files)

The Savoy band, Boston, 1948 (*photo Robert Parent*)

With Mezz Mezzrow (and Jimmy Archey's trombone), Nice, March 1948

At the piano with Dick Wellstood, Boston, 1948 (*photo Robert Parent*)

Sid Catlett's birthday party at Storyville, 1950: (left to right) Sid, George Wein, Hoagy Carmichael, John Field (*photo Robert Parent*)

Johnny Hodges blows my soprano, Storyville, 1950 (*photo Robert Parent*)

Colonel Bogey and *The Stars and Stripes*, with a little jazz thrown in here and there. Everybody was happy except the poor bastards who had to carry our rifles and back-packs. Well, tough – they were lucky to have such a great band, small as it was!

I was politically conscious at the time and very left-wing in my thinking. In 1948, while at the Savoy, I'd campaigned for Henry Wallace, who had been Truman's vice-president but was running for president. My involvement included giving a lecture on jazz with my band at Wellesley College under the auspices of the American Labor Party. I was probably the only soldier at Fort Dix with a subscription to *The Compass*, a left-wing newspaper. This led to some difficulties. It was the McCarthy period, and all recruits were required by the army authorities to sign a document called the Attorney-General's List, certifying that they weren't members of any of the organizations on the list, all of which had been labeled subversive. I refused to sign, with the result that I was investigated by the CIA. They did a very thorough job, going to my family and friends and questioning all sorts of people about my background. They found nothing to incriminate me, but it was still police-state stuff – not what you'd expect in America.

During basic training I auditioned for the Band School at Fort Dix and, to my great relief, since this was the time of the Korean War, I was accepted. The Ninth Army Band School trained bandsmen for eight weeks before they were assigned to bands. Practically all the professional musicians on the East Coast who were drafted ended up at Ford Dix, and I met a lot of musicians from different backgrounds. Instead of being shipped to Korea after eight weeks, I was assigned permanently to the school as an instructor. It was particularly gratifying because after the Chinese entered the Korean War many bandsmen found themselves reassigned as stretcher or ammo bearers. My job was to teach musical theory and harmony. To do this I got out my old textbooks from Juilliard and Eastman, managing to stay a chapter or two ahead of my students. Although it was not helping me find myself as a jazz musician, I was gaining experience playing a lot of different kinds of music, which stood me in good stead in years to come. I was intrigued with my tenor sax and worked hard at it, but it wasn't really my voice at the time. I wanted to play like Coleman Hawkins and Chu Berry and Ben Webster, but, I guess because I still lacked a sense of my own worth, I couldn't seem to pull it off. The big, fat, masculine sound was the kind of tenor sound I wanted, but it didn't come out that way. Now in 1987 I'm playing tenor again, but this time I feel I can do it.

A Warrant Officer who was a jazz buff came over from Governors Island on an inspection tour and heard my little combo at Fort Dix. He liked what he heard and had me transferred to Governors Island, where I joined the First Army Band. I was given the position of solo clarinet with the concert band, replacing Phil Phatt, who was leaving the army to join the San Francisco Symphony. The solo clarinet chair in a concert band is pretty demanding, as you have to play all the transcribed violin parts. I was woefully inequipped for the position and felt way in over my head. The player next to me could see that I was having difficulty, and he suggested I went to his teacher, Leon Russianoff. I followed up his suggestion and started an association that has lasted for many, many years. Leon was a small, bespectacled man with a worried look on his face, but possessed of great warmth and dedication to teaching. I had found another master to help me along the rocky road to self-awareness! Different from Bechet as night is from day, but a man whose knowledge I respected and one who treated me with kindness and patience, much as Sidney had done. Leon taught at Banner Music, a music store on the fourth floor at 48th Street and Broadway. Banner was the hang-out for all the reed men in New York in the jazz, legitimate and club-date fields. Here there were seemingly endless discussions about reeds, mouthpieces and horns every afternoon. It was here that I met Stanley Drucker, another student of Leon's, who always sported a cigar and a swaggering tough-guy attitude. Stanley was the youngest player in the New York Philharmonic and the fastest guy on clarinet I'd ever heard. Today, Leon, who still teaches at that same studio on Broadway, insists that Stanley and I are his best pupils, which is as fine a compliment as I can imagine. A few years later Leon took on a young student named Penelope. She was extremely tall. I used to see Leon and Penny at clarinet recitals and the contrast in their respective heights was quite startling. Soon Penny became Mrs Russianoff. She is a psychiatrist who became famous for playing herself in the movie *The Unmarried Woman*. She brought out a zany, humorous side of Leon that had been simmering beneath the surface of respectability. Today the Russianoffs are among our most favorite people.

Leon is a classical clarinet teacher with a great appreciation of jazz and I studied with him continuously for over five years, going through the whole classical repertoire and developing my skills as a legitimate clarinet player. His teachings led me further and further away from the New Orleans roots of Sidney Bechet and Johnny Dodds where I had started. My playing became much more polished and refined, but much less full of passion and feeling. If you listen, for example, to my 1960 album *New Clarinet in Town*, you will hear how much I was influenced by legitimate clarinet technique. The playing is clean and pure, but rather clinical. The things that I was learning from Leon and my teachings from Sidney were not really incompatible, but I couldn't figure out how to combine them at the time. The final trappings of the Bechet style had now fallen away completely and I was left with nothing. I was out on my own, well and truly, but still with no personal voice or identity or any clear sense of direction.

SIX

Oblivion isn't so bad

When I came out of the Army in 1954 I went to the Manhattan School of Music under the GI Bill of Rights. I still didn't know what to do and this seemed to be a good way of filling the void, but I found it to be a very unrewarding experience. My classmates were all music majors, but many possessed little aptitude for music. They were typical of the sort of musician turned out in thousands by the college conveyor-belt system, competent readers and technicians but with no originality or creativity, and certainly no knowledge or appreciation of the history of jazz. They couldn't phrase a melody, hear the harmony, or feel the beat. And, what's more, they were being taught by people who were no better. The old adage of "Them that do, do – them that don't, teach," is perhaps more true in the field of music than any other. What was even more significant was the fact that these students were destined to be the next generation of music educators, a fact not calculated to inspire one's confidence in the future of music! The atmosphere at Manhattan didn't give me the inspiration my studies with Sidney had. I felt I had to get away from it. I still wanted to be a jazz player. I wanted to be as serious about it as my idols were. Bechet was serious, Louis was serious. It wasn't some little fun-and-games hobby they did. They had something to say and they wanted to say it. The Manhattan School of Music was not a place where I could say what I wanted to say!

What came along next was a reunion with John Glasel and Eddie Phyfe, two of my old friends from the Wildcat days. We all retained our love of the early jazz while developing interest in later forms. We didn't think that there was as much disparity between the two styles of music as the fans and critics would have you believe. Our feeling was that there was a oneness to the whole music that we could demonstrate musically. We had respect and affection for, say, *Royal Garden Blues*, but we wanted to play in it a new way that reflected some of the postwar developments in jazz. Alternatively, we could play something that was much more contemporary, but instead of that unison style we could do it in three-part harmony or in a freewheeling ensemble combining elements of traditional and modern. The more we talked about it, the more attractive the idea began to seem, so, with the addition of Eddie Hubble on trombone, Tommy Goodman on piano, and Bob Peterson on bass, we formed a co-operative group known as the Six.

I was the musical director in the sense that I called the tunes, and, in general, I also directed the arranging assignments. Glasel did a lot of the arrangements for the first edition of the group and Tommy was also a good writer. Eddie Phyfe was in charge of publicity, and John, who had recently graduated from Yale, was in charge of contracts and union business. Our début was in a series of Sunday afternoon concerts at Childs Paramount, a huge cavernous basement restaurant in Times Square, but our first steady engagement came through the good offices of Jimmy Ryan. He had been a good friend right from the Wildcats days and had always had a soft spot for the "Westchester Kids," as he called us, and so, when we told him about our band, he said he would give us a listen. Jimmy had been a Broadway hoofer. His main claim to fame was that he had danced in the Jerome Kern show *Roberta*, starring Bob Hope. He loved the Broadway life, the theater, and the people. I knew this, so when we went to his club one afternoon to audition it was with a program of Kern, Gershwin and Cole Porter numbers. He liked what he heard and immediately offered us a six-week engagement.

Ryan's was the hub of the dixieland movement, and this period in 1955 was the height of its revival. All the college kids would flood into New York, particularly at the weekends, to listen to their favorite music at Condon's, Nick's and Ryan's. The initial reaction of the audiences to our group was one of bewilderment. Although they were hearing familiar melodies, they were being played in a style that didn't sound like dixieland to them. They were so very sure about what they wanted to hear and couldn't understand what we were doing. When we played at Café Bohemia, the home of hard-bop music in the 1950s, we had the same problem in reverse. It was a mixed black and white audience and, right from the start, they were distressed because ours was an all-white group. The fans were used to hearing Art Blakey, Max Roach, Hank Mobley and that bunch, and they were equally bewildered to have in front of them this bunch of "ofays" playing *Royal Garden Blues* and such things. Like the audience at Ryan's, they were absolutely sure what they wanted to hear. We didn't use the tenor/trumpet unison, and it sounded strange to them. In an effort to sell the group, we pooled our resources and produced a record. We peddled it round the record companies and eventually sold it to Norman Granz, who issued it on the Norgran Label.

After playing Café Bohemia we got ourselves an agent, a friend of Eddie Phyfe's from Cleveland. Although he got us several prestigious bookings, such as Music Inn and the Newport Jazz Festival, most of the dates were at little clubs around the country. Wherever we went, whatever type of audience we played to, it was always the same story. Jazz had become completely and utterly divided and we sounded familiar to neither camp. I remember an experience when our agent booked us into a Chinese restaurant called the Grange in Hamilton, Ontario. We followed a banjo-playing duo who wore propellor beanies on their heads and sang risqué songs. Although they had featured some dixieland groups at the club, we were obviously not what the owner had expected. We realized this during the first set when we saw him head for the phone with a worried look on his face, obviously calling our agent to complain. Upon querying the oriental gentleman at the end of the set as to how he liked the band, we received the blunt reply, "Too much nigger music." It was all so frustrating for us, and after several cancellations we were left stranded. We realized it wasn't going to work, and some of the guys started to drift away. Sonny Truitt, Bob Hammer and Bill Britto had joined us by then on trombone, piano and bass respectively, and with the new line-up we recorded two albums for Bethlehem, a small but active East Coast record company in the 1950s. The second of these albums was titled *The View from Jazzbo's Head*, which was a play on the title of a current novel called *The View from Pompeiis Head*, and a tribute to Al "Jazzbo" Collins, a well-known New York disc-jockey who dug what we were trying to do.

The Music Inn in Lenox, Massachusetts, was in a summer resort adjacent to Tanglewood, where the Boston Symphony was in residence every summer. Its owners, Phil and Stephanie Barber, were jazz fans who wanted to present a jazz program as a contrast to the classical program at Tanglewood. The engagement was an interesting one. We were the band in residence for three weeks, and once each week we gave a concert with a guest artist. Pete Johnson was the guest one week. After the concert we wanted him to stay and jam with us because we'd been so elated with his playing. His reply to our pleadings was, "Oh, no. I gotta get back to Buffalo for my milk route." The great Pete Johnson was a milkman because music couldn't provide him with a living!

Finally, after two years of knocking our heads against the wall, we too had to accept that we couldn't make a living with the Six, and we disbanded. Had I not stripped myself so completely of the Bechet image, I suppose I might have been tempted to go back to the old format of the Wildcats, but I felt there had to be some light at the end of the tunnel and, if I continued studying and searching, I would surely find a way that would be Bob Wilber and no one else. It would have to be my own statement, though – I didn't want to be anybody's protégé. I wasn't looking for fame or fortune; I was simply looking for my own voice, and I felt that if I found that voice the other things would follow. There had been so many changes in my musical character that my sense of direction was becoming less and less, and, as it did so, my belief in my ability to get up on the stand and say something musically was also declining. It was a very confused period for me. When the opening for a clarinet player at Eddie Condon's came up, I took the job and stayed there for two years. In a sense, it felt like a retrogression to me musically. I had a lot of respect for the Condon guys and there was really nothing else for me to do. I wasn't a studio musician who could get the jingles and record dates, and I had no name in modern jazz, where young musicians like Gerry Mulligan and Stan Getz were establishing themselves along with black players like Clifford Brown, Sonny Rollins and so on. There was really no place for me to go except Condon's. If I hadn't had the cushion of my bank balance, I suppose I'd have taken up the flute – an absolutely essential double to do the freelance work around New York. I could have done very well, because I was always a pretty good reader, but I just had no eyes for the flute. There was a great deal of studio work for musicians in those days, playing backgrounds for popular singers. There was also television and jingles, areas in which people like Dick Hyman, Bobby Rosengarden, and many of the old players of the big-band era like Yank Lawson,

Cutty Cutshall and Lou McGarity were doing well, with two or three dates each day. I had the ability to do it, but I had lost the easy confidence I had felt under Bechet's wing. The realistic thing to have done would have been to take up the flute or oboe in order to get the freelance work, but somehow I resisted it. I just wouldn't give up my dreams.

In my own way, I was busy. I was playing at Condon's in the evenings and continuing my legitimate clarinet studies with Russianoff during the day. In addition I was studying tenor with Joe Guidice, a colleague of Leon's, and, needless to say, doing a great deal of intense practicing. I felt isolated, however – on the periphery of life. The refuge I'd sought in the world of jazz was not solving my problems or making me happy. It seemed like it was always the other guys who were doing the good gigs, getting the big write-ups, meeting the beautiful women. I had no close friends, only acquaintances, relatives and my fellow musicians. With them, the old camaraderie I'd so warmed to was proving to be superficial as the jobs became scarce and the competition tougher. The jazz world wasn't the happy paradise it had seemed ten years before – the joint wasn't jumpin' any more.

An incident that occurred during this period was recalled to me recently in a letter from a neighbour, Fradley Garner, who lived across the hall. His sister was getting married and they needed a witness. Fradley knocked on my door and enlisted my services. His father was a veterinarian, and as the service was about to start he received a call from a distraught lady – her parakeet, Herbert, had fallen off his perch and was lying on his back on the bottom of the cage and making strange wheezing noises. Fradley's father explained to the lady that he was busy and would come by her apartment in a couple of hours to minister to the ailing bird. Just as the couple were exchanging vows the phone rang again. It was the same lady, obviously extremely upset. Through her tears she cried in a voice we could all hear in the still apartment, "Cancel the house call. Herbert's just died!" The main reason why Fradley remembered the incident was it was the first time he'd ever seen me smile.

Meanwhile, there was this job at Condon's. I'd first listened to Eddie's records in the Commodore Music Shop as a kid, and I had seen him at Nick's and the Town Hall concerts in 1944 and 1945. Our Westchester gang loved Condon, Pee Wee Russell, Brad Gowans and all those others who were our anti-establishment cult heroes. Later on I played with Eddie at Ryan's in the jam sessions that always ended each Sunday afternoon session. The closing number was always *Bugle Call Rag*, which for some reason, after everybody had played a break, always went into *Ole Miss*. There would be 16 or more guys packed on that stand some Sundays. Eddie would direct the whole proceedings and when you had his favorites, like Pee Wee Russell, Sidney Bechet, Bobby Hackett, Billy Butterfield, Hot Lips Page, Wild Bill Davison, Bud Freeman, Lou McGarity and Jack Teagarden all blowing together, the sound was awesome. All the guys respected Eddie, who, although he wasn't a great soloist, was a first-class rhythm guitarist and could direct a jam session like Toscanini conducting the New York Philharmonic. What with taking weekly lessons on clarinet and tenor I needed a lot of practice time and a place where I could spend many hours without disturbing anybody. I asked Eddie if I could use the club during the daytime when it was empty. "Why not, kid," he said, "Just see Bill – he cleans up during the day." The club was a big place with a whole string of rooms down in the cellar, like catacombs. At one time, in the Prohibition days, it had been a speakeasy called the Howdy Club. It had an elaborate trap-door arrangement in the basement, so that when there was a raid all the whiskey could be concealed very easily. It was a great place to practice. I'd spend hours blowing away in the basement with Bill upstairs vacuuming, cleaning the tables and polishing the bar. There had been a string of clarinet players at the club, starting with Tony Parenti in 1945. He was followed successively by Peanuts Hucko, Pee Wee Russell and Edmond Hall. Pete Pesci, the manager, called me with the offer of a job when Hall left in 1956 to join Armstrong's All Stars. Pesci was a rough, tough guy who didn't know much about music, but he knew how to manage a nightclub efficiently. His staff of waiters were all Italians, some with rather limited command of the English language. They would come up to the bandstand with requests for songs while we were playing. I remember one night when a customer requested *Come rain or come shine*. The waiter's version was slightly different – "'A-comma rain' or 'A-comma shine' – either one." On another occasion a request for *That's a Plenty* became "That's a Parenti" – and that's what the tune was called from then on! During the 1950s, when entertaining on the company expense account was at its height and the tips were flowing, they would take a month off in the summer and return home to Italy. I'm sure they made a lot more money than we, the poor musicians, did.

It was a strange relationship between Pesci and Condon; possessing such different personalities, they were always falling out with one another. Pete used to take command whenever Eddie went on a drinking spree. Condon wouldn't show up for a couple of weeks and then he'd suddenly appear, all business-like. On one occasion Eddie was making a record of songs associated with Bix Beiderbecke. He wanted to use Bobby Hackett, always a great admirer of Bix, but Bobby was under contract to another label, so there was a problem. When Hackett mentioned this to Condon, Eddie replied, "No problem, Bobby – we'll just call you Pete Pesci." I remember the review in *Downbeat*: "Who is this Pete Pesci on cornet? He shows great promise."

At the time I joined, Wild Bill Davison would lead the band whenever Eddie was socializing with the customers or was absent on a spree. The other guys were Cutty Cutshall, George Wettling and Bob Casey. Bob left after he decided to move to Florida. The management, who were always trying to cut corners, decided that we should carry on without a bass. When business got a little better I recommended Leonard Gaskin, with whom I had done some record dates. It turned out to be a long run for Leonard – everybody liked him. I enjoyed working with that band. Wild Bill and I were good friends and George Wettling was a nice, easy-going guy except when he'd had too much drink; then he'd manage to make himself as objectionable as possible. He'd always call me the next day, and I'd hear this quiet, sheepish voice asking, "What did I do, Bob? What happened?" He couldn't remember a thing. George's wife was equally naughty when she had a few drinks too many. She was a big lady whom we nicknamed "Sea Biscuit" after the famous race-horse. She'd come sashaying into the club and start table hopping, telling everyone what a lousy drummer George was. Occasionally she would look up at the bandstand and shout various epithets at her husband, like, "Why don't you get off those drums, you bum?" Eventually there developed a hard and fast rule at the club that George could only have the job if his wife didn't come in.

We began to hear rumors that the English promoter Harold Davison was interested in taking the band to England. At that time, the British musicians' union applied a strict reciprocal rule regarding work permits, so, in order to accommodate us, Freddy Randall's band had to come to the States. Joe Glaser took care of the Stateside business. Although there was no demand for British bands and nobody had ever heard of Freddy Randall, Joe was able to arrange a tour because he was Joe Glaser. I'm sure it couldn't have been a happy experience for the British guys – Glaser sent them out to the boondocks, booking them anywhere just to comply with the exchange rule. They arrived in the States before we left and came in Condon's one night. We all felt sorry for them; they obviously realized that the only reason they were here was because six bodies had to be in the States while we were in England. As it turned out, our tour got off to a disastrous start. We took the overnight plane to Heathrow. Condon and Dick Gehman, who collaborated with Eddie on the book *We Called it Music*, had been up all night carousing and were somewhat the worse for wear. Eddie came off the plane with his hat askew, holding aloft a jug of whiskey. All the photographers and reporters were there, and when one guy asked Eddie how many quarts of whiskey he had drunk during his lifetime, Eddie's facetious answer was just what the question deserved – 6833 quarts! The next day all the London newspapers were full of reports of this American jazzman who had drunk 7000 quarts of whiskey, graphically illustrated by photos of Eddie at the top of the portable stairway, unshaven, hair flying in the wind and listing precariously to port (no pun intended).

We checked in at the Cumberland Hotel at Marble Arch, grabbed a little shut-eye and then went to a press conference at a restaurant in Soho at 5.00 p.m. Unfortunately Eddie arrived late. He still hadn't been to bed. He'd been met off the plane by his old friend Ernie Anderson and, together with Dick Gehman, they'd gone pub crawling, with the result that Condon was exhausted and suffering from jet-lag and a hangover. The reporters were put off by his decidedly diffident manner; he seemed to be dreadfully high-handed with them. As a result the British press, although often praising the band, had few kind words to say about its leader.

We started the tour in Scotland. We caught the Royal Scot to Glasgow sans Condon, who decided to stay overnight in London and fly up the next day. We arrived in Glasgow on a cold and misty morning. As we were having lunch at our hotel, Eddie breezed in with Anderson and Gehman in tow and ordered his "lunch" – his famous hangover cure, "the juice of two quarts of whiskey." We were sharing the tour with Humphrey Lyttelton, who, since I had last seen him at the Nice Festival, had become famous in England as a result of the trad boom. The audience, expertly warmed up by Humph's band, were in a receptive mood. When we came on they were puzzled by Eddie's casual manner and didn't really know what to make of him. He had always viewed the microphone as some sort of adversary to be approached warily, if at all, and in his advanced state of exhaustion his remarks, invariably witty, were unfortunately totally unintelligible to his Scottish audience. There were cries of, "Aw, play the guitar," and, "Why don't you go home and sober up?" The less knowledgeable fans in the audience had assumed they were going to hear a great guitar virtuoso. When, after the opening number, Eddie handed his guitar to Ernie Anderson standing in the wings, they were totally mystified. The band, having played together night after night at the club, was tight and cohesive and saved the day, but nevertheless our opening night left us with an uneasy feeling about the whole tour.

Our next concert was in Leicester, and it was there that an incident occurred that Eddie never allowed me to forget. After Lyttelton's opening 60-minute spot, the Condon band was introduced one at a time to the audience. When the name "Bob Wilber" was called out, nothing happened. There was backstage panic – I was nowhere to be found. The audience was beginning to get restless when to the rescue came Bruce Turner, Humph's clarinet player. While all this was taking place I was back at our hotel, fast asleep. We'd had a tiring trip by bus from Glasgow and I'd gone straight to bed, leaving instructions with the desk clerk to call me an hour before concert time. The girl forgot to call me. When I woke up and looked at my watch it was already past seven; the first performance of the double concert started at six! In a total panic, I jumped out of bed, pulled on my clothes, grabbed my horn, and ran downstairs to call a taxi. It should have come as no surprise to me to discover that taxi drivers are the same the world over.

"Take me to the concert."

"Which concert, mate?"

"The Eddie Condon concert."

"The Eddie who concert?"

"The Eddie Condon band, from New York."

"Where is this 'ere Condon bloke playing?"

"I don't know, but surely you must know."

By trial and error, we eventually arrived at the concert hall just as the band was about to go into *That's a Plenty*, our big finale. Now that band contained some of the fastest living and hardest drinking legends of jazz, such as George Wettling, Wild Bill Davison, Cutty Cutshall, and Gene Schroeder, not to mention Eddie himself. It appealed to Eddie's sense of humor to recall in later years that the only member of the group who ever missed a concert was the young, serious and sober Bob Wilber. Bruce Turner, however, was a capable deputy. In fact he was the main topic of interest in the newspaper reviews the next day. I got to know Bruce quite well on the tour. He had been playing dance music on the boats in order to come to New York to study with Lee Konitz. When he was warming up his alto in the dressing room, he sounded just like Konitz, but on the stage his clarinet sounded like Edmond Hall, and his alto like Johnny Hodges. Finally I said to him, "Bruce, I don't understand. You sound just like Lee Konitz backstage but on stage it's all Hall and Rabbit. You're a great musician but I haven't heard Bruce Turner yet."

"Dad," he said, "you wouldn't want to hear that!"

The tour continued with concerts in Edinburgh, Manchester, Bristol, Plymouth and, finally, London. While checking into the hotel in Bristol, a bunch of us were getting our room keys at the reception. The hotel lobby had a tiled floor, and as we were standing there we became aware of the sound of water hitting a stone surface. We turned round and were horrified to see Wettling standing by the elevator, relieving himself. Humph, with great presence of mind, realized the receptionist would see what was going on and have us all thrown out. Leaning across the desk and spreading his arms apart so that his coat obscured the view, he engaged the gentleman's attention with a long, involved query delivered in a loud voice. Meanwhile George concluded his ablutions, got into the elevator and disappeared. We never did find out whether the hotel staff solved the mystery of that pool of water by the elevator door.

The final concert in London at the Queen Elizabeth Hall was a great success. Afterwards Humphrey Lyttelton wrote a summary of the tour in the *Melody Maker* and, with his permission, I am reproducing his article.

One of the advantages of touring with an American band is that one automatically receives all the press cuttings relating to their performance. The comments on the Eddie Condon tour have been richly entertaining. One theme runs through almost all of them – Eddie's own somewhat nomadic role on the stage. As one Scottish commentator chose to put it – "Eddie Condon's All Star Band, brought with it a dapper little mascot – Eddie Condon."

Needless to say, the now legendary "Silent Guitar" caused a certain amount of comment. Some writers seem to have acquired the notion – from what source I cannot think – that Eddie Condon came here as the world's greatest guitarist. No one who has read Eddie's own autobiography, *We Called it Music* will imagine that this description found any favour with him. Nothing could be more devastating than his own self-deflation when referring to a famous Louis Armstrong session – "They let me sit in a corner and hold my banjo."

According to Dick Gehman, his friend and collaborator in the book *Eddie Condon's Treasury of Jazz*, he deals crushingly with any heavy-handed attempts at flattery from effusive customers at the Condon Club. If someone tells him how effective his guitar is in the rhythm section, he is apt to give him his stoniest glare (the one without the twinkle), and say, "I knew the whisky was strong in here – but not that strong." It must be said too, that when he put down his guitar after two or three numbers, not to take it up again, there were no complaints from the rest of the band.

Opinions about his role as compere and organiser are mixed. In many places, where he inadvisedly spurned the microphone, his wisecracks fell on the stoniest ground. A pity, because when he was on form and when he found a good-humoured member of the audience who could act as a stooge, he was very funny. Even his routine announcements were quite unpredictable. One fact which, by virtue of his permanently belligerent, Cagney-ish expression, might have escaped some observers is that he remained, even in the face of ill-natured heckling, permanently good-humoured. On one unfortunate occasion, some members of the audience threw pennies onto the stage, and one actually whizzed past Eddie's nose, causing him to recoil. Straight away he walked up to the mike. "You shouldn't throw those things, you know. You're liable to hit someone in the eye and knock his teeth out."

Summing up, one could fairly say that those writers who knew their jazz accepted and appreciated Eddie's role as master of ceremonies.

The most receptive and appreciative places were London and Edinburgh, from which you may draw your own conclusions. Comments about the rest of the band varied. Once again, total ignorance begat a certain amount of disappointment. The West Country critic who asserted that Condon has "long preached purity in traditional jazz" (did you ever hear such rubbish!) naturally went away disgruntled. "All we got was a 'pop' concert", he grumbled. On the other hand, the music appears to have had the most curious effect on one listener North of the Border. He said in relation to Cutty, "*Sentimental Journey* featured ex-Goodman bandsman Cutty Cutshall. The smooth, liquid flow from his tenderly handled trombone crystallised in the Cutshall-created cathedral chill to form the bluest of blue stalactites above a hushed audience's head." I must say I liked Kingsley Amis in *The Observer* about Wild Bill, whose cornet "constantly seemed about to produce not just notes but a wisp of black smoke or a shower of gravel." I am less enthusiastic about his school-boy assessment of Bob Wilber – "whom any half-dozen British practitioners might have replaced with advantage." The spoilsport curtails our merriment by withholding their names. I know at least two eminent British practitioners who agree with me that Wilber was the most exciting and impressive musician in the group.

The visit to England was a very satisfying experience for me. I had always been something of an Anglophile, but the tour left me with a warm feeling for the people, not only the musicians but the ordinary men and women I came in contact with every day. In particular, the women, who seemed to relate to men in a courteous and respectful way, appealed to me. There was something very feminine and sexy about it in contrast to the hard-boiled "Don't mess with me, Buster" aura that so many American women exude. I couldn't completely pin it down, but I knew there was something different going on and I liked it. The English women made me feel that I was really a man, and in a very real sense it set the stage for the relationship with the Sheffield lass who was to become my wife.

When we got back to New York I recorded an album with Eddie titled *The Roaring Twenties*. It was basically the Condon house band, except that in some numbers Billy Butterfield replaced Wild Bill and Vic Dickenson took Cutty's place. It was recorded at the big 30th Street Columbia Studios and was a fun session. At the end of *That's a Plenty* you'll hear a group of four-bar breaks by the front-line guys, with the rest of the band coming and riding it out. George knew that Eddie would point to him for the last break, and he was ready. When setting up his drums for the session he'd noticed a set of timpani sitting nearby in the corner, so when Eddie gave him the nod George jumped up from his stool and ran across to do the break on the kettle drum. It broke everybody up. In fact on the end of the tune you can hear somebody laughing: it's James Jones, the author of *From Here to Eternity*, whom Condon saw at the club the night before and invited to the session. Eddie was in great spirits that day. The whiskey was being passed round and he was making all kinds of humorous comments that came across on the record. For instance, while Vic was taking a solo, Eddie solemnly announced, "Victor – on Columbia." During a bass solo on *Wolverine Blues* you'll hear him say, "Bob Wilber, take that cup of coffee away." My next date at the 30th Street Studios was when Columbia Records asked Wild Bill to do a follow-up to the album he had made with strings. Bill's idea was to use the Condon house band, backed by strings, playing beautiful arrangements by Deane Kincaide. It was titled *With Strings Attached*, and it was the first time I'd recorded with strings. For a jazz man, to feel that warm cushion of violins, violas and cellos behind you can be quite thrilling. My own playing gives one a glimpse of the metamorphosis of my musical thinking since the Bechet days. There are some pretty moments, but it all sounds very tentative – I still had a lot of wandering in the wilderness before me.

Eddie loved the atmosphere of his club. When it was downtown in Greenwich Village, he lived on the North side of Washington Square and walked to work in five minutes. When New York University bought up all the property in the area, Condon's had to move. Eddie and Pete spent weeks trying to find a suitable location uptown and eventually settled on the Hotel Sutton on East 56th Street, where Turk Murphy had run an ill-fated venture for a short while. Turk had found some angel who had a grandiose scheme of opening up clubs all around the country using Turk's name. The idea was that Turk's band would be continually touring from one club to another. The scheme was over-ambitious and soon collapsed leaving large debts outstanding. Eddie and Pete paid off the bills owed by the ill-fated Bourbon Street and took it over for the new club. The original Condon's had had fantastic acoustics. The distance from the bar to the stand was at least 150 feet and you could stand at that bar and hear perfectly. The only amplification was a mike on the piano. The room at the Hotel Sutton, on the other hand, turned out to be very dead acoustically. It was completely carpeted and there was no resonance at all. In all the years I played there I was never happy with the place. It always seemed as if you were fighting to project your sound. You blew your lungs out but the sound just reached the end of your horn and dropped to the floor. Over the years Eddie began to lose interest, and became less and less involved in the club and in the music scene as a whole. The nature of the club had begun to change when Eddie's style of jazz ceased to be the rage with the college kids. The place started to become a hangout for all sorts of people from the sports world – players, reporters, announcers. They were encouraged by Pesci, who was a great sports fan and loved the idea of having all these well-known golfers and football players in the club. It also became a hangout for politicians. I remember Bobby Kennedy was there one night with a bunch of his cohorts. They set up a big table at the back of the room with four or five telephones, and throughout the whole evening they were busy wheeling and dealing, totally oblivious to the music, while we were blowing our guts out on the stand. And then there were the women. I began to notice all the exceedingly beautiful women who seemed to be at the bar every night, and it didn't take me long to realize that there was a high-priced call-girl operation going on. All very convenient, with the hotel upstairs.

In the early 1960s the Twist swept New York and jazz went further into the doldrums. Pesci's wife was crazy about the Twist, and she was always telling the musicians that jazz was dead. She finally convinced Pete that this was the coming thing, so they removed tables from in front of the stand and put in a dance floor. They had our band, led by Max Kaminsky, playing Twist music, and pretty soon all the call girls and the football players were twisting like crazy. The whole character of the place changed dramatically within a short period of time. Eddie had been away from the club sick for about six weeks, and it was on New Year's Eve that he decided to come by and check things out. He had his own set route to enter the club that never varied – in through the hotel entrance, across the lobby, into the kitchen past the cash register and out into the club alongside the bandstand. I remember glancing down and seeing Eddie standing there, his mouth wide open, with a look of utter bewilderment and shock on his face as he gazed out at the bedlam – streamers, balloons, whistles, paper hats, call girls and football players twisting away, the musicians blowing their lungs out on some rock song, with yours truly honking away on tenor. He thought he was in the wrong place. What had happened while he was gone? After the winter of the Twist Condon's rapidly went downhill. The following Christmas Eve at midnight there wasn't a single customer. There wasn't any point in staying open, but we couldn't leave without Pesci's permission. He was off partying somewhere. Finally he called in and we musicians staggered wearily out of the club at 1.30, not having played a single note.

Some of the jobs that Eddie had over the years almost defy belief. When Paul Whiteman was having trouble with Bix because of his drinking problem, he engaged Eddie (of all people) to try and keep Bix on the straight and narrow path. Similarly, Eddie was hired as an extra banjo player on the Fats Waller *Minor Drag* date. His job was to produce a stone-cold sober Fats at the studio at 9.30 the following morning. Eddie spent the whole night making the round of the clubs with Fats, just to keep track of him. He got Fats to the studio on time, but what a state they were both in! Then there was the occasion quite a few years later when Eddie was in hospital with troubles caused by alcohol. His wife Phyllis, thinking to shock him out of his need to drink, went to see him with a list of all the jazzmen who had died from booze. Eddie surveyed the list, looked at Phyllis, and said, "Not a bad group, but it wouldn't work – no drummer!" Later, when I was with the World's Greatest Jazz Band, George Wein presented a concert at Carnegie Hall with our band and a group led by Eddie in conjunction with the Newport Jazz Festival. It was a disastrous concert for us. Yank Lawson was greeted backstage by a bunch of his English fans, who presented him with a bottle of 100% proof vodka, and innumerable toasts to Anglo-American friendship followed. Billy Butterfield had flown up from Florida on a flight that featured free drinks, and he was poured off the plane by a relieved stewardess. The result was that our trumpet section was almost non-existent. Lee Wiley came out of retirement, and also on the bill were Teddy Wilson, J. C. Higginbotham and Joe Thomas. Eddie had been ill and not active for some time. As a result Phyllis was extremely nervous, fearing that Eddie might not be up to leading the group. As a form of insurance she brought along a large thermos filled with vodka. As it turned out, Eddie had no problem at all. He led the band like an angel and was the perfect Master of Ceremonies, but Phyllis was so nervous that by the end of the concert she had emptied the thermos herself and was smashed!

Eddie was a free spirit, without any overblown ideas of his own importance. He didn't like the negotiating and business side of music and as a result he sometimes let us down. He was, however, a marvelous leader on stage, with impeccable taste and a great ear for the good things of jazz. He had the ability to put together splendidly compatible players and make great records. His contribution to jazz, particularly in the United States, has been unjustly ignored in recent years, but in the long term the name of Eddie Condon will be very important. He created a school that was basically inspired by the great musical happenings in Chicago in the 1920s and, out of that, developed a style which perhaps reached its apex in the late 1930s and early 1940s. It wasn't dixieland, but a free-wheeling form of small-band jazz that had a distinctive sound all of its own. Neither was it an all-white movement. Eddie had his favorites, both black and white. He loved Hot Lips Page, who appeared in many of the Town Hall concerts, Bechet, Sid Catlett, Billie Holiday and James P. Johnson. It would seem from his records that the groups were predominantly white, but most of the players who understood and fitted in with the style just happened to be white. His records stand as a testimony to a marvelous style, and Eddie was the one who put it together.

Although I enjoyed working with Eddie, I felt when I joined him in 1956 that it was a step back musically for me. By then the style had passed its great creative peak. Inevitably, it had become formularized, which is something that seems to happen to all creative movements as time passes.

Eddie had a long fight with bone cancer, a particularly painful disease, and the word got around that he had not long to live. Ralph Sutton, who was in town and staying with me, went with me to the hospital. We entered his room and there was Eddie, all skin and bones, unshaven and with tubes attached to him. We didn't know whether he was just lying there with his eyes closed or whether he was unconscious. I very quietly said, "Hi, Eddie. It's Bob and Ralph."

Eddie opened one eye, looked at us and said, "You know, oblivion isn't so bad."

Two days later he died.

SEVEN

Clarinet à la King

After my two years with Condon I got a job in the fall of 1957 working with Bobby Hackett at the Henry Hudson Hotel. The hotel was adjacent to the Colisseum, a large new convention center on 57th Street, which had just opened. The hotel management, sensing the opportunity to revive their fading fortunes, decided to open up a long-unused ballroom with a dinner and dancing policy. Hackett, who had been working on staff at WABC in comparative anonymity, had suddenly shot into the spotlight with the success of Jackie Gleason's *Music for Lovers* record. The album, which featured Bobby's horn over a background of syrupy strings, was the biggest selling LP ever released at that time, with the result that Bobby, who since the late 1930s had been a well-known name in the jazz world, was now a pop star.

In 1939 the Rockwell–O'Keefe organization had decided to launch Bobby in the role of bandleader. He gathered together all his old pals, Eddie Condon, Pee Wee Russell, Brad Gowans, George Wettling and Max Kaminsky. From a musical point of view, they were good choices, but business-wise, he was just asking for trouble. All these guys, including Bobby himself, were some of the hardest drinkers in the world of jazz. The band was totally disorganized, a financial disaster. Glenn Miller came to Bobby's rescue by giving him a job in his band on guitar. Glenn used to give Bobby $50 spending money each week, and the rest went to paying off the debts; it was hard living on 50 bucks, but it did get Bobby out of hot water. He also got opportunities to play cornet with the band. On one occasion, when they were playing at some small-town dance-hall, the ballroom manager came up to Glenn and said, "If you don't stop the guitarist fooling around with that bugle, I swear I'll fire the whole goddam band."

Bobby was a lovely man, a very gentle soul who had nothing bad to say about anybody. Even when a friend, exasperated by his perpetual good nature, asked him what he thought about Adolf Hitler, Bobby paused for a moment and replied in his deep voice, "Well, you gotta admit he was the best in his line." (!) He had a zany sense of humor, a funny way of looking at life, but also a definite paranoid streak. The two great dangers as far as he was concerned were the Mafia and Communism. He always used to refer to the *New York Times* as the "Uptown Daily Worker." For many years he was afraid to visit Europe because it was too close to Russia and the Communists. He was a New Englander by birth, born in Providence, Rhode Island, and the one place he loved more than anywhere else was Cape Cod. He always had a dream of setting up a deal whereby he would have the house band at one of the places on the Cape and never again have to leave. Unfortunately, he was not a good businessman. He always seemed to get in with the wrong partners; inevitably things went wrong and Bobby would have to go back on the road to retrieve his fortunes.

He was a small, frail man, and he had to gear his playing to his physical limitations. Although he worshiped Louis Armstrong, he just didn't have the physical strength to play a trumpet with Louis's big, commanding sound, so he played it in a very gentle way. It was a small sound in person, limited in volume, but on record it sounded big and fat. There was a unique fluidity to his playing and, coupled with his flawless harmonic ear, it enabled him to flow in and out of the changes with amazing ease and grace. I found that playing with Bobby was a whole learning process – he was a teacher without knowing it. A consummate musician who paid meticulous attention to all the details in the music, the subtleties of harmony and the little melodic twists, he believed in respecting the composer's intentions. He used to say, "The guy wrote it this way and that's the way we oughta play it. Before you make your own variations give the people the original version." He certainly taught me to respect the song I was playing.

The band Bobby led at the Voyager Room in the Henry Hudson Hotel in 1956–7 was an interesting one. Instead of a string bass it had John Dengler on tuba and bass saxophone. John walked up and down the tuba like a four-in-a-bar bass, and he was very good at it, able to grab a breath without destroying the line. There was a lot of doubling in that band. As well as the two previously mentioned instruments, John played a quite respectable cornet. Dick Cary was the pianist and doubled on trumpet and peck horn, a small version of the baritone horn in the tuba family. Ernie Caceres, the great baritone sax player, doubled on clarinet, and Tommy Gwaltney, who was basically a vibraphone player, also doubled on clarinet. Throw in Bobby Hackett's trumpet and there was a tremendous capacity for different sounds, allied to very adventurous writing by Dick Cary. When everybody was playing their horn doubles in a concerted ensemble, drummer Buzzy Drootin had his work cut out keeping the rhythm going. I was the replacement for Tommy Gwaltney, who left to work at a club in Washington. It was not until after Bobby had offered me the job, and I had accepted, that he sprung on me the fact that I would have to play vibes. I hadn't really appreciated just how important the vibraphone sound was to Bobby – he wanted it in place of strings for the ballads. When I told him I'd never played the instrument, he told me not to worry and suggested I take a few lessons from Freddy Albright, one of the top percussionists in New York. It was a crash-course which taught me the bare essentials, just enough to scrape by. With Freddy I was studying on a full regulation keyboard, and when Tommy left he naturally took his vibes with him. The only vibraphone available for me was one belonging to Dengler, who prided himself on having at least one of practically every instrument ever invented. Whereas the usual vibraphone goes down to F below middle C, John's had a cut-down keyboard that ended on middle C. On the opening night I was playing this unfamiliar instrument. We were on the air and I was sight-reading the arrangements with my eyes glued to the music. I went for a note below middle C but hit only air. With nothing to stop it, my left arm continued to descend and I almost fell off the edge of the bandstand.

I was amused years later to read a review in the *Melody Maker* of an airshot recording by the band, which said, "Wilber's vibraphone is less authoritative than Tommy Gwaltney's." Positively the understatement of the year! We used to do things like Monk's *Off Minor* and way-out things by Dick Cary, who was very adventurous in his harmonic approach. He used to listen to a lot of Stravinsky and Bartók, and incorporated their ideas in his voicings. I did some writing for the band, too – some Ellington-type originals. There was a health club at the hotel with a swimming pool, massage room and sauna. Every Tuesday Dizzy Gillespie came in for a swim followed by dinner, and afterwards he'd sit in with the band, more often than not on piano, which he played in the same quirky fashion as his horn but with fewer notes. Listen to his piano on Parker's *Billie's Bounce* and *Now's the time* – that's how Dizzy sounded. On one memorable evening we had Coleman Hawkins as guest. He'd been working at the Metropole, where his horn was stolen from the band room. He could always get a brand-new tenor from Selmer anytime he asked, but to replace his old Link mouthpiece was another matter. The Berg Larsen he was trying was giving him problems, and occasionally a loud squeak would mar his usual cavernous tone, but I didn't care. To be on the same bandstand as one of my idols was a thrill. It took me back to that night when Denny and I missed the last train and wound up at Kelly's Stables listening to *Body and Soul* at two in the morning.

The job at the Henry Hudson Hotel finished in March 1958 and, after one final week at Storyville in Boston, the group disbanded. The big convention trade the owners had hoped for at the hotel had not materialized, and except for the weekends we were playing to a sea of white table-cloths. Joe Glaser, Bobby's agent, wanting to capitalize on Jonah Jones's great success, was sending out trumpet players with three rhythm everywhere. Hackett was perfect for this commercial formula, and so a noble experiment in jazz ended. Back in New York one day, I got a call from Jay Feingold, Benny Goodman's manager, asking me if I was interested in a band that Benny was putting together for a package tour that included Dakota Staton and the Ahmad Jamal Trio. He said Goodman would like to hear me play, so I went along with my tenor to the Carrol Studios on 41st and Ninth Avenue, where Benny was holding auditions and rehearsals for a band of five saxes, four trumpets, three trombones and rhythm. There was a fair amount of tension in the air. A number of us were auditioning that day and you felt you were on trial. When it was my turn to sit in the section, Benny pointed at me to solo, and seemed pleased with what he heard. He kept noodling on his clarinet and leading the band, continually sifting through all the musicians there. Teddy Wilson and Cootie Williams were in the studio; I had the impression that Benny was auditioning them too!

I was in a state of awe at the prospect of this job with the legendary Benny Goodman, and afterwards, when Jay took me aside to tell me that I had the job, I was elated. He gave me a full rundown of the rehearsal dates and the tour schedule together with the road-sheet, and for the next three weeks we were involved in intensive rehearsals. Benny was relaxed, obviously enjoying the idea of putting a big band together again and intrigued with the new arrangements he had commissioned from Bill Holman, Shorty Rogers and Gil Evans. Bill had done a chart on *After you've gone* which sounded more like Kenton than Goodman. Nevertheless, Benny enjoyed the new sounds and worked hard to get the charts right. He seemed in an affable mood, particularly with me. Some of the other guys fared less well, however, and I began to appreciate why the legendary "Goodman Ray" – Benny's blank, unsympathetic stare of disapproval – had always had a demoralizing effect on his sidemen. The only two guys who had worked with Benny before were Roy Burns on drums and Turk Van Lake on guitar. The lead alto was Herb Geller and second alto was Vinnie Dean; both were ex-Kentonites. My fellow tenor was George "Babe" Clarke and the baritone was my old friend Pepper Adams, well known by then for his work in the bop field. In the brass section were Rex Peer on trombone, John Frosk, a powerhouse lead trumpeter, and Taft Jordan, who had started out with Chick Webb and was with Duke in the 1940s. Scott LaFaro, who later became such an influential player with Bill Evans, was on bass. It was an interesting mixture of old and modern styles, racially balanced and with no really big names. I think that Benny had had such an unfortunate experience with the all-star band he had put together in the early 1950s for the disastrous tour opposite Louis Armstrong, that he was happy to have eager, young unknowns who were excited and thrilled to be playing with him.

So one sunny fall morning we all met at the Hotel President on West 48th Street. Parked there was a Greyhound bus with the words "Benny Goodman and his Orchestra" emblazoned along the sides. Off we went. Our first concert was in Troy and afterwards, in an unusual display of generosity, Benny took the whole band to one of the leading restaurants in Albany, where, in a private room, we were served beautiful food and wine with recordings of Bach and Mozart being played in the background. A pattern was established on that first night in Albany whereby the band would stay in one hotel, invariably a good one but not the best, while Benny would stay in the top hotel. We traveled by bus but never accompanied by Benny, and we really never thought anything about it, just taking it for granted that when we reached our next destination Benny would be there in his dressing room. On that opening night in Troy we played all the new arrangements and they were received with polite applause, if not wild enthusiasm. The second concert was in Rutland, Vermont, and I remember it vividly. It was the first time Benny had played there since his halcyon days of the late 1930s. During the sound check an elderly couple came up to the bandstand and asked us, "Where's Harry? What's happened to Gene? Isn't Jess playing tonight?" We played all the new arrangements in the first half and the audience was absolutely stunned – they were expecting the Fletcher Henderson sound and what they heard was so totally different. The applause was lukewarm at best. Benny was obviously upset and when he came off the stage he growled, "These goddammed modern arrangements. That's what's killing the music." He ordered Jay Feingold to take them all out of the book and we opened the second half with *Don't be that way*. The applause was deafening and Benny was happy once more. All those expensive new arrangements we had rehearsed so carefully were never to be played again. That night I learned how important the roar of the crowd could be to a big star.

I began to have more personal contact with Benny as he became conscious of the fact that I was a clarinet player. He used to invite me into his dressing room to ask about reeds. The whole floor would be strewn with them. He would open up a box before the first half, select one reed and throw the rest away, repeating the process before the second half. I found this incredible because he would never give a reed a chance to break in. He just consumed them like cornflakes. Vido Musso once told me how Benny was always saying, "Hey, Vido, let me try your reed." He would put Vido's reed on his mouthpiece and say, "This is a good one," and keep it. When he called a number that had clarinet parts for the sax section, Vido wouldn't have a reed. Benny, seeing that Vido wasn't playing and forgetting that he had taken Musso's reed, would give his hapless victim "the ray." After this happened a few times Vido got pissed off and decided to fix Benny. One night, when Benny wasn't looking, he took off the barrel of his clarinet and switched it with the one from Benny's horn. Benny never noticed and kept on playing, so the next night Vido switched the top joints. Benny played on. The bottom joint then followed, and it finally ended up with Vido having Benny's horn. After a few nights Vido, his revenge complete, told Benny good-naturedly what he had done. With any other sideman instant dismissal would have followed, but Benny, who liked Vido to the point where he tolerated Musso's almost total lack of reading ability, thought the whole episode was a marvelous joke and laughed uproariously.

Our tour gradually headed down South. Although this was 1958, there was still a high degree of segregation in that part of the country. The band bus carried all the musicians, as well as Dakota Staton and her trio and Ahmad Jamal and his trio. At the various rest stops we made, it was clear from the hostile looks we received from the southern Whites that they didn't approve of what they saw. When we stopped overnight, we first of all had to pull into the black section and leave off all the black musicians and singers at some funky, rundown hotel, while the rest of us went across town to some better-class hotel. Benny was in a relaxed mood, enjoying the music. He seemed to be emerging from a long period of intense concentration on classical music and wanting to recapture the raw, hot quality of his 1930s playing. He particularly liked to stretch out on *King Porter Stomp*, some nights playing ten or more choruses in a row. Benny had an amusing way of first introducing the sextet and then beckoning to so many of us to come down front that the "sextet" would end up consisting of nine or ten musicians, all lined up across the front of the stage. We did catch a few glimpses, however, of the darker side of his nature as, for instance, the night when we were on stage and Benny was counting off the next number. When Benny counted, he took a long time to get the tempo exactly where he thought it should be, so there was quite a long, almost embarrassing, silence. As he was almost ready to count off he knocked over his music stand with the bell of his clarinet, and his conductor parts went flying all over the stage. Benny just stood there. He never spoke a word but beckoned imperiously to Jay Feingold, who was standing in the wings. Jay hurried out and, scrambling all over the stage on his knees, picked up the music, sorted it out, and put it back on the stand. All the time Benny just stood there with his clarinet under his arm picking his nose. Meanwhile you could hear a pin drop – the audience sat in stunned silence, as embarrassed as we musicians sitting on stage were.

The *esprit de corps* of the band was very good. The sax section frequently got together in its own time to rehearse parts that were giving us difficulty. The bus was comfortable and, with the exception of the black players, we stayed at first-class hotels. We had an occasional night off to off-set a case of the "roadies" – a musicians' term for the numbing fatigue that usually sets in on a tour of one-nighters. The show opened with the Ahmad Jamal Trio, followed by Dakota Staton, and then the big band played after the intermission. I enjoyed Jamal's trio, in particular the wonderful bass of Israel Crosby, whose roots went back to the early years of the swing era when he played and recorded with Benny and Gene Krupa. The drummer, Vernel Fournier, was from New Orleans and had some of Zutty Singleton and Baby Dodds in his playing. The big band provided the background for Dakota Staton. It was the only time on the whole tour when I had a clarinet solo, and I used to wait every night for that one opportunity. On our nights off I'd join the black players and we'd head for the black section of town known as "Soulville," where we'd "scoff up a storm" with good southern cooking and then enquire about a club. There always seemed to be one spot in every town where we could sit in. The sitters-in invariably included Pepper Adams and Scott LaFaro, who always astounded the local musicians with their incredible technique on their respective instruments. I was keenly interested in joining in, because I'd been associated with traditional jazz for so long that I wanted to show that I could play in such company. During one stop-over in Indiana, we found a little after-hours club that had a trio of exceptional musicians, completely unknown outside of local circles. They were the Montgomery brothers – Wes, Buddy and Monk. We were particularly knocked out by Wes's guitar with those unusual octave passages that became his trademark.

I had never played in a big band before, except in the army. The tour was a great thrill and a learning experience for me, not only to be playing all the things I had loved as a kid but also to be able to observe Benny close up. I was under Benny's wing. He obviously liked me, but I didn't feel as secure as I'd felt with Sidney – Benny was so unpredictable! He seemed to be striving to recapture some of the drive and fire of his earlier playing and also trying to move away from the influence of Reginald Kell, which had changed not only his concept but also his actual physical way of playing the clarinet. For a number of years Benny had been studying with Kell, who was a very influential, albeit controversial, classical clarinet soloist from England. He had a very distinctive way of playing, with an extremely voluptuous vibrato and a very romantic, almost feminine, approach to the instrument. It was very beautiful when Kell did it, but when Benny tried to emulate him, it just didn't sound like Benny. Goodman had always had that gutsy Chicago edge to his playing, the thing that Tesch and Pee Wee had. It had always been an important part of his style, so when he changed to the mellow, almost effete, sound he'd developed with Kell, it was beautiful but it wasn't Benny. Kell also got him to change the angle of his fingers on the keys and to change his embouchure from single lip to double lip. With the double-lip embouchure the upper lip is folded over the top teeth, whereas with the single-lip embouchure the teeth touch the mouthpiece; theoretically, the double-lip embouchure opens the throat and makes a larger chamber in the mouth in order to produce a bigger, rounder and more mellow sound. It works fine in classical music, where the player is sitting and can support the bell of the clarinet on his knee. Without the teeth on the mouthpiece, however, there is no firm grip, so when Benny used the double embouchure when playing jazz and moving around in front of the band it just didn't work. It was an altogether too delicate way of playing and Benny was never really able to adapt it to jazz. His attempt to combine the delicate approach of Kell with the hard-driving style he'd had since his youth in Chicago was a failure. As a result Goodman lost a lot of confidence in himself. Benny finally realized the Kell influence was detrimental to his playing and tried to do something about it. Throughout the tour he was continually changing from one embouchure to the other, trying to get back to his old way of playing. In truth he never did. To listen to the remakes of *Clarinet à la King*, *Mission to Moscow* and *Benny Rides Again* we recorded at the end of the tour and compare them with the versions from the 1940s is instructive. We hear the tragedy of a great artist who got perhaps as close to perfection as anyone in jazz and then lost it. Certainly the old bravado returned, but never the steely perfection that had been his hallmark. Many people blame Kell for ruining Goodman's playing, but Kell always maintained that he told Benny, "Don't try to play like I do. You're Benny Goodman."

I enjoyed working with him. I was somebody who could listen to him play and tell him his reed sounded bad without having my head chopped off. I wanted to study him and figure out the secret of his magic. He had this fantastic, natural genius which he didn't really understand himself. From his first studio recording of *Clarinetitis* in 1929 at the age of 17 to the incredible perfection of the 1945 sextet version of *After you've gone*, Goodman never turned in a bad performance, at least on record anyway. He had that marvelous relaxed way with a pop tune, indeed with everything he played in the swing era. He could translate whatever came into his head directly to the clarinet. He breathed and talked on the instrument to the point where the clarinet seemed to disappear and all you heard was Benny. His best playing was done when he was totally unconscious of trying to play, when his whole being was motivated by the feeling of swing. If the band was swinging, Benny would start playing and it would happen – the phenomenon that disciples of Zen have attempted to describe in writing whereby the conscious mind ceases to control (or interfere with, as they would say) the flow of mental and physical activity, resulting in a perfect symbiosis of thought and action. To achieve this state of perfection in jazz requires musicians who are compatible, and Benny, always conscious of this, picked his sidemen with loving care. In the 1940s Mel Powell inspired him tremendously, and in the old band, when Gene Krupa and Jess Stacy got a rolling kind of groove going on the medium-tempo things, Benny responded with the most lyrical playing ever heard on the clarinet. Charlie Christian was another source of inspiration and, indeed, Benny's first meeting with Christian was a perfect example. John Hammond had discovered the brilliant young guitarist from Oklahoma and had been trying to persuade Benny to audition him, but Benny was not being very co-operative, particularly after being told that Christian played electric guitar. Eventually, in desperation, John sneaked Charlie onto the bandstand one night. When Benny stepped out, he was taken aback to see sitting amongst his immaculately dressed musicians a figure in purple trousers and yellow shirt, wearing a stetson hat. Benny had no option but to start the performance, so he gave the downbeat on *Rose Room*. Charlie's propelling beat and fantastic ear for melody soon had him joining in and matching Goodman stride for stride. It's on record that *Rose Room* that night lasted for 40 minutes, with Benny on a real high. The partnership of Goodman and Christian, which was tragically cut short by the guitarist's death from tuberculosis, lasted less than three years but produced the most swinging performances of Benny's entire career.

I'd behaved myself on tour. I'd done nothing to incur Benny's displeasure. I was just a tenor player in the sax section who was given an occasional nod from Benny for a brief solo. It had been a safe harbor where I could do my work and not be exposed or have too much responsibility. All I had to do was to play my part well, keep my nose clean, and stay out of trouble. I was never subjected to any of Benny's eccentricities. I was always afraid of something like that happening, so I kept out of his way and gave him no cause for venting his spleen on me. As a result my relationship with him was always a cordial one. I had a great desire to do some arrangements for the band; I wanted to write beautiful charts like the Eddie Sauter and Mel Powell things. In my heart I knew I had the ability, but I didn't have the confidence and couldn't persuade myself my efforts would be anywhere near as good.

I felt very grateful when, at the end of the tour, Benny indicated that he would like me to work with him again, although nothing specific was lined up. Meanwhile it was back to the New York freelance grind, chasing around for odd jobs here and there, picking up the scraps left by the older, established clarinet players. I always got depressed when I returned from those tours on the road and found my old problems waiting for me. I was angry with myself for my inability to go out and force my way on the New York music scene as I had done in the Wildcat days. I was angry with the fans who had deserted me when I had moved away from Bechet in order to find myself. New York was my Nemesis, and I was still looking for scapegoats to blame for my inability to crack the Big Apple.

I suppose it was a form of escapism from the harsh reality of the city that prompted me to move out to Rockland County, where I bought a nice house surrounded by lawns and trees. I borrowed the money to purchase the property from my mother. Although it started out as a loan, it ended up as a gift because of my inability to keep up the repayments. It was so ironical that, although I had rebelled against the wealth and privilege of Scarsdale, it kept coming back to bale me out of my difficulties. Financial aid was gratefully received, but it did nothing to bolster my self-esteem. I sank deeper and deeper into this fantasy world, living the life of the country squire but without having any solid position in my career. Incredibly for an American boy, I'd never learned to drive a car as a teenager. The war-time shortage of gasoline coupled with my lack of confidence in my ability conspired effectively in this regard. It was essential to have a car in suburbia, so in preparation for the move I took some lessons at a driving school and passed my test on the second attempt. My first car was a Volkswagen that my parents had purchased in Germany and brought back to the States as a gift. I'd always liked foreign cars, and after driving the VW into the ground with the countless trips to and from New York City I bought a Peugeot and, a few years later, a Volvo. I even indulged myself in a second car, a huge eleven-seater Land Rover. In a way the four-wheel drive vehicle was a necessity, for I lived down a long country lane which passed through a farm and then crossed a stream onto my property. The stream was a catch-all for the surrounding hills and during heavy rains would flood its banks. This, coupled with the snowdrifts which I had to plough through after a blizzard, made my country hide-away inaccessible at times except with a four-wheel drive vehicle. The Land Rover which had already seen a lot of wear when I purchased it, was constantly breaking down and consumed gasoline at an incredible rate. Nevertheless it was a prestige symbol to me. It made me feel that I was somebody, a feeling that I wasn't getting from the music business.

In early 1959 I got another call from Jay Feingold. The band was reassembling for another tour, this time in the Northeast, but reaching out into the Midwest as well. There were a few new faces in the band, including Russ Freeman on piano, but by now I was a solid, established member. It was just the band with no supporting acts. The vocalist was Betty Bennett, a good singer, but it soon became obvious that Benny was not happy with her segment of the program, in which she did some of her own songs with just the rhythm section. It wasn't Benny's usual format for a singer, and in his own mind it seemed to over-emphasize her position with the band. When we played at the University of Iowa, a very good close-harmony college group comprising three guys and a girl was given a spot on the bill. A few nights later at our next venue we were amazed to see this girl backstage sans her male associates. In the first half of the show that night Betty did her usual solo spot. In the second half Benny introduced the girl from Iowa, who came on and sang a couple of songs. At the end of the concert Benny acknowledged the applause, brought out the girl for her share, but omitted to call Betty. This became a regular routine until eventually Betty did what any normal person would have done in the circumstances. After her solo stint she changed into street clothes and went back to the hotel. What, she thought, was the point of hanging around if Benny didn't call her out for a bow? The final concert of the tour was in Pittsburgh, at the Old Mosque where the Pittsburgh Symphony played. At the end of the evening Benny went through his routine of acknowledging various people in the band, including the girl, for applause. This time, however, he called out, "Betty Bennett, ladies and gentlemen. Come on out here, Betty." Benny knew full well that Betty had not been staying around for the second half, and apparently he took some sort of sadistic pleasure from knowing that the word would get back to Betty that she had not been there when asked to take a bow.

Countless musicians have had the experience of Benny making things so uncomfortable or intolerable for them that they felt their only option was to quit. The guitarist Ben Heller once said he knew his days in the band were numbered when Benny started placing him and his guitar behind the drums. Then there was Joe Rushton and his bass sax. When Benny first hired Joe he sat out in front of the sax section. His next seat was with the saxes, then he was moved back amongst the trombones and finally back with the trumpets. Joe said that when he ended up behind the trumpet section he knew it was time to go. There was, in fact, method to Benny's madness. The musicians' union rules require that a bandleader who fires a sideman has to pay the musician's fare home, but there's no such obligation when a man quits, so over the years Benny saved himself a lot of money.

While on the tour we played a concert one night in Austin, Texas. After the show a local musician came backstage to chat with us. He told us all about this fantastic whorehouse just outside Austin: "All you have to do is jump in a cab. All the drivers know where it is." After the mind-numbing boredom of the long bus journeys we had been having it was decided that some relaxation was called for, so that night a bunch of us piled into cabs in a state of great excitement, imagining the pleasures in store for us. They took us to a kind of roadhouse with a bar and a jukebox – nothing fancy but a nice, jolly atmosphere about it. We sat there, eyeing the girls as they paraded around, while the madame passed among us seeing that we were all supplied with drinks. I'd been quite excited about the escapade because my idea of whorehouses came from reading jazz books that gave descriptions of places like Mahogany Hall and all the other famous pleasure palaces in Storyville. This joint wasn't anything like that. It was a very functional place that looked as if it might have been converted from a motel – no beautiful piano with Jelly Roll Morton or Tony Jackson playing, just an ordinary garish looking jukebox. As we sat there drinking, the madame was called to the phone. She returned laughing, saying, "Just had a call from that hotel you guys are staying at. Some John wants me to send over two girls immediately." A silence descended on us as we sat looking at each other. Might it be, could it possibly be, Benny?

I didn't get the girl I wanted. I'd had my eye on one particular blond ever since we arrived, but, being the backward sort of chap that I was, one of the other guys grabbed her while I was trying to screw up my nerve. I ended up with someone else but, never having been through this kind of routine before, I didn't know what to expect. In retrospect it was all so disappointing. The first thing I had to do was to go into the bathroom and have a thorough wash. When I returned I was asked to say precisely what I required. I didn't really know what she meant, so she very quickly ran through the whole catalogue in a very matter-of-fact sort of way. During the subsequent proceedings the madame kept wandering in and out of the room. "Is everything okay?" I cricked my neck as I tried to turn my head towards her to assure her that it was, but no sooner were activities resumed than she reappeared to urge her employee, "Be quick. There's another customer waiting." After that experience I decided my cat-house days were over. I went back to fantasizing about Lulu White and Mahogany Hall!

After our last concert Jay Feingold came round to each of us individually and told us we would be recording the following week. When we turned up at the studio, Scott LaFaro and Roy Burns were missing – in their places were George Duvivier and Shelly Manne. Clearly this was the reason why Benny had not told us collectively about the studio date. I don't know why Benny was dissatisfied with those guys, particularly Scott, who was a magnificent bassist. One night, riding the bus through the cornfields of Iowa, Scott and I were sitting together listening to some Bechet recordings being played on the radio as a tribute to Sidney, who had died the day before. Scott had originally started out on clarinet, but he'd never heard Bechet before. After one of Sidney's classic performances on *China Boy* he turned to me and said, "Jesus, that guy plays what Benny tries to play."

As I have said before, I got on well with Benny. I think he used to get lonely up there in his penthouse apartment on 66th Street. I wouldn't hear from him for months, and then one day he'd call up, on the pretext of wanting to play duets, but really because he wanted some company. One time he was getting ready to take a sextet into Basin Street East and wanted me to come up because of some Cole Porter number he needed an arrangement on. I sat down at the piano with the sheet music and said, "Let's see, Benny. What's a good key for this on clarinet?"

"Oh, no," said Benny, "it's not for the clarinet. It's a vocal arrangement I want. I'm going to sing it."

In the fall of 1959 I had a job with Benny working in the Thanksgiving Day parade sponsored each year by Macy's department store. One of the features of that year's parade was the Goodman Orchestra playing on a float. They didn't want to pay Benny's price for the full band, so they settled for the sextet. The weather was freezing and our small group was huddled on the float, wearing overcoats, mittens and scarves. It was altogether too cold to play, so Benny told the organizers to get one of his tapes and the group would mime to it. Some minion was sent for a tape, but it was by the big band. So there we were, moving through the crowds lining Fifth Avenue, six musicians simulating the sound of a 16-piece band. I watched the faces as we moved along – none of them realized that we weren't really playing, though it seemed incredible to me that they couldn't hear it was the sound of a big band blaring from the loudspeakers. Ah well, I was learning not to over-estimate the perception of the audience for this music I so passionately believed in.

Benny Goodman was the greatest natural clarinet player who ever lived. He heard a sound on the clarinet that nobody else heard in any kind of music, and he had a concept of the instrument that was so musical, like a singer's voice. He played with incredible ease on an instrument that is extremely difficult to play in a free, relaxed way, but it was done so effortlessly that he made it seem like the easiest thing in the world.

You can hear in his playing all the things that influenced him while he grew up in Chicago in the 1920s. His early training at Hull House and his studies with Franz Schoepp, the principal clarinetist of the Chicago Symphony Orchestra, provided him with a discipline to which he added the inspiration and experience that came from listening to all the jazz greats of those early days. You can hear Pee Wee Russell in Benny's occasional use of the growl, and Frank Teschemacher in the sharp, jagged lines and punchy attack. You can hear Jimmie Noone, and Johnny Dodds, and Don Murray, the marvelous clarinetist who played with Bix Beiderbecke, and you can hear Bix and Louis Armstrong too. It didn't take long for Benny to bring all these influences together and to form his own distinctive style. It is amazing to hear the gutsiness, fluidity and control displayed by Benny on his 1927 recordings of *Clarinetitis* and *That's a Plenty*. Here was a boy no more than 17 years old, but already an accomplished virtuoso who had listened to and learned from all the best things that had gone before and who was already a distinctive voice. That record alone should discourage anyone from trying to play the clarinet!

My first memories of Benny were the big-band recordings of the 1930s, when his playing had a rough edge to it; it wasn't as polished as it later became, but there was a tremendous warmth and excitement to it. By the time he left Ben Pollack in 1930 and began freelancing around New York, he'd mastered the clarinet technically. Whereas his earlier playing was full of notes, he now began to edit and to understand how to play the melody as a commercial way of reaching an audience. He developed this marvelous way of treating a melody with such restraint that he literally forced the listener to say, "Gee, what a beautiful song." There are so many examples of this, particularly with the trio and the quartet, where his way of playing numbers like *The Man I Love* and *Body and Soul* made them his very own and showed the way for all jazz clarinet players of the period. After the swing era ended the clarinet went into an eclipse from which it has never really recovered. There was such perfection in Benny's playing that it seemed as if there was nowhere else to go with the instrument. In the 1940s Buddy DeFranco came along. Although he had started out with the Goodman influence, he was determined to do something different. Buddy was influenced by Charlie Parker and the bop school and extended his chordal knowledge so that he consciously used harmonic complexities that weren't part of Benny's vocabulary. But yet Buddy, for all his technical expertise and knowledge, never achieved the naturalness that characterized Benny's playing. That's the best word I can use: it was so natural, with never a feeling of technique for technique's sake. Everything was purposeful, and at its best it had that marvelous rhythmic drive and hotness. Neither was there any hint of sentimentality when he played pretty tunes. He showed how to play pretty without the saccharine quality that marred Jimmie Noone's ballad playing.

My favorite period of Benny's was the early 1940s. I think that a prime reason for his brilliance in those years was the competitive factor. Artie Shaw had erupted like a Roman candle in the late 1930s and was a very big star after the success of *Begin the Beguine*. In 1939, disgusted with the hysteria of the jitterbugs, he walked off the bandstand and flew to Mexico, only to come back the next year with a big hit, a tune he'd picked up south of the border, called *Frenesi*. By then he definitely posed a threat to Benny's position as number one swing clarinet. Artie was smart enough not to play like Benny. He had his own sound, very lyrical, and of course he had his gimmick of always ending on a high note, sometimes as high as double high C. Although I was never influenced by Shaw, I've had a lifelong admiration for his musicianship and his great integrity. I think it was this competition from Artie that spurred Benny on to the brilliance of his playing during his period with Columbia Records. You can hear that brilliance in the various versions of his sextet, where first he had the inspiration of the great Charlie Christian on guitar, the young George Auld playing tenor, and Cootie Williams playing that marvelously hot, pungent trumpet, and later on Red Norvo and Slam Stewart and the brilliant Mel Powell on piano. Then there were the arrangers: Eddie Sauter adding new colors and new sounds to the big band, and Mel Powell, whose arrangements were simpler but always swinging.

In the mid-1940s the popular music scene was changing. The big bands were gradually falling apart because the postwar economic conditions could not support them. A contributing factor was the disastrous recording ban imposed by union leader James Petrillo in 1941 which lasted for a year and a half and steered public taste towards the singers and away from the bands. This was when Benny's playing started to develop some of the problems that plagued him in later years. The downward curve in his career, along with all his frustrations, began around 1946. He never thought the swing era would end; like practically everyone else in the music business he thought it would go on forever, and couldn't understand what was happening. His attitude was: "I'm doing this thing better than anyone else and better than I've ever done it before. So what's happening? What am I doing wrong?" The fact was that, with the competition from Artie Shaw and the sweeter style of Glenn Miller plus the popularity of the singers, Benny was no longer the kingpin he had been. His bewilderment was apparent when the band was working at the Paramount Theater. Yank Lawson, who was playing for Benny during that engagement, remembers the situation: "Frank Sinatra had just left Dorsey to work as a single and was on the bill with Benny. Benny had heard vaguely about this kid who sang with Dorsey, and after leading the band through a few numbers he introduced him. When Benny heard the roar go up, he turned to us and asked, 'What the hell is going on? What's all that noise about?' It was totally incomprehensible to him that a boy vocalist should elicit such audience response." For Benny, it had always been a question of telling someone to hire some boy to do a few songs.

When Columbia failed to renew his contract in 1946, he moved to Capitol, but there was no improvement in his record sales and it was almost in desperation that he turned to bop as a means of renewing his popularity. It was a disaster. Despite the fact that the bop band was a very good band, it just wasn't Benny. Although he continued to play with all his technical brilliance, there was a coldness about it that is all too apparent from the recordings of that period. Then, in 1948, along with many other bandleaders, he finally gave up the struggle of trying to maintain a big band. In effect, he said, "Screw it. I'm fed up with jazz anyway. I'll concentrate on classical music." In beginning his studies with Reginald Kell, Benny was running away from his difficulties in the jazz field. (He was also undergoing extensive psychotherapy at that time and had a permanent psychiatrist on his staff.)

Benny had difficulties in coping with his incredible success, which became more and more evident as his popularity waned. I've talked with musicians who knew him in the Pollack days. They describe him as a really likeable guy and say that the change in his character came only after the success. Up to that point he had been just a great musician for whom there had been nothing but music. He had poured everything, his whole soul, into playing that music, when suddenly he was catapulted into a position of great responsibility and public visibility. He simply wasn't equipped to deal with the resulting pressures, as very few of us would be. Where other musicians might take refuge in drink or drugs, Benny isolated himself from his fellow human beings and surrounded himself with people who ran all his affairs for him. While all his feelings came out in the warmth of his music, they were not reflected in the way he dealt with people. There was also a problem about money. He never quite believed he had as much as he had, and, coming from a very poor background, he always seemed afraid that his wealth might disappear. Mel Powell told me of an incident in the 1950s when Benny went into a Las Vegas casino with Mel and proceeded to buy a one-dollar chip. He put the chip down and stood there with perspiration pouring from his brow as he watched the roulette wheel spin round!

In 1953 Joe Glaser had the idea of a package tour featuring Louis Armstrong and Benny. Right from the start Benny saw himself as the star of the show. Here was the opportunity he had been waiting for, to re-create the 1930s band and to re-establish himself with the public. Always ready for the opportunity to put down any rival, he displayed his cavalier attitude at the first rehearsal. He kept Louis and the All Stars sitting around the studio for three hours while he rehearsed his own band. After he'd finished Benny announced, "That's it, rehearsal's over. Sorry, Pops, we didn't have time to get to you. See ya tomorrow and we'll give you some time then." The totally calculating Benny had deliberately kept Louis hanging around. Armstrong knew it and he was furious. Unfortunately the one thing that Benny had overlooked was the fact that, while he had been relaxing at his estate in Connecticut rehearsing chamber music, Louis had been riding high with the All Stars. With Armstrong fired up by the treatment he had received from Benny and determined to top him, the result was inevitable. From the first concert it was obvious that the All Stars were going to be the big hit with the audiences. Benny couldn't stand it. His total paranoia took over as he vented his spleen on John Hammond, the tour manager. This was the parting of the ways for John, who had worked so hard for so many years in guiding Benny's career, making decisions for him and helping him in every way possible. Nobody knows to this day whether it was a heart attack that Benny suffered or whether he just fainted from all the tensions, but he bowed out of the tour and Gene Krupa took over.

Benny retreated once more to his home in Connecticut. From then onwards his whole career consisted of an occasional reappearance for a recording or concert, and then he would retreat yet again into seclusion. The recordings were a pale reflection of his earlier brilliance, the concerts, although always well attended, were for the most part lacklustre. His concert at Carnegie Hall in 1978, celebrating the 40th anniversary of the famous 1938 appearance, was acknowledged by all to have been a disaster. The tour of Russia in 1962, while receiving much publicity, was uninspired musically. In fact the animosity of the band towards Benny was so great that upon their return to the States they went into the studios and recorded an album with Phil Woods doing the clarinet solos!

It would have been the ideal time for Benny to do what Isaac Stern did so gracefully when at a public ceremony he handed over his mantle to the younger players. There is nothing wrong with retiring gracefully, but Benny was psychologically incapable of taking that final step. It's very difficult to come to terms with the fact that you are over the top, and the natural tendency is to try and hang in. In a way, there is an element of self-delusion about it – you know that you are not playing at your former level, but you try to convince yourself that, with the right reed, you can get it all together again. It was simply an emotional thing for Benny, because there was nothing else he had to prove. His rise from rags to riches was one of the great American success stories of the 20th century. He was a respected jazz artist and a classical virtuoso performer, a megastar adored by millions of fans. For so many years, music had been everything to him. He had told himself so often, "I've got the world in a jug and the stopper in my hand. I don't need friends. Go away, don't bother me." But now that the crown had slipped he discovered the truth. He had nothing. Sure, there were the millions in the bank, the beautiful penthouse on 66th Street, the priceless antiques and paintings – but there were no friends. Certainly, when I was there the phone never rang.

It was the true time for reflection. He could have told himself that there was no reason for him to be nasty, and paranoid, and fearful. He could have got out his list of all the people he had ever known professionally, all the people he had insulted, whose feelings he had hurt, or to whom he had been rude and cruel. He could have phoned those people and said, "You know, I was a real son-of-a-bitch. I was too possessed with myself, too full of ambition and greed. I know I didn't treat you nicely. I want to say I am truly sorry for what I did to you. I'd like to be friends with you because I respect and admire your talent and think you're a fine person."

The sad thing is that nobody would have believed him.

EIGHT

A cry for help

After the spring 1959 tour, I got yet another call from Jay Feingold, asking if I wanted to do a South American tour with Benny. I thought long and hard about the offer, but by this time I had already promised Max Kaminsky that I would join him at Condon's. I only played tenor with Benny and, although I liked the tenor, it was strictly a secondary instrument for me. I still considered clarinet my main instrument, and of course I never got any real chance to play it with Benny. I figured that if I stayed with him I never would. I think, with hindsight, that had I taken the offer I would probably have been in line for his next big tour, which was the one to Russia. Financially, the job with Maxie wasn't as good, but in a way I was looking forward to playing clarinet in a small jazz band – I felt like a fish flipping back into water.

Also working in Maxie's band would be Dill Jones, the Welsh pianist I had first met at the 1948 Nice Festival and who was a very good friend right up to his death in 1984. At one time I had a trio with Dill on piano and Clyde Lombardi on bass, playing both classical music and jazz. Clyde was a marvelous player who took on the practically impossible task of playing cello parts on the bass for things like the Brahms and Beethoven trios. Dill was also a good friend of Dr John Horton and John's wife Pug. The Hortons were from Sheffield, England, but for some years had lived in Albany, New York. One night they came into Condon's to see Dill and hear some jazz. Dill introduced me to his friends. I was immediately struck by the exotic beauty and lovely modulated voice of this English lady, who turned to me, saying, "So, we finally meet." Although I was puzzled by this comment, my introduction to her brought back all the feelings about English women that I had experienced on my visit to England in 1957. I was surprised, after chatting to her and returning to the bandstand, to hear Max invite her up to sing. She called out *St Louis Blues* and suddenly, in place of that lilting, cultured accent, I was hearing sounds of Bessie Smith and Ma Rainey. It really knocked me out; it was such a total contrast and utterly unexpected.

While John Horton, a trombone player himself, was busily engaged in conversation with Cutty Cutshall, Pug explained that she had written to me back in 1947 at the time I was studying with Bechet – hence her opening remark which had so mystified me. A little bell started to ring in my head. Could it possibly be? I recalled a series of fan letters from an English girl which I'd saved in a shoe box in the attic of my parents' home in Scarsdale. The next time I was up there I rummaged around the attic until I found the dusty old box. As I undid the string and took off the cover I remembered Harry Crawford passing on to me letters postmarked "Sheffield, England," and addressed to me care of the Commodore Music Shop. I sat on the floor and settled down to re-read the letters.

Dear Bob Wilber.   I read about you studying with and living with the great Sidney Bechet. How marvellous for you. I would love it if you could get me his autograph and a photograph of the two of you together. Do you know other musicians I like such as Eddie Condon, Jimmy McPartland and Wild Bill Davison and would you be able to get me their autographs as well? I am fifteen years old and I love jazz music. It is my ambition to go to America but I don't know whether I ever will. Do you know of any American musicians who might be coming to England as I would love to meet them and talk to them about my own favourites, Sidney Bechet, Jelly Roll Morton, Louis Armstrong and Bessie Smith? Could you let me have a photograph of yourself?

I turned to the next letter.

Dear Bob Wilber.   Thank you for sending me the photograph. I wish we could hear as much jazz in England as you can in America. Last week my friend Diz Disley and I walked four miles to hear a record of "Tishomingo Blues" by Bunk Johnson. We played it over and over again. Have you heard that record?
  In the past month, I've been to twelve jazz clubs but because I'm only fifteen years old, some of the places wouldn't let me in so I had to stay outside and try and listen through the doors and windows.

  I sat there trying to contrast mental pictures of a jazz-crazy English teenager with the beautiful, sophisticated woman I had just met at Condon's. Why, out of all the fan letters I had received over the years, had I kept those particular ones? As hard as I tried to convince myself that this was the hand of fate, that old familiar self-doubt within me kept saying, "Wait a minute. She's a beautiful woman and you're only a guy behind a horn. Don't try and make any time with her because she's only going to stamp on you, and you know how rotten you feel about being rejected." The next time we met at Condon's I was polite and friendly but totally cautious, and when she invited me out for coffee after the job I respectfully declined and offered what I thought was a reasonable excuse. I was totally scared, because I couldn't believe that she could find anything attractive about me apart from my playing. Perhaps those feelings weren't altogether misplaced because several years later, Pug, as she was known to her friends, told me her recollections of our meeting in Condon's. She said, "I had been fascinated by you ever since seeing a photo of you in 1947 and reading about Bechet's love for you. Then, in 1960, when at last I met you at Condon's, you were standing at the bar, a small figure hidden behind the collar of a raincoat, looking for all the world like a turtle with horn-rimmed glasses. I was conscious of being well dressed and, as Dill introduced us, I remember looking down from the height of my high-heeled shoes and trying to convince myself that this was indeed the beautiful, golden-haired boy I had seen in that photo. It wasn't until later, when I heard you play, that you seemed to emerge as the person I remembered. David off the stand but Goliath on it. I was fascinated. As you played, your personality began to emerge, totally different from the frightened little man I had finally met."

Despite all my misgivings, I was fascinated by Pug from that point onwards. She was always there, somewhere, in the back of my mind, but of course she was married to a successful doctor, had children, and a whole life of her own in Albany. I had enjoyed meeting her, but, although we exchanged an occasional letter or phone call over the next few years, there was nothing that was in any sense bringing us together.

In 1963 I got a job at a new club in northern New Jersey, just over the state line from Rockland County. The owner, who ran the local funeral parlor, had been looking for some excuse not to have to go home and face his complaining spouse every night, so he bought an old Victorian mansion with the idea of converting it into a nightclub. He fixed it up like the Gaslight Club in New York, a very successful operation which employed a group of scantily clad girls as waitresses and a three-piece band. The bulk of the clientele consisted of tired businessmen who could revivify their flagging spirits by ogling the girls while imbibing great quantities of booze. The customers were encouraged to join in with the band. They were provided with wooden swizzle sticks, which they would tap frenetically on their glasses, the veins standing out on their flushed, perspiring brows as they sang *Melancholy Baby* and *Ace in the Hole* at the top of their voices. Hardly an ideal gig – but many a good jazz player has worked this type of club in lean times. Charlie Queener, a pianist and composer who played with Benny Goodman's band in the 1940s and later at Nick's, had worked at the New York Gaslight Club for years. He was asked by the new owner to put together a trio for the New Jersey venture. Charlie called me and the guitarist Carl Kress. Carl had first achieved notice in the early 1930s as one half of a guitar duo with the late Dick McDonough. He was very busy in those days doing radio shows and recordings. By 1934 Carl had moved to Long Island and bought a half-interest in the Onyx Club on 52nd Street, which was just becoming famous as "Swing Street." He purchased a yacht and used to commute daily by boat from Massepequa to Manhattan across Long Island Sound. Between the radio shows, recording and running the club, it was a long day and Kress was not averse to an occasional drink to help keep him going; Carl's route across the water after he had closed the club at four in the morning could be considerably more circuitous than his journey in. By the time I met him in the 1960s the nightclub venture had gone down the drain years before, the radio days were over and the yacht had been sold. He still had his old home in Massepequa, however, and did not mind commuting daily to northern New Jersey in his ramshackle old car for the sake of a gig. Carl's fortunes may have suffered, but not his guitar playing. His basic style was chordal rather than single-string. He had a unique way of plucking his bottom string, which was tuned lower than normal to give the effect of a walking bass.

The Gaslight Club gig started in September and continued into the spring.

That fall I started doing the "Jackie Gleason Show" with Max Kaminsky. Every Tuesday, when the show was taped, I'd send another clarinet player to cover for me at the Gaslight. My sub was a clarinetist by the name of Robert Wilber who lived near the club. He'd been around New York for years. In fact I sometimes used to get his phone calls and mail. He'd taken to using the name Ardie, after his initials R. D., to avoid the confusion over the names. An attractive feature of the gig (to me) was the "Gaslight Girls." We put on a little show every night – the girls would sing "boop-be-doop" type songs, do a little patter and finish off with a finale featuring the Charleston. The bosses' office, which was used by the girls for changing into their costumes, was also our band room. It was the scene for much light-hearted banter and hilarity. The girls, who spent the evening exposing tantalizing areas of flesh to the customers, were quite unconcerned with us three males in their dressing room. One girl in particular fancied me and had a charming way of inviting me to join her in her car during her ten-minute smoking break. Smoking was the last thing she had in mind!

After a few months Charlie left to return to the New York Gaslight Club. I took over leadership, and got my old friend Dill Jones to join us on piano. Carl and Dill hit it off immediately. Carl would pick up Dill in Manhattan every evening and they'd drive out to the gig, fortifying themselves at a few bars along the way. It was an interesting trio. Between the Roaring Twenties musical fare we'd sneak in some of Carl's originals and arrangements for the three instruments of Beiderbecke's *In a Mist* and Strayhorn's *Chelsea Bridge*. Besides clarinet I was playing tenor, still searching for an identity on the instrument. There was the Freeman–Young–Miller approach and the Hawk–Chu–Webster approach; I liked both but couldn't figure out how to combine them.

One night we had a blizzard. I lived less than ten miles from the club and could make it home, but with the heavy snowfall it was out of the question for Carl and Dill to drive into town. I suggested they stay at my place, but they weren't ready to leave – the boss was in a drinking mood that night and wanted company. I left the three of them, arms entwined and vowing eternal friendship, and drove home. The next night my fellow musicians showed up at work, tuxedos very crumpled and looking rather pale and wan. As best as they could remember, they'd left the club about six o'clock that morning, the three of them leaning on each other for support as they staggered through the snowdrifts. Passing his funeral parlor, the owner had a brilliant idea. Suddenly realizing his wife would not take kindly to his bringing his pals home, he suggested they could spend the night at the funeral parlor. It sounded like a fine idea – the bitter cold was beginning to counter the warmth from the alcohol – so the boss unlocked the door, let the guys in and staggered on home. Kress and Jones found themselves in the "viewing" room, where the only places to sleep were on the floor or on three chairs put together. Neither prospect seemed very palatable, so they explored further. Opening a door, they discovered the storeroom where the coffins were kept. Unable to locate the light switch, they felt around in the dark until they found two empty coffins, then climbed in and fell asleep. Next morning when the owner's assistant opened up for the day's business he was terrified to hear snoring noises emanating from the store room. In a panic, he called his boss, who said, "Don't worry, Joe. That's just a couple of friends of mine. Let 'em sleep. We'll go ahead with the viewing this afternoon, but don't show any coffins today!"

Then there was this job with Gleason. Maxie had known him from the days when Jackie had been just a scuffling comic around New York. Jackie liked Maxie a lot, and the idea of having Maxie in his organization appealed to him. Apart from Max and myself, the band included Cutty Cutshall, Morey Feld and Angelo de Pippo on piano and accordion. We didn't play on the actual show – that was the job of the studio orchestra. Our job was to play for the audience in the studio while the technicians were setting up the cameras and lighting. It was a very enjoyable gig and we had a lot of fun. Before the beginning of our second season on the show Jackie took the whole organization out on a promotional tour, drumming up interest for the new series. We flew to Los Angeles, and from there boarded a private train which worked its way back to New York, stopping at all the major cities en route. It was like a circus coming to town. We usually arrived at a town late morning to be greeted by the mayor and his entourage, with full radio and television coverage. Then we would be taken to a hotel and be fêted at a big luncheon. Gleason would make a speech, and entertainment would follow until about 4.00 p.m. After that we returned to a big party on the train, with dinner, music and dancing, while moving on to the next city and a repetition of the whole thing.

Jackie got to like these parties so much that whenever he did a benefit out of town he'd hire a private club car on the train and take along all his cronies, the Glea Girls and Maxie's band. We always used to arrive first at the station to set up. Nobody else would be there except Gleason busily supervising the loading of all the food, champagne and drink from the "21" Club, tremendously excited at the prospect of the approaching party. As the train left the celebrations took off, with everybody getting happy and the band really hot. Meanwhile Jackie's initial enthusiasm was beginning to fade. After a few drinks he'd start thinking about things that were troubling him, such as lawsuits, alimony, weight problems, etc. Without fail, as the train pulled into the station with the band wailing, everybody dancing in the aisles, laughing and shouting, Jackie would be slumped in his chair, fast asleep.

Once a year he used to do an all-music show. Although he didn't know much about jazz, he enjoyed it, so there was always a high jazz content. I remember once when the bill included Roland Kirk, the blind saxophone player whose talents extended to playing three horns at the same time – two of them weird-looking contraptions, named the manzello and the stritch, which he had invented himself. They decided to do an arrangement of one of Roland's numbers, and the staff arranger wrote a background for the huge string orchestra. We were all in the rehearsal studio, Jackie was conducting and Bobby Hackett had just finished playing. "OK," called Jackie, "who's next?" They led out Roland Kirk with his dark glasses and three horns dangling from his neck, an altogether strange sight. Jackie was still looking at the score as he said, "OK, we've got Roland Kirk." He turned round and saw Kirk, and his eyes popped out of his head as he yelled, "What's that?"

Somebody said, "It's Mr Kirk, Mr Gleason."

"Get that thing out of here," Jackie shouted, "I can't have that on my TV show." They led Roland out of the studio, leaving Jackie yelling, "Get me Stan Getz."

After that second season Gleason retired and moved to Florida. CBS eliminated the staff orchestra, and Maxie's little band was out of a job. I wasn't doing any steady work, just picking up an occasional jingle date or dance gig. The schism between traditional and modern jazz was total, and, to make things worse, rock-and-roll was bigger than ever. Work was very difficult to come by – to get a gig you really had to hustle – and, as usual, that was something I found difficult to do.

One thing I did get involved in was the Music Minus One records. They went all over the world and made quite an impact. Even to this day amateur musicians come up to me and tell me how they play alongside me using these records. The idea originated with a guy named Irving Kratka, who later started Inner City Records and built it up to quite a big deal by buying up defunct labels and recordings that had never been issued. His original concept was of a rhythm section playing popular material for aspiring singers to practice with, and it was very successful. He came up with the very appropriate name of "Music Minus One." In so many areas, the right name for the product is often the difference between success and failure, and this name was just perfect. It also had an additional advantage in that it could be abbreviated to "MMO," so easy to say and with no loss of identity. Irv decided to expand the concept and do a dixieland-style record for those who wanted to play that kind of music. I had originally known him when he had been a drummer around New York in the 1940s, when the Wildcats were the focal point of the traditional movement. He came to me because of our association and friendship in those early days, probably thinking that I would do the job for less money than others, but knowing that I had the tools to do this rather specialized kind of assignment. To present a jazz performance with one part missing was not something that could be done off the cuff; it needed great planning so that the home player felt he was really a part of the band. It was an important psychological feature of the project to make the player have the feeling that if he didn't play his part well the performance wouldn't make it and he would be letting the group down.

I made arrangements of popular dixieland numbers and did two albums with an all-star band that featured Bud Freeman, Vic Dickenson, Buck Clayton, Panama Francis, Dick Wellstood and Abdul Malik. I later found out that, in order to get more mileage out of the project, Kratka repackaged the albums as straight jazz records. I remember seeing these albums in a record store and thinking to myself, "My God. What are people going to think about this? They'll think Wilber must be crazy, having the band play backgrounds with no solos." I regarded the action as very unethical on Kratka's part and told him so. Nevertheless, over the next few years I was involved in a whole variety of MMO recordings. At least it gave me the opportunity to write original music, as a result of which I was able to get into ASCAP, the American Society of Composers, Authors and Publishers.

One Wednesday afternoon, down on the union floor, I got a break in the form of a Friday night out-of-town gig with Les Elgart's orchestra. On the way to the job in Buffalo, New York, with the drummer, guitarist and me wedged into my little VW, we ran into a major blizzard. Pretty soon trucks and cars were stalled all over the thruway, but by barreling around them through the drifts we finally made it to Buffalo, the only car in the band that got through. By then it was midnight and the dance promoters had gone ahead and hired a local band, so we looked for a motel and fell into our beds, totally exhausted. The next morning I drove the guys to the airport, where they caught a plane for New York. The guitarist, Ralph Patt, was also the manager, and he had to hire a band to go to Harrisburg, Pennsylvania the next night to play a dance gig. Meanwhile the leader, Les Elgart, was marooned at a gas station on the thruway – my VW had got through but his $30,000 Maserati didn't make it! Still exhausted from the drive up the day before, I started to wend my way home. Discovering that the thruway was closed, I tried every secondary road I could find, usually ending up having to turn back because of a truck stalled in the snow, blocking the road. By nightfall I'd made it to Batavia, New York, and that was the end of the line. Nobody had gotten further south, and as a result every hotel and motel in town was jammed to capacity with stranded truckers and motorists. Cold and hungry, I stopped in a diner. I explained my plight to a sympathetic waitress, who said she knew a lady nearby who had a small room in her attic that she might let out for the night. For a sizeable fee the arrangement was made, and after a few hours' sleep I was up early to make a second attempt to get home. By morning the blizzard was over and the sun was out, but it was bitterly cold, with high winds blowing the snow into huge drifts. The thruway was still closed, but by a winding, twisting route through one small village after another I gradually worked my way south. At one point I fell asleep at the wheel and banged into an oncoming car, denting both of our fenders. About ten o'clock that evening (it was now Sunday) I drove wearily down my driveway – not having played a note the whole weekend or having made a single dime!

Another snow storm caught me again a short while later when I had a Friday night concert with Jimmy McPartland in Yorkville, the German section in the Upper East Side of Manhattan. As I got into my car to drive home to Rockland County it was snowing hard, and the covering on the ground was getting deeper and deeper by the minute. When I reached the George Washington Bridge, the entrance was blocked and I couldn't get on. I continued up the West Side drive, but the car kept getting stuck in the snow, making it necessary to dig the rear wheels out and start again. At last I managed to get off the highway at Mosholu Parkway in the Bronx, where I finally had to abandon the car under the elevated railway tracks. It was now a major blizzard. I was frozen, and, after getting some coffee to thaw me out, I found a phone box. I got a small room in a hotel near Grand Central Station and took the subway downtown. The next morning I heard on the news that all the bridges and tunnels out of Manhattan were closed. I stayed in the hotel all Saturday and finally was able to take a bus home on Sunday afternoon. On Monday I went back into the city to look for my car. It was totally covered by snow, but I managed to dig it out and drive it home. I staggered into the house utterly exhausted, and went to bed feeling ill and feverish. With no sign of improvement the next morning I called the doctor in. After examining me he announced that I had the mumps. This is normally a childhood ailment, but for some reason it seems to raise a smile when an adult is the victim. For an adult, however, it can have serious consequences. My temperature kept rising and rising, until the next day it reached 105 degrees; this was accompanied by a very sore throat and a painful swelling of my testicles. The doctor gave me some antibiotics, saying, "If this doesn't work you're going in the hospital." Well, it did work: my temperature came down, but a long period of convalescence followed.

The mumps left me physically debilitated and mentally depressed. I finally recovered and, once more, faced the joyless task of scrambling for gigs. I would jump into the VW on Wednesday mornings and drive down to the union headquarters in New York, determined to get a job for the coming weekend. The offices of the musicians' union were on 52nd Street between Broadway and Eighth Avenue, in the same building as the famous Roseland Ballroom. Every Wednesday afternoon from one o'clock onwards the dance floor of the Roseland was given over to the musicians to congregate and mingle in their efforts to find themselves work for the weekend. The contractors roamed the floor assembling bands for dances, weddings and barmitzvahs. The exchange floor, as it was known, was absolutely full by two o'clock, the air thick with smoke and everybody milling around. There were well-defined sections of the floor where different types of musicians would congregate – over here would be those who did the Latin work and over there would be those doing the society-band work – the Lester Lanin, Meyer Davis kind of thing. Yet another section would contain the more hip musicians, the jazz guys trying to fix up with one of the dance bands going out to play at a college or resort. This was the end of the dance-band era. The people who hired these bands thought they were getting a regular organized group, like they would have in the 1930s and 1940s. Little did they know, and the bookers did nothing to disillusion them, that all they were getting was a makeshift band, hastily put together and fronted by a well-known leader who had a library and an agent and nothing else. The agent would book a date and then get a contractor to go down to the exchange floor and put a band together. I used to hang around, hoping upon hope that some contractor would come up to me, saying, "Hey, Wilber, we could use you Saturday night. Are you busy?" or that I'd hear my name coming across the loudspeaker, "Paging Bob Wilber, wanted for such-and-such a band for Saturday night."

I usually waited in vain, and by four o'clock, when most musicians would have got themselves fixed up, I had to accept the inevitable fact that yet another week had passed by without a gig – not even a lousy club date playing music I hated. I wasn't a part of the Latin or society groups and neither was I a part of that group of jazz musicians who were working the big-band gigs. The only area I felt a part of was the dixieland field, where there was an occasional gig, but there were so many of the old-timers still around I only got a call when they couldn't get the older clarinet players with the famous names. I ended up working with people such as Stan Rubin, a clarinet player out of Princeton who had a college band called the Tiger Town Five. He had gained notoriety in the early 1950s by being asked to play with his band at Princess Grace's wedding in Monaco. It was a big publicity event on which Rubin very smartly built a whole career. I hated that job, playing fourth tenor in the band of a very limited musician who had a fantastically over-inflated opinion of himself and who saw himself as the successor to Benny Goodman and Artie Shaw. The sheer frustration of knowing that I was a damned good clarinet player reduced to playing such a role in the band of a musician like that was almost unbearable.

Another similar job was with Sol Yaged, a clarinetist with a limited amount of talent which he used to pursue a lifelong ambition to be a carbon copy of Benny Goodman. He built a reputation and a following around the New York area leading a band playing the numbers that Benny had made popular. Here I was, again, just another tenor player in his band at the Metropole Cafe. The Metropole was a long bar on Seventh Avenue, and working there was one of the low spots in my life. The band room was located three floors above and you had to walk up dirty, dingy, urine-smelling stairs to reach the room where you kept your instrument case and coat. The bandstand was over the bar, a narrow ledge that stretched from the front door to the back of the club – some 50 feet. Looking outside from the bandstand you saw all the drunks, junkies, prostitutes and bums wandering by. Some of them would come in and stand at the bar, staring up at us until they were chased out by the bouncer. We played alternate half-hour sets with another group from nine until three in the morning, and they were long, long evenings. The sheer misery of it all was in such sharp contrast to the experience of Christmas that year out in Scarsdale with the family – the beautiful Christmas tree and the presents. There was such a warm feeling of being with my family and being treated with love and kindness, superficial as it was. Then, with the party at its height, I had to get in my car and drive into town, back to my gig above the bar at the Metropole, playing for all those low-life people. I stood there in that dreadful, sleazy atmosphere on Christmas night, wondering whether I would ever get my life together, wondering whether there would ever be a relationship between the life I had grown up with, and the life I now had. They seemed so separate, so far apart from each other.

Despite the fact that I still couldn't talk to my parents about my problems, there was nevertheless a definite feeling of security in their home and in their affluent life, where everybody was nice, where the food and wine flowed, and the manners were gentle and refined. Family get-togethers were usually during a holiday, when everybody was cheerful and happy and there were never any sharp words spoken. It was all a matter of "Isn't life wonderful? Isn't it marvelous to be together as a family?" One felt absolutely obliged to fall in with this kind of mood. For anyone to have put a damper on it would have been ungrateful and unchristian. Although it still felt phoney to me, there was something comforting about it all. My parents never realized I was unhappy because I never let on that I was.

Although at the time it had seemed the right thing to do, my decision to leave the Savoy band after two years of great adulation was the first step down the road to the obscure state in which I found myself 15 years later. The band had settled into a safe, commercial formula, but for me the excitement had gone. With the explosion of interest in dixieland music, amateur bands began to spring up all over the East Coast, playing for parties, fraternity and college dances, wearing straw hats and striped blazers. It had nothing to do with what Louis, Sidney and Jelly were saying in their music, but the public loved it. It became increasingly difficult to be given serious consideration as a jazz artist because of being associated with music that was becoming more and more the province of the amateur. I remember taking part in a benefit at the Central Plaza for a musician who had fallen on hard times. A bunch of us, all well-known jazz players, were on the stand having a real jam session when Conrad Janis came in. Conrad was a well-known actor who led a band and played trombone for kicks; he was a big draw at the Central Plaza, but he completely destroyed the good feeling when he took out his trombone, and, instead of joining in as a fellow player, he jumped on to the top of the piano, swinging his slide through the air and blowing at triple forte volume. He immediately trivialized the whole proceedings, but the fans went wild. It was an opportunity for razz-ma-tazz that Janis took advantage of; he couldn't play very well – nobody thought of him as a serious musician – so he took the other route. He made the serious players look inconsequential.

Turning my back on Sidney and trying to lose the Bechet image been had another major psychological step, and the ultimate decision to sell my soprano had been akin to cutting the umbilical cord. As the loss of identity developed, the self-confidence and belief in myself diminished. The most trivial things began to upset me. For instance, I had always been told, particularly by women, that I looked younger than I was and, although most men would take that as a compliment, it began to depress me. I had always had this feeling about myself that I was just a boy and not a man, and the remarks only reinforced this hang-up. I wanted to be thought of as a strong, mature male, not as a young boy. I was in such a negative state of mind that I turned down the chance to play with Louis Armstrong and the All Stars. I was called by Joe Glaser on two separate occasions and offered the clarinet chair – first when Edmond Hall left, and then when Buster Bailey died. I can clearly recall those telephone calls from Joe: "Hey, kid. You wanna play with the Armstrong All Stars? We'll start you out at $500 a week, and if ya do well ya can end up makin' a grand like some of the other guys."

At that time this was the highest-paid job for any sideman in the whole field of jazz. It was necessary, however, to sign on for a full year. It was strictly a road band; when you were with Louis you had to pack your bags and leave home, perhaps being away for almost the whole year apart from an odd day here and there. But this was Louis Armstrong, my great idol. On each occasion I returned Joe Glaser's call, telling him how honored I was to be offered the job but that my circumstances were such that I couldn't accept. All that Joe said was, "OK, kid. Thanks. Goodbye." In retrospect, I suppose I should have taken the job. After all, I was an itinerant musician and it was as such that I had to make my reputation and earn my living. But I was in the classic dilemma of the New York freelance musician – not working very often but afraid to leave town because I might miss that all-important call from a contractor, record company or producer which might put me on the road to that mythological state called "success." Without my investment portfolio I certainly wouldn't have been able to ignore such a chance. I should have jumped at it because money was the least of my problems. Whether, in retrospect, it would have changed things for me is difficult to say. Originally, when the group included people like Barney Bigard, Edmond Hall, Peanuts Hucko, Buster Bailey, Jack Teagarden and Trummy Young, the tag "All Stars" had meant precisely that. Later on, musicians who were not big names began to come in and the group developed into nothing more than a background for Louis. I might have gained some notoriety that would have helped my career, but who knows? Joe Muranyi spent all those years with Louis and when he left he became the house clarinetist at Ryan's, which paid practically nothing.

And then there were the business people in whom I put my trust. I desperately needed to reach some kind of public, but I despaired of being able to do anything artistically and getting anyone to accept it and market it. The only thing to do was to put myself in the hands of a producer who would come up with an idea. I told myself that these guys were in positions of power in the music industry; they knew the business, they knew what would sell, and they knew how to market it. I figured that if I was flexible enough and gave them exactly what they wanted, something was bound to happen. I didn't really believe in the underlying philosophy of trying to do something that the public wanted and hitting it big regardless of quality and integrity, but I had run out of options. My first opportunity came through Bill Randall, a very influential disc jockey in Cleveland, Ohio, whose program was widely regarded as a barometer of public opinion in the record business. Bill was an intellectual, interested in philosophy and psychology, but his heart was in jazz and particularly in the music of Bechet. He had heard an English recording of *Petite fleur*, a Bechet number, by Chris Barber, featuring Monty Sunshine. He had also gotten wind that an American company had acquired the rights, and, being an astute guy and knowing the market, he sensed that the song had potential. So he called me in Scarsdale on Christmas Day: "Bob, I've been watching the British market, and *Petite fleur* has begun to take off. I know of your great interest in Bechet and if we move fast we can get a cover record out over here. If you can put a band together for a date tomorrow, I'll fly in from Cleveland and we'll do it."

I quickly rounded up the guys and the next day we recorded *Petite fleur*. Bill immediately took it round to MGM and they snapped it up. We waited for things to happen but unfortunately, due to a shake-up in the management, the company sat on the recording for six weeks, and by the time they released it it was too late. The Chris Barber recording was a smash hit and it flooded the market. The company probably never lost a moment's sleep over the opportunity they had let slip by, but I did. In truth, our recording was not as good as Barber's and my clarinet was not as good as Monty Sunshine's in projecting the feeling of Sidney's tune. In fact Monty did a fine job; it was a marvelous performance. I was in the middle of my studies with Leon Russianoff and my jazz sound was rather academic, rather inhibited and certainly not at all like Sidney's. It was a pity, for I was the natural one to have done it. I could have done it in 1948 but not in the 1960s, totally confused and searching for an identity as I was.

Dave Kapp, the younger brother of Jack who founded Decca Records, was another person who thought he could do something for me. After his brother's death Dave established himself as a record producer. His boast was that he could take anyone and turn them into something big, provided they did exactly what he said. Dave used to come into Condon's, and one night he invited me to his office for a business talk. When I arrived he played a recording of *Midnight in Moscow* by Kenny Ball and told me that trad was going to be the next big fad, even taking the place of rock-and-roll. All I had to do was change my name to "Bobby Wilber," record the material he would find, and do exactly what he told me. A typical record producer, absolutely sure of himself and of his own omnipotence! I recorded a few sides using the house band from Condon's. The material was mostly country-and-western tunes and folk songs. Kapp released a couple of singles but nothing ever happened. The Kapp brothers grew up in Chicago in the 1920s, and heard Louis at the Sunset Café and Jimmie Noone at the Apex Club. They went into the record business in the early 1930s with Bing Crosby as their big star. I never knew Jack, but Dave really loved hot jazz – though he made his money in commerical music. He liked the idea of being able to take jazz and make a commercial success of it. That's why he was so excited about the trad-jazz movement. Like so many people in the record business – John Hammond, Bob Thiele, the Ertegun Brothers and Jerry Wexler – he was in it because of his love of jazz as a kid.

Dave Kapralik was another, a publisher who wanted to feature my soprano in front of a gospel choir. He came up with a really corny piece of music for the session called *Everyone's gone to the moon*. He had me record the melody on soprano, then he re-recorded it with the soprano playing the melody again, but slightly late. Then he did it a third time so that he had an overlay, giving the whole thing a souped-up, ethereal sound. He put it out with an original of mine, *The Tender Ways of Love*, on the other side, but again absolutely nothing happened. Mr "Know it All" then moved on to his next project, which was the planning of a campaign to turn the fighter Mohammad Ali into a big singer! I once met Ali in Kapralik's office; he seemed like a nice guy, but hardly a singer.

If there was any lesson I learned from those experiences, it was that nobody really knows what the public wants, and that if an artist goes out with any such pre-conceived idea it's a recipe for failure. What really happens is that everyone does what they do best, and if the time and the place are right you may succeed. The big audience in popular music is the young people – those from age 14 to 24. Music means more in people's lives during that period than it does later on, and the young have money to buy records – before marriage, kids, car payments and taxes change the picture.

One pleasurable experience I had at that time involved Billy Strayhorn. I felt honored when I got a call from Billy in 1966 inviting me to join a band that he was putting together to play Duke's music at a concert for the Duke Ellington Society. I felt particularly pleased because, apart from the french horn player Willie Ruff and the drummer Dave Bailey, I was the only member of the band who was not an Ellington alumnus. The concert was very successful, and a couple of days later Billy called me again asking me to record with him at the Victor Studios on 23rd Street. When I got there I was thrilled to find the Duke himself in the control booth, acting as A & R man for the date. We ran down the arrangements and began to record. Every once in a while Duke would come out from the booth with a little scrap of music paper that had some notes on it for a clarinet part. He kept handing the sheet to me, saying, "Let me hear this. What's it sound like?" After I played the notes Duke would say, "OK, man, thanks," walk back to the booth, and the recording session would continue. He kept coming out every 20 minutes or so with a few more notes added to the part or a few alterations made. "OK, what's this sound like now?" Obviously he was in the middle of some composition and wanted to get the clarinet part right. Nobody knew what happened to those recordings until they recently turned up in a batch of tapes donated by Mercer Ellington to a Danish radio station. It was common practice for the Duke, however, when he had fallow periods with his band, to take his musicians into the studios and record, paying the men for the date out of his publishing company funds. It was his way of keeping the band together. When we finished recording our numbers from the concert there was a little time left, so Duke came out into the studio and said, "Hey, fellahs, let's play some blues. Who's got a riff?" Clark Terry came up with one. Duke and Billy sat down together at the piano, sketched out a routine and we recorded two more sides.

"Stray" or "Swee'pea," as Strayhorn was known, was a gentle, lovable guy, content to bask in the radiance of Ellington's fame and quite happy to take a back seat, despite the importance of his contribution to the world of Ellington. We all missed him when he died of cancer a few years later.

There was one more sting left in the tail of this particular period of my life. It was late autumn and all the leaves were on the ground. I was coming home from a gig, and as I approached the house I could see the gutters filled with leaves and the rain water overflowing and running down the walls. I got out a long ladder and climbed up to clear the gutters. The ground was quite wet. I hadn't secured the ladder properly and suddenly I felt it slipping from under me. I came crashing down to the ground some 18 to 20 feet below. Although I was lucky enough to fall into bushes rather than onto concrete, I nevertheless put out my hands to try and cushion the fall and immediately felt a sharp pain. When I came to I found that I had broken both my wrists! The doctor set the wrists in plaster, gave me some painkillers and sent me home. A couple of days later, when the effects of the drugs began to wear off, I started to think about the importance of those hands to me as a clarinet player. What on earth could I do, what on earth would I be, without them? In something of a panic I went into town to see a specialist to make sure that everything was all right. The specialist I saw was the consultant for the New York Giants football team and took care of all their bone injuries. He took one look at the plaster casts, and I'll never forget the words that followed: "The first thing we must do is to break these casts and re-set your wrists. The casts are set all wrong. The way they've been set will leave your hands angled out to each side when the bones knit together."

What a shock! If I hadn't gone to that specialist my career as a clarinet player would have been finished. The doctor broke the casts and re-set my wrists. The new plaster casts ran all the way up to my armpits, making it difficult for me to perform the simplest tasks. The sound of my clarinet was not heard for some considerable time, and as I sat around waiting for nature to take its course I had all the time in the world to reflect on my life and ponder over my problems. My future seemed bleak and the problems of the music business insurmountable. I began to feel that a solution was beyond my own capacity and that maybe I should seek help. What had happened to me? Why had my career, in fact my whole life, reached such a dead end? I felt I needed an objective person whom I could talk to, who'd give me some advice on how to straighten out my life. I asked my doctor to recommend someone and he made an appointment for me with a psychiatrist. My decision to see him was based on the realization that I hadn't succeeded, a difficult thing to say to yourself. I finally had to admit, "I can't make it on my own. I need someone to help me."

It was an admission of failure.

Part III. Hope

NINE

Picking up the threads

The psychiatrist my doctor had recommended was an old gentleman who lived and practiced on West 86th Street in New York, opposite the Museum of Natural History. He had gone to Vienna to study dentistry, but had switched to psychiatry after hearing a lecture there by a new professor by the name of Sigmund Freud. He was sympathetic to my musical interest, having played violin in what he euphemistically termed "a jazz band" in order to pay his way through medical school. Over the following months he gradually began to implant in me better feelings about myself. I discovered how guilty I had felt at rejecting my parents' wish that I go to college and enter a normal profession. I also found out that I was subconsciously accepting my lack of success as just punishment for turning away from Sidney's influence and striking out on my own. By dispelling these illusions I began to believe that I could really do something with my life. I began to see I was a real man, that I had something to offer the world with my playing, composing and arranging skills. His advice was: "If you want to do something, then go out and do it. If you want to play this or write that, then do it. Don't waste a single thought on doubting your own ability. Stop turning your cheek when other people hurt you. Stick your fists out, don't always be on the defensive."

It was a long slow process, but I began to see glimmerings of light at the end of the long, dark tunnel. Almost imperceptibly the confidence in myself, both as a human being and as a musician, began to return. I think you can hear this change in my subsequent recordings. In those first stages of my rehabilitation I was fortunate to be working with Bobby Hackett, who was always a support to me, a sympathetic and non-threatening friend. We worked through the summer of 1966 on Cape Cod at a place called the Rooster. I lived at Oldfields with my parents. While it was all very pleasant I still didn't sense that I could talk to them about my problems. Vacations at Oldfields were always a continuous round of good times, as the gushing comments in the guest book at the end of each guest's stay always indicated. Who was I to put a damper on all this joy and happiness?

It was a good group with Bobby, myself, and Dave McKenna on piano. The drummer and bass player, whose last names I can't recall, were Dave and Bob. Bobby always introduced us as "three Bobs and two Daves – the only royal flush in jazz." The proprietor was the son of the owner of Reisenweber's Café, the first place the Original Dixieland Jazz Band played in New York in 1916. He remembered crawling under the piano as a kid to listen to the band, and he told us of the tremendous impact the band made as people flocked there to listen and dance to the new "jass" music. Notwithstanding our boss's enthusiasm for jazz, the Rooster was a typical Cape Cod operation, where you could never be quite sure of getting paid. It only needed a couple of weeks of rain on this holiday peninsula and instant panic set in; everybody would be fired, the whole place redecorated and a new operation opened up with a different entertainment policy. Bankruptcies were a dime a dozen. Not even George Wein, who opened the Summer Storyville on the Cape with attractions like Erroll Garner and Dave Brubeck, could make things pay, and he gave up after two summers. That fall Bobby started bringing me on his record dates. We were working at Condon's, and Verve Records wanted him to do all the old dixie warhorses with a big band, so we made an album titled *Creole Cooking*. After 20 years I had grown sick and tired of playing the same 20 songs of the standard dixieland repertoire, so I tried to do something different and unusual in the arrangements. For instance, on *Do you know what it means to miss New Orleans* I feature Dave McKenna on the first chorus in 3/4 time. For the bridge, I have Cutty Cutshall and Bob Brookmeyer doing a duet in 4/4 time, and then we go back into 3/4 time for the last part. On *Royal Garden Blues* I introduce the B flat strain in long meter, making it 24 bars rather than the usual 12. It gives a stretched-out Basie feel to the tune. When we revert to the 12-bar structure on the shout chorus at the end, the thing really romps. In a sense it was like some of the things we did with the Six, playing the familiar stuff in a different way.

In the spring of 1966 I had a gig with Bobby playing at the Dream Room on Bourbon Street in New Orleans. On the plane I struck up a conversation with an attractive lady sitting next to me. When we landed we claimed our baggage together and shared a cab into town. We went first of all to her hotel, and after she had checked in I suggested she came downtown to my hotel, which was considerably less fancy than the one in which she was staying. One thing led to another and very soon we were in bed together. It was obvious my therapy was producing results. I returned to New York in a carefree mood, with a new sense of confidence. That my amatory adventure had occurred in New Orleans, the cradle of jazz, somehow seemed symbolic – I'd originally gone into jazz for the freedom it offered me.

My next job of any importance was with Bob Crosby in 1967, playing at the Steel Pier in Atlantic City. The Pier was a famous old venue in the heyday of the big bands and I was excited at the prospect of playing there. This edition of the Bob Cats was a good band and included Yank Lawson, Matty Matlock and Bob Haggart. Crosby's usual practice was to try and get as many of the original members as possible and then use substitutes for any chairs he couldn't fill. It was basically the Bob Cats' sound but included occasional vocals from Bob which nobody took very seriously. He used to stand on the bandstand and wave his arms round; it meant very little but he was a very pleasant fellow. He knew he was no great shakes as a singer and he was very realistic in attributing his success in the music business to the name he shared with his famous brother. He had no illusions about that – he just loved the kind of music his band played and enjoyed being on the bandstand with them.

On our first day in Atlantic City we had to be at the pier by one o'clock in the afternoon. As we walked towards the ballroom I began to hear a strange sound building up, like the chattering of a huge flock of magpies. When we entered the building we found a crowd of about three thousand youngsters, mostly girls, excitedly talking away. It seemed very strange, not at all the kind of audience I'd been expecting. Then I noticed various signs that read "Appearing Today," "One Day Only," followed with the name of a lollypop rock group. I realized that we were just the filler for these big-money pop groups. When we got out on stage the kids were still chattering away, consuming cotton candy, ice cream and chocolate bars. We opened up with *Muskrat Ramble* followed by *Tin Roof Blues*. The kids seemed to be oblivious to the music, barely acknowledging our presence with an occasional glance. The only thing that attracted their attention was Bob's son, Chris, a young man in his early 20s with long hair who occasionally sang a vocal. They liked him, but the rest of us were nothing more than background music. When we came off stage after the set we noticed outside the stage door a long black limousine disgorging scruffy young men with guitars and amplified basses, who went directly on stage and set up their equipment. As soon as the curtain went up, three thousand young girls started screaming at the top of their voices. The band launched into its big hit, which was impossible to hear because the screaming was so loud. The minute the band stopped, the screaming stopped. No applause, just silence. Then the band went into the "B" side of their hit record and the screaming started again, only to end once more in abrupt silence when the music stopped.

This procedure was repeated for three of four more numbers, all of which ended abruptly with no announcements. The curtain closed, the musicians trooped off the stage, piled in their limousine and drove away. They were followed by their van, loaded with electronic gear. This went on for two whole weeks with a different group each day – always the same routine. It gave me an insight into the state of the music business, but the really curious thing was that the kids didn't actually hear the music. I realized that this wasn't music to listen to but music to be part of, to "do your thing to," as the expression goes. The audience was there, the group was there; they were all involved together but in a strangely impersonal way. My God, how the world was changing!

The next engagement we had was four weeks with a four-week option at the Hilton Hotel in Chicago, the old Stevens Hotel – for many years reputed to be the largest hotel in the world. The only drawback was that it was a seven-nights-a-week job, no night off. It was an easy gig because all we had to do was to play 20 minutes of dance music before the ice show, another 15 minutes during the show and a final short dance set when the show ended. Bob Haggart put the band together for Crosby. It was a good group. Besides Yank, Hagg and Matty we had Cutty Cutshall, Dave McKenna, Cliff Leeman, and Billy Cronk on bass, with me taking Eddie Miller's part on tenor. It was frustrating, however, because there wasn't all that much to play, but working seven nights a week meant you were completely tied down. I used to pass the days visiting museums, attending the Friday matinée performances of the Chicago Symphony Orchestra, reading books and generally hiding away. Every day I'd walk over to Frank Wells's little shop to see how he was getting on with my clarinet mouthpiece. Wells is a guy who is famous for customizing mouthpieces. It seems like every clarinet player I meet has gone to him at one time or another. After seven weeks, however, he still hadn't got what I was looking for – maybe I really didn't know myself what I wanted. During the whole engagement Cliff Leeman never left the hotel. He simply took the elevator from his room down to the club and back up again after the gig. He had all his meals sent up to the room and delegated various members of the band, usually me, to go out and get cigarettes and booze. At the end of four weeks the management took up the option, but the band rebelled – another four weeks of unfriendly skaters, Crosby's jokes and no night off seemed like purgatory to us. Crosby pleaded with his sidemen and we begrudgingly agreed to do another two weeks.

It was a very turbulent time in politics. Martin Luther King was assassinated while we were there. When Yank heard the news on the six o'clock bulletin he was really shocked. He went down to the bar for a drink. The bartender greeted him with, "Well, they finally got the black bastard, didn't they?" Yank, who is a very big man, reached across the bar, seized the offending party by his lapels and shook him like a rag doll. As the news spread, riots broke out in the black section of the South Side. The general fear was that they would spread to the area along Lake Michigan where all the fancy hotels, stores, offices and apartment houses were. The lake front symbolized the dominance of the white power structure in Chicago and would have been a natural target for looting and burning.

That night the management wouldn't allow the staff to leave the hotel. After the gig, where we played to an empty house, we sat up in Crosby's room, looking out at the angry red glow in the sky as the fires raged on the south and west side of town. As we watched we got an insight into Crosby's naïveté; he was a delightful man but completely out of touch with what was happening in the world. As we discussed the race problem, he offered the following comments: "I can't understand all this rioting. The Blacks have a good life in this wonderful country of ours. They do very well. I just finished a tour of the South and I didn't see any poverty at all."

"But Bob, don't you read the papers?"

"Oh, that stuff's all communist propaganda. The United States is the greatest country in the world and the Blacks know it."

"But Bob, where exactly were you?"

"My agent books me on the country-club circuit. I was playing the finest clubs in the South. Nothing but black people waiting on tables and bartending. They're all doin' fine, earning good money." Bob had no idea of the realities of life in the 1960s.

This was the year of the presidential election, and Richard Nixon was running for office. He had set up his campaign headquarters in the Blackstone Hotel, next door to the Hilton. Shortly after the riots President Lyndon Johnson was flying to Chicago to address a meeting of leading businessmen at the Hilton. The hotel was swarming with security men. One of the guys in the band had a friend who worked for the Associated Press who had set up a press room in the Blackstone. One night he invited us to go up and see what a press room was like. We'd all had our share of drink, but Dave seemed more affected by it than the rest of us. As we wandered round the room he was sounding off: "Fuck Nixon. To hell with Lyndon Johnson." When Dave was in his cups a favorite expression was "Rigore, Rigore." Apparently he was referring to Igor, Dr Frankenstein's assistant in the famous tale of horror. Two FBI men, mistaking Dave's harmless exuberance for a threat to national security, moved stealthily towards his six-foot plus frame, guns in underarm holsters ready for use if necessary. As the two of them grasped Dave's arms, gently and firmly, one of the men said, "Let's not say any more nasty things. You've had a big night and now it's beddy-bye time. Be a good boy and come with us." With Dave still mumbling "Rigore" they propelled him out of the press room, down the elevator, out of the Blackstone, across the street to the Hilton, up the elevator and to his room. After depositing Dave on the bed they locked the door and stood outside on guard. He was not let out until Johnson had arrived, given his speech and left the next day.

I have my own particularly sad memory of that hotel. I walked into the bar one night and was shocked to see my good friend Cutty sitting there with a beer and a whiskey in front of him. He'd had an alcoholic problem for years and had been told by his doctor to keep off the booze if he wanted to live. Cutty had decided to give up. He just didn't want to live. That was in April and he died the next summer. We were working at the Colonial Tavern with Eddie Condon, and Cutty didn't show up for the Saturday matinée. The night before he'd been in a jolly mood – drinking, to be sure, but playing great. After the first set Eddie got worried and called the hotel. They got no answer on Cutty's phone, so Eddie said, "You'd better get the police and break the door down." They found Cutty, still in his tux, lying peacefully on the bed. He'd passed away in his sleep.

It was interesting talking to Yank and Bob about the old days with Bob Crosby. They had originally been colleagues in the Ben Pollack band in the early 1930s, but when Pollack started to use the band's salary to promote the career of his girlfriend they started getting short money on paydays, so the band decided to quit *en masse*. There had been a tight camaraderie in the band, so Bob and Yank, along with Ray Bauduc, Nappy Lamare, Eddie Miller and Gil Rodin, decided to stick together and form a co-operative band. They went to the Rockwell–O'Keefe Agency, who recognized that the guys had the nucleus of a good band but advised them they needed a frontman with a name. Various names were put forward, one of which was Jack Teagarden. Jack was the one the guys really wanted, and while Jack himself was keen to join he had signed a contract with Paul Whiteman that he couldn't get out of. After considering Johnny "Scat" Davis, whom the guys rejected, the agency finally came up with Bob Crosby, a young kid singing with the Dorsey Brothers Orchestra, and younger brother of Bing. They admitted that Bob wasn't a great singer, but they felt they could build up his name because of the success of his famous brother. "Just take him on as a sideman. He'll stand in front of the band but he won't really be the leader. He'll be just another member of the co-op." What eventually happened, with the band riding high and its Decca records selling well, was a meeting of the co-operative at which Gil Rodin announced to the musicians, "Fellahs, we're changing the structure of the organization. From now on Crosby will own 50% of the band and the rest of us will own 50%." They took it because the band was on the crest of a wave and they had no other option than to resign, but it was a bitter pill for them to swallow. There were some people in the band, like Billy Butterfield and Vernon Brown, who were not members of the co-operative but were on a straight salary basis. When Yank found that the non-members were making more money than the members, who were paid on a percentage of the gross, he quit and joined Tommy Dorsey.

I met Bing in 1970 when I was with the World's Greatest Jazz Band. For two years in a row he asked us to play for the annual stag party the night before the opening day of the Pebble Beach Golf Tournament that he sponsored. When we arrived on the first occasion, Bing's brother Harry was waiting for us in a white Rolls-Royce. Our plane from Los Angeles had arrived late. Harry told us he had sent Dean Martin out to the airport to meet us, but when the chauffeur opened the car door Dean fell out on to the tarmac, completely blotto. Finding that the plane was late, the chauffeur bundled the well-known performer back into the car and drove back to town. When we arrived at the venue and set up we found ourselves in a relaxed male atmosphere, with golfers, sports fans and celebrities from the film world drinking and gabbing. We played a few numbers and then Phil Harris joined us for a couple of songs. Bing came out and they did a couple of scat vocals together, all totally relaxed and informal. During one of their duets I looked over to the side of the stage and saw Harry James. He had a Martini in his hand, and at the end of Bing and Phil's number he walked out on to the stage and asked Yank to hold his drink and lend him his horn. Taking the trumpet he put it to his lips and launched into Armstrong's opening cadenza from *West End Blues*. Now as every trumpet player knows, that cadenza is extremely difficult to play even when cold sober, and Harry was hardly in that state, but damned if he didn't miss a single note. A truly phenomenal player. I thought he was the greatest there was on trumpet until, at the age of 14, I discovered Armstrong.

Bing was a very convivial, low-key, relaxed and friendly man – very like the image the public had of him. He worked with our band and enjoyed every minute of it, in no way treating us as underlings.

Yank told me that the Crosby Band hated swing music and riffs. They wanted to play authentic New Orleans music. The arrangements were written in such a way that, even with the extra brass and reeds, it would sound like a small band. Haggart told me that one of his biggest problems in writing for the band was the fact that the baritone saxophonist, Gil Rodin, an astute businessman who managed the band, was a mediocre player. Bob devised ingenious ways of voicing so that, without Gil being aware of it, his part was buried, unheard and totally unnecessary. If there was some important client in the audience, Gil could just put down his horn and go over to speak to him and he wouldn't be missed. Rodin went on to become a vice-president of Universal Pictures.

The band had fascinated me as a kid because it was different from any of the other big bands. In a sense it was perhaps the first revivalist band of all, the first band to take a look back to the 1920s and find inspiration in the music of Oliver, Morton and Armstrong. Interestingly enough, it was, like all the later revivalist bands, white. In the 1930s the black musicians weren't interested in looking back, they were into riffs and swing. They were in a great hurry to make progress musically and socially, and what had happened ten years earlier meant nothing at all to them. The New Orleans musicians like Morton and Johnny Dodds who couldn't shift their style to fit the new sound were consigned to obscurity by the cruel hand of "progress." When you look at the history of American popular music as documented on records, starting with the Original Dixieland Jazz Band in 1917 through the Goodman Band of 1937, the rapidity of the change in music was staggering, far greater than the change in the last 20 years. When Goodman's 1938 Carnegie Hall Concert opened with a tribute to the Original Dixieland Jazz Band, it was considered comic, something to laugh at, something from a different world. Among those in the audience that night at Carnegie Hall was Johnny Dodds, who was in New York for the first time in his life to record some sides for Decca – the first time he'd been in a recording studio since the early 1930s. What must Dodds, who was ekeing out a living running a cab company in Chicago with his brother and only playing occasionally, have thought to see Goodman, whom he remembered as a kid in short pants hanging around the bandstand at Kelly's Stables ten years before, being the recipient of such adulation and applause in that sacrosant temple of American Culture? At least the Crosby band remembered the old music and were determined to keep the sound alive. Interestingly enough, Crosby's take-over of the band and his postwar success in television could have made his sidemen totally jealous of him, but it didn't happen that way. To this day Bob still gets jobs and always calls Yank, Haggart and the rest. They take his gigs when available, happy with the music, happy to be together. Crosby deserves a lot of credit for inspiring that kind of loyalty.

Yank has been a very good friend to me. He was an avid tennis player in his youth, and during the 1930s, while working with Crosby at the Blackhawk Restaurant in Chicago, he used to work out at the tennis club with Don Budge, the top American player at the time. In the late 1960s, while playing a jazz party in Odessa, Texas, Yank decided he'd be better off out on the tennis court rather than sitting around the hotel pool, drinking all afternoon. Looking round for a partner he spied me, and persuaded me to do the same. Not having played since my youthful summers in Prouts Neck, I somewhat reluctantly agreed, and to my surprise found that I had a good feeling for the game. It was another step in developing my sense of self-worth, and to this day I always take my tennis racket along on my travels.

Yank is still a fine trumpet player, liked and respected by everyone. He has a knowledge of the music business second to none and an inexhaustible fund of stories. Although a few years back he stopped drinking for good, he still likes to tell about a contest he had with another trumpeter when they were doing radio shows back in the days when live bands were used. They first of all did the show for the East Coast and the Midwest. Then, because of the time difference, they took an hour off and did the show all over again for the West Coast. Having an hour to kill, the musicians always headed for the nearest bar. This often resulted in the second show being quite different from the first. In those post-Prohibition days heavy drinking amongst musicians was quite the norm, and there were quite a few who never survived the era. But there was plenty of work around and the musicians could afford to be carefree and irresponsible. The poor conductor would often plead with his musicians to keep their socializing under control so that the second show wouldn't be a complete shambles. On this particular night an argument developed between Yank and another trumpet player as to who was the better drinker. Their section-mate said, "Let's resolve this. I'll buy you guys as many Martinis as you can drink and we'll see who can really hold his liquor." Yank won. He downed 21 Martinis in the hour and then went back to play the second show. His fellow brass-man, who lapsed into unconsciousness on his 20th drink, was laid out in the back room to recover and was conspicuously absent for the West Coast broadcast. When I asked Yank how the show sounded he grinned and replied, "I can't remember."

It's an ironic fact that during the 1930s Depression, with so much suffering and people out of work, musicians were riding high, making records, playing on radio and touring with bands. It seems when people are in bad straits and there is a lot of trouble in their lives, music means a lot to them and they appreciate it for bringing some light and joy to their existence. Indeed, one of the great reasons for Benny's success was his music expressed joy at a time when people didn't have a great deal to be happy about. The whole music business thrived at a time when the country was suffering. It wasn't until the postwar era, when people with money in their pockets began to place more emphasis on materialistic values, that good music, the food for the soul, began the downward curve that still prevails today.

In 1966 a very significant development in my career occurred when I discovered a little curved soprano saxophone in a music store. It gave me an idea of doing something with a soprano sax that was different from Bechet. From the very first notes I played on it, I heard a definite difference from the straight soprano sound I was used to. My first influence was Johnny Hodges. At first I stuck pretty much to the lower register, trying to get a sound like Hodges on alto. As I developed confidence on the horn I saw the possibility of combining the Armstrong influence with that of Hodges, owing to the similarity of range and sound of the soprano and trumpet. After all, the great musical love of my life had always been Armstrong – above everyone else he was my inspiration for playing jazz. The more I got into it, the more I began to feel that this was the distinctive musical identity I had been looking for. After all those years of wandering and searching I was beginning to have a sense of who I was musically. A forcefulness, a sense of purpose that had hitherto been missing from my playing, began to appear. At the same time my clarinet began to free up, sounding less up-tight and self-conscious than it had for years.

A major boost to my confidence came along in the form of Bill Borden, the former arranger of Claude Thornhill, who ran Monmouth Evergreen Records. At his invitation I went to his office, and could hardly believe my ears when I heard him say, "Bob, we'd like you to do an album featuring the music of one of the Broadway or popular composers in a jazz style. We've compiled a list of possibilities. Would you like to do the project and, if so, which composer would you like to do?" Bill had learned about me from his former Thornhill colleague Rusty Dedrick, with whom I had worked on an Irving Berlin project and subsequently on an album devoted to Harold Arlen. My work on those albums had apparently impressed Bill, resulting in this most generous, open-ended offer. Would I like to do it? These weren't the usual record executives telling me exactly what they wanted – they were actually giving me a wide range of choice! It was a thrilling moment for me because it was the first time in many years that someone had expressed confidence in me, a confidence that went far beyond my mere aptitude to play an instrument. It was a vote of confidence in my ability to put together the musicians, to write the arrangements, to conduct the date, to do everything with no strings attached. I was elated, and determined to show all those people who thought of me as just another clarinet player at Condon's that I was capable of a lot more than just playing in a jazzband every night till four in the morning.

I threw myself into the assignment with enthusiasm and high hopes. I wanted the record to showcase the composers' music, but in a jazz vein. I also wanted my fans to hear my new soprano sound and to ascertain the difference between it and the Bechet sound I'd been so closely identified with in my early years. After considering Waller and Ellington, I thought about Hoagy Carmichael and his association with Bix. I thought about *Riverboat Shuffle* and *Washboard Blues* and his other jazz compositions, not to mention his great popular tunes, and I concluded that Hoagy was the natural choice. The album turned out to be an artistic success and was nominated for a Grammy Award in 1970. The Grammy, similar to the Oscar in the movie field, is awarded for musical excellence in various categories every year by the National Association of Recording Arts and Science. Its main offices, reflecting the three centers of the music business in the United States, are located in New York, Los Angeles and Nashville, Tennessee. That year the West Coast members all voted for another nominee, Quincy Jones, who was riding high in his first year in Hollywood. Quincy's record won, but at least my album got its due recognition and I was proud of it. It also, incidentally, started a come-back for Maxine Sullivan, who sang on five tracks.

It didn't completely open up things for me because, unfortunately, it wasn't a commercial success. Bill Borden, after his youthful years in music, had spent most of his adult life running the family business. His little record label was a labor of love and he didn't have the staff or the marketing knowledge to sell a lot of records. Although it would have been nice to have a big seller, the really important thing for me was the feeling of achievement it had given me. It was also a prime example of what can happen when a company is willing to give complete artistic freedom to the artist. The usual attitude of a record company is, "We know what the public wants, so do it our way. You want a record that sells, right? Listen to us and you'll have a hit." All poppycock, of course, but the average record producer's belief in his ability to read public taste is absolute. The musician ends up feeling that his principal function is to make money for the record company, not to make an artistic statement. It was ironic, however, that those who gave me artistic freedom to make a record that was nominated for a Grammy didn't have the marketing ability to make money with it, whereas those who did have these skills were never prepared to give me the freedom.

I felt I was making some progress with my life following the visits to the analyst, certainly so in the music field, where I could feel the confidence returning and where my soprano was developing into a real voice. I was still not ready for the ultimate step of saying, "I am a leader. I want my own band." That didn't come for quite a while, but at least I was now beginning to enjoy playing jazz again.

One of the busiest musicians around in 1969 was Yank Lawson. As well as playing at Condon's, Yank was working on staff at NBC, holding down a permanent place in the "Tonight Show" band. One of the advantages of the television job was that musicians could bring in an original piece of work. In exchange for allowing the bandleader's publishing firm to publish it, he'd play it on the "Tonight Show" as a filler, and the composer would get a credit with ASCAP. Thanks to Yank's efforts, I used to compose little pieces of no more than two minutes in length, orchestrate them for the band and have them played on the show. One day Yank approached me with a proposition. Would I be interested in joining a band a friend of his was putting together? That friend was Dick Gibson, a very unusual and interesting man of great talent and vision. In his early days he had been an all-American football player and later coach at the University of Alabama. He started his business career as a financial investor with Lehman Brothers, one of the biggest banking firms on Wall Street, and following that became a business manager for the *New York Herald Tribune*. In the 1960s Dick moved to Denver, where he found a dentist with an idea for cleaning teeth by means of a pressurized-water system. He interested a group of investors, who formed a company to market the product, calling it Waterpik. With the help of an effective advertising campaign, the Waterpik became a very popular and successful product. His company was subsequently bought by a big conglomerate, Teledyne, and all the original investors, including Dick, emerged with a very handsome profit.

Having grown up in Mobile listening to jazz, Dick loved visiting the jazz clubs in New York. When he moved to Denver he really missed that part of his life, so he started putting together little jazz parties at Aspen, up in the mountains. He invited a dozen of his favorite musicians from New York, people like Wild Bill Davison and Teddy Wilson, and persuaded a group of his wealthy Denver friends to join him in footing the bill. Arrangements were made with a local hotel, and for three days everybody had a marvelous time with jazz music, socializing, eating and drinking. From then on it became an annual event. Dick then contacted the manager of Elitch Gardens, a famous amusement park in Denver. It included a dance hall where Benny Goodman had played on his original tour out to the West Coast in 1935. Benny's hot, swinging band had been a dismal failure there; the Elitch crowds were used to sweet bands like Wayne King and Guy Lombardo. Dick's proposal was: "Let's go 50–50 on a deal. If I bring in some of my favorite musicians from New York, will you let them play here at Elitch Gardens for three consecutive weekends in the summer? I'll see it gets plenty of publicity in the newspapers and on radio." The deal was made and for several years, starting in the summer of 1966, the Nine Greats of Jazz (later ten) were a very successful attraction. The musicians all liked Dick, who was an extremely generous man. He arranged accommodation for them in the homes of his friends so that they saved on hotel bills and he recorded the evenings at Elitch Gardens, put the records out on his own label and shared the proceeds among the musicians.

Following the sale of the Waterpik company, Dick felt in a position to pursue his great dream of forming a band, to be called the World's Greatest Jazz Band. When Yank approached me to join the band I jumped at the chance. The first rehearsals were a great thrill. Bob Haggart had taken the best pop material of the era – songs by the Beatles, Burt Bacharach, Simon and Garfunkel, Jim Webb, etc – and arranged them in a style tailor-made to the talents of the players. The original band consisted of Yank and Billy Butterfield on trumpets, Lou McGarity and Carl Fontana on trombones, Ralph Sutton on piano, Morey Feld on drums, Bob Haggart on bass, Bud Freeman on tenor, Clancy Hayes on banjo and myself on clarinet and soprano. (Clancy was supposed to bring his guitar for the contemporary things and save the banjo for the dixieland stuff, but somehow the guitar never made the trip from San Francisco.) It was all so creative and new and the musicians were fired up by the musical challenge Haggart's arrangements presented. To hear Bud Freeman romping through *Mrs Robinson* or to play the arrangement of *Sunny* that Bob had tailored around my soprano was really exciting. While I was heartily sick of all the old warhorses, I wasn't ready to move away from my roots and play modern jazz. I felt that this was a very creative way of playing traditional jazz with a fresh, contemporary feel. Our library was extensive. The book included, in addition to the contemporary material, Haggart's famous originals like *South Rampart Street Parade* and *What's New* and some of the things I'd written for the Hoagy Carmichael album.

The ten-piece band could roar with the impact of a large orchestra, but with such great players could also improvise freely like a small group. Somehow all the varied material we played from different eras coalesced into a distinctive and unique sound, not like the sound of any other band before it.

In the fall of 1969 Gibson came to New York and persuaded the management of the Riverboat Room, deep in the bowels of the Empire State Building, to hire the WGJB (as it came to be known) for a three-week engagement. Dick was indefatigable in the promotion of his dream band. He hired a press agent to publicize the event and on the opening night he laid on a big party, with champagne and caviar for the press, jazz critics and everyone of importance in New York. He got the band guest shots on all the big TV shows – Steve Allen, Ed Sullivan, the "Today Show" and the "Tonight Show." Another of his early achievements was in signing a contract with Sol Hurok, the top promoter of classic music and ballet in the world. All Hurok's acts were prestigious people in the classical field, and for him to take on a jazz group was unprecedented. It was a very impressive connection for the band to have in its formative stages.

The Hurok organization did a good job in promoting us, so that in general our dates were pretty successful. We had problems on one tour, however. Hurok had booked us as part of a concert series in Ohio, each venue presenting six Hurok attractions. Unfortunately the attraction preceding us was Van Cliburn, the famous classical pianist from Texas who had made such a tremendous impression when he visited Russia and won the International Piano Competition in Moscow. His fee for his appearance on the circuit a month before us had been astronomical. All the venues lost money, and in order to pay him off they had to appropriate funds from their subscription tickets. When we got to Ohio, the promoters were dependent upon filling the house in order to pay us. Unfortunately we hit a bad streak of weather and the audiences who'd turned out for Van Cliburn the month before stayed home. The promoters ended up with half-empty houses and not enough money to pay us. We were eventually paid, but the Hurok office ended up by taking a loss. It's still difficult to book jazz as a cultural event because of the sneaking suspicion that still exists among many patrons of the arts that somehow jazz is not quite respectable.

The second stage of Dick's dream then began to take shape as he looked around New York for a permanent home for the band. For many years the Roosevelt Grill in the Roosevelt Hotel had been the headquarters for Guy Lombardo's band, but it had been empty for years. The hotel was contemplating selling the room to a bank for one of their branches, but by using all his charm Dick convinced them that the WGJB would be the ideal tenant to revive the entertainment potential of the room. No sooner were we installed than cracks began to appear in the seams of our smooth-running machine, owing to cash flow problems that Dick was experiencing because of fluctuations on the stock market. Gradually large debts accumulated. There was no means of paying them off, and things were looking pretty bleak for the band as the crowds failed to materialize. Then there came on the scene a wealthy playboy from Phoenix, Arizona, named Barker Hickox, who was looking round for something to make life a little more exciting. He became very interested in the band, and stepped in to rescue the whole operation just when Dick was having difficulty meeting the pay-roll.

It was a very emotional meeting in Colorado Springs, with Gibson, Hickox and the co-leaders, Lawson and Haggart, when Hickox took over. Dick said, "Well, Barker, welcome aboard ship. Glad to have you with us. All I want out of this deal is the same salary as the rest of the guys and I'll continue promoting my band."

Hickox eyed him with a cold stare and said, "Gibson, we don't need you any more. You're out." Hickox took over the whole operation, and also formed the

World Jazz Record Company. Although he had unlimited financial resources, he had no talent at all for promotion, in direct contrast to the dynamic ability of Gibson. Typical of Barker's approach was a tour on the Northwest that he set up. Flying across the country in his private plane, he and his pilot stopped off at a whole succession of little towns, where he hired the local hall and stuck up a few posters around town before flying on to the next place on the map. At the end of our 20-concert tour he invited the whole band to a sumptuous dinner at Trader Vic's in Seattle. During the evening he stood up and said, "Here's a toast, gentlemen, to a marvelous tour. I lost $25,000 but it was great fun." In truth the tour was insane, an utter disaster. We played in little towns where they neither knew nor cared anything about jazz.

One prestigious job that Hickox did get for us, through his strong connections with the Republican Party, was President Nixon's first inaugural ball in 1970 at a fancy hotel in Washington, DC. We alternated with the band of Lester Lanin, the leading society band in America, and right from the start it developed into some sort of competition. Lester is always a very uptight, nervous man, but on this occasion even more so than usual. The reason was that during the evening the president's party would be visiting us, and Lester wanted to be sure that, when it arrived, it would be his orchestra on the bandstand and not us. All through the evening a battle of wits went on between Lester and Bob Haggart. When Lester's band was playing, he placed an upright sign on top of the piano reading "Music by Lester Lanin" and left it there when the band finished its set. Bob, who stood with his bass by the piano, noticed the sign and placed it face down, so that during our set it was not in evidence. When Lester came back he was very angry to see the sign face down and immediately restored it to its original position. When we came back Bob placed it face down again, and so on. By the time the presidential party arrived, Lanin, who had been reduced to a nervous wreck by the sign business, was further dismayed, having just finished his set, to hear the sound of the approaching entourage. Our band's ability to play the traditional ruffles and flourishes as the president entered the room was considerably impaired by an accident that occurred earlier in the evening. While making an announcement Yank had tried to raise the microphone to his considerable height, but it refused to budge. When he finally gave it an extra jerk it suddenly shot up and hit him on the lip. Any more playing was out of the question and for the rest of the evening Billy was our only trumpet player.

During one of our breaks I was watching Lester leading his band in his usual nervous fashion, when a portly, beribboned colonel and his lady came dancing by. As they passed Lester, the colonel inadvertently stepped on Lanin's foot. I saw Lester grimace visibly as 250 pounds' pressure crushed his small pedal extremity encased in its delicate evening pump, but Lanin quickly recovered his aplomb. As the colonel apologized, Lester, with a beaming, cringing smile, gushed out, "My pleasure, sir." The Uriah Heep of the music business!

Another amusing incident in my years with the WGJB occurred at a country club in Palm Springs. We were doing a tour of one-nighters and, to fill a break in our schedule, one of Dick Gibson's wealthy friends threw a party at his club and hired the band to play. We flew in from an engagement in Anchorage, Alaska, and were met at the airport in Los Angeles by a fleet of limousines which drove us across the desert to the plush millionaire's resort. After cleaning up at our hotel we went over to the club, where we had an early dinner with our host. He was quite relaxed and was looking forward to the evening, but his wife was running round, worrying whether everything would be all right. She was in a highly nervous state, excited but apprehensive as she confided to us: "It's going to be wonderful. The only thing I'm worried about is that we have two members here who are always causing problems. They're just born trouble-makers. We had a private party last month and these two drunken guys gate-crashed and upset everybody. I certainly hope nothing like that happens tonight." She turned to her husband and said, "You know who I mean, dear. Your two pals, Hoagy Carmichael and Phil Harris."

We finished our dinner and set up the stand. Ralph Sutton was in an unusually convivial mood and we wondered what had happened. It turned out that after dinner Ralph had wandered into the club bar. There he'd met Phil Harris, who greeted him like a long lost buddy and proposed numerous liquid toasts to their eternal friendship. On top of the Martinis and wine he'd had during dinner, Ralph found it impossible to stand upright and collapsed on a sofa at the back of the ballroom. We realized that we were going to be without a pianist that evening, but as this kind of thing had happened before we just went ahead without the piano. I was doing my solo on Hoagy's *One Morning in May*. It sounded a little empty without Ralph's usual brilliant accompaniment, but suddenly I heard some very strange chords behind me. The chords were right but it didn't sound like Sutton at all. I looked round and there was Hoagy Carmichael sitting at the piano, his head weaving from side to side, obviously four sheets to the wind. He looked up sheepishly at me and said, "Ish shat OK, man? I wash jush tryin' to help." Meanwhile I looked back at the drums and saw that Gus Johnson was no longer on his usual perch. In his place on the ten-foot high riser was Phil Harris, slashing away with a huge smile on his face. He went for one big cymbal crash, missed the cymbal, lost his balance, and fell backwards off the drums. The unthinkable but inevitable had happened – Carmichael and Harris had done it again!

Ralph Sutton and I were room-mates on the road. I couldn't have had a better "roomie" than Ralph. We were both partial to silence and could go for hours without talk. Our conversation consisted only of what seemed important. That might seem rather uninteresting, but our room represented a haven of peace and relaxation in the constant whirl of our professional life. One just has to be impressed with Ralph's musicianship. He has impeccable technique and, with his tall build and large hands, gets a huge sound out of a piano – the larger the instrument the bigger the sound. I found, in writing original compositions for the band, that if I just wrote the melody and chord symbols, it would take a while for Ralph to figure out what I intended. Realizing the problem, I wrote out complete piano scores and Ralph got the idea immediately. He's got the finest knowledge of Fats Waller's stride piano of anyone around, but his beat is less ragtimey, more like Basie in its feel. His repertoire has always tended to be rather narrow in that it favors repetition of much of what he has done before. Fortunately the material, like the Lion's *Echoes of Spring* and Meade "Lux" Lewis's *Honky-tonk Train*, is great stuff, and his fans never get tired of hearing Ralph play them. It's a pity in a way, because there's a great creative player lurking behind those horn-rimmed glasses, and all he needs is someone to stimulate him and push him. He's a natural talent and doesn't need constant practice to stay consistently brilliant. For many years he never even owned a piano. Jack Lesberg gave him his when he was moving to Australia. I was visiting Ralph about six months after he'd acquired the instrument, and when I asked him how he liked it he took me into the living room. There was the piano and bench in the corner of the room covered with plants and flowers. His wife, Sunnie, had decided that the piano was the ideal setting to display her greenery. Ralph didn't mind – he never practiced anyway. He didn't need to.

Dick's idea of having a permanent home for the band in New York was an excellent one. The Roosevelt Grill was the perfect room, but it just didn't work – the business wasn't there. It was at the time when the fear of getting mugged and robbed in New York was at its height, and people just weren't going out at night. Besides that, interest in jazz seemed to be at a low ebb, and consequently the band had to do a lot of touring to stay together. As well as extensive coverage of the United States, we undertook tours of South America and Europe. Our visit to England was an artistic success but a financial disaster. The arrangement was that the promoter would pay for the package in the form of two checks, one before the tour started and the other after it ended. The second check bounced sky-high. Our promoter, a Scotsman from Aberdeen, had helped the Harold Davison Agency book dates in Scotland for one of their attractions. When the Davison people suggested to him that they would help book the WGJB in England, he was very high-handed about it, saying, thank you, but he didn't need their help. It was a big mistake, as the promotion and publicity in England turned out to be abysmal. Fans who called the Hammersmith Odeon in London, where we were doing our opening date, were told by the box office that they knew nothing of such a concert. This type of thing continued to happen throughout the tour, and in a way it was a relief to return to the States. That summer we had quite an experience at the Newport Festival. The festival had originally started out as a cultural event with lectures and seminars plus the live music, and in that form it had been a very pleasant affair, but gradually over the years its character changed. With the introduction of rock groups into the program, hippies started to converge on Newport from all over the country with their tents, cheap wine and drugs, taking over the town and antagonizing all the local residents.

This particular summer the festival was held in a big field, around which a fence had been constructed, with the stage and stands in the middle. At the back of the field, outside the arena, was a hill where people could sit and look down on the bandstand and listen to the music. It was occupied by thousands of hippies smoking pot and drinking wine. One of the leading rock groups at the festival was Sly and the Family Stone, comprising ten people who appeared on stage in all kinds of exotic costumes, supported by numerous technicians backstage manning all the electronic equipment. As the frenzied sound of the group boomed out through huge 20-foot high speakers, the hippies on the hill got more and more worked up. Gradually the feeling began to spread among them that they ought to be inside the arena instead of being shut out on the hill, and they started moving down to the perimeter fence, which was protected by guards with huge wooden clubs. A very ugly confrontation seemed to be building up as Sly and his group finished. We were standing around backstage when George Wein ran up, obviously in a highly agitated state. "Look, you guys, we got big trouble. You've got to get out there and quiet them down." Meanwhile, in order to try and placate the hippies, some of them had been allowed into an area directly in front of the stage usually reserved for critics and reporters. As I stood there I looked down through a jungle of microphones and cables into a mass of bodies writhing like maggots. They in turn were staring up at us through glassy eyes and shouting, "Hey, look at the old guys." The sky was gradually darkening, there was an angry glow that indicated an approaching thunderstorm, and all around the perimeter the hippies were advancing on the guards standing ready with clubs raised. It looked as though they would surge forward at any minute and push over the fence, and then all hell would break loose. Luckily at that point the heavens opened up and the rain came down in buckets, defusing an explosive situation. It was such a relief that none of us onstage or in the audience minded getting soaked to the skin – particularly George Wein, who knew that a riot would have wrecked his future as a jazz festival producer. Later than evening I bumped into the manager of the rock group, none other than Dave Kapralik who had tried to convert me into a cult figure and Mohammed Ali into a pop singer!

If anyone were to plot a graph of the World's Greatest Jazz Band it would show a brilliant start and a gradual decline. Right from the beginning its biggest asset was the Haggart arrangements of contemporary material. Project 3, the first company to record us, were smart enough to realize that the pop stuff was a marketable commodity. The nationwide airplay following our first release confirmed the accuracy of that assessment; our jazz versions of *Sunny* and *Mrs Robinson* got far more airplay than anything else the WGJB ever recorded. Unfortunately, Enoch Light of Project 3 didn't have the facilities to market records on a big scale, and after two LPs we moved over to Atlantic Records and the Ertegun brothers. In a way, that was perhaps the start of the decline. Ahmet was the businessman of the organization, always looking for a mass audience, while Nesuhi was the nostalgic jazz fan who affectionately remembered the old Bob Crosby band. He was the one who was really interested in us and he supervised our first recording session in Los Angeles. Sadly, Haggart's arrangements of contemporary music meant nothing to him; all he wanted was the old Bob Cats' sound. When the results reached Atlantic's marketing people, they couldn't understand why Nesuhi was recording all that "old stuff" and they just threw it on the market, with no effort at promotion. Besides, Atlantic Records was totally black-oriented; the whole foundation of the company's success was based on the black sound and the selling of that sound to a white audience. All the salesmen related to Aretha Franklin and Ray Charles, but certainly not to us, and as a result the marketing of our product was virtually non-existent.

If only somebody in the music business could have seen the potential of the WGJB a lot of people would have made a great deal of money, but it didn't happen that way. Lawson and Haggart became categorized victims of their own fame, forever associated with Bob Crosby, the Bob Cats and dixieland music, but that was not what Haggart and Gibson had in mind. The original concept was something unique in jazz, a massed-group sound from six horns and four rhythm that combined traditional jazz with the beauty and freshness of contemporary music. The business people had neither the vision nor the courage to give it the big push it needed. Gradually Yank and Hagg backed off and started to play safe, catering to the hard core dixieland fans, the loyal audience they could trust, who only wanted to hear the old favorites like *South Rampart Street Parade* and *Big Noise From Winetka*. The big world out there that wanted to hear *Mrs Robinson* and *Sunny* was an unknown entity, but that was where the potential and the future really lay. Haggart knew this but was fighting a lost cause, because the attitude of the musicians had also begun to change. They were so vain that they objected to putting on glasses to read music in concert and club situations, so music stands and arrangements gradually got left off the stage. The attitude became, "Oh, let's not bother. Let's just go out and jam." It was basically the drinkers in the band who couldn't be bothered. The heavy boozer is always battling the effects of alcohol, either drunk or hung over, and when one is in that state it's so much easier to say, "What the hell. Let's just go out and blow." Increasingly the presentations developed into an opening number of the full band followed by an endless procession of soloists trooping out on to the stage to play with the rhythm section. Haggart never said anything about it, but it really broke his heart because he had put so much thought and effort into it. There was also the additional handicap of having a co-leader who, in those days when he had a few drinks, got belligerent. Yank would call the tunes while Bob was standing at the back playing bass. When Yank was "under the weather," all he wanted to play was *Jazz me Blues* and *Tin Roof*. He may have pictured himself back at the Blackhawk with Crosby!

Gradually the excitement I felt began to subside as I saw the band sinking into a repetitive, routine pattern. I had been with the organization for six years. I liked the guys, all excellent musicians, and there was a security which had been important to me as I emerged from my depression of the 1960s, but now I was getting bored with it and could see that it wasn't going anywhere. It reverted to what it had been back at Elitch Gardens, a very good dixieland band, but that wasn't the reason the band so excited me. To some extent, the problem with the WGJB was that it happened ten years too late. It should have been organized when most of the members were in their 50s rather than their 60s. At that time, however, Haggart was deeply involved in the lucrative jingle business and Yank was on staff at NBC, earning big money. They didn't want to know about going on the road with a band, but that's what they should have done. The reason they eventually did was because the whole world of freelancing and jingles started to change. Singers like Bob Dylan and Joan Baez didn't use large orchestras for backing, and jingles were becoming more and more rock-orientated. The large staff orchestras at all the networks were all disbanded, leaving a large group of musicians who either retired or scrambled for the theater and club-date jobs available. That was why so many people went back into jazz – people like Dick Hyman, Milt Hinton and Bobby Rosengarden. The world in which they had made a lot of money had disappeared. There was a whole new generation of producers and contractors into the sounds of rock music. This is something that is always happening in the commercial music business – every ten years or so there is a turnover of producers, contractors and musicians reflecting the current "in" sound.

Despite everything the WGJB continued to be a viable commodity in the jazz world. Through its recordings and tours it had established a world-wide following. Even when it started to sound old and tired, it was still something unusual. Ralph Sutton left first, in 1975, then Bud Freeman and then me. We all had the feeling that we were treading water and needed a change. The band continued for a number of years afterwards, touring all over the world with varying personnel, but more and more as a pick-up unit with whatever musicians were available. The World's Greatest Jazz Band, the brainchild of Dick Gibson, a dedicated jazz fan who really believed in its name, never made back the money that Dick, and later Barker Hickox, poured into it. But it was a noble failure which, because of its very existence, contributed to the revival of interest in jazz in the 1980s.

TEN

Rediscovering Bob Wilber

A person who catches the public's fancy and becomes a recognized figure must have an image that is fairly simple and direct, one that the public can comprehend. I had been wandering through the musical wilderness in a very confused fashion for many years and the public did not know what to make of me. The abandonment of Bechet, the change from soprano sax to tenor, the idealism of the Six, were all factors that contributed to my disappearance as a public figure in jazz. Throughout the late 1950s and early 1960s I was doing nothing that was calculated to restore my image. I remember seeing a jazz encyclopedia of the period and reading the sections on Pops Foster, Jimmy Archey and Tommy Benford, all of whom were described as having played with Bob Wilber's band. There was no section on Bob Wilber, however. When I subsequently spoke to the author he said quite simply that there was no interest in me at that time. It was as though I had ceased to exist.

The psychiatrist represented the turning point, and I think people will detect the effect upon me as a musician by listening to my subsequent recordings. For instance, on *New Clarinet in Town* from 1960 you hear a detached, clinical performance that lacks the spontaneity and conviction essential to a great jazz performance. My album with Ralph Sutton, *The Night They Raided Sunnies* on Blue Angel from 1969, is the first evidence that things were on the mend. The clarinet is freer, less inhibited, and there is the sound of some happiness there. The Hoagy Carmichael album was the big breakthrough, however. I began to get a focus on myself, an idea of who I was, and I started to believe I had something to say. The recordings with the World's Greatest Jazz Band clearly revealed a new Wilber at work. The band represented my big opportunity to get things together again. I was working with friends, playing music I enjoyed, writing arrangements, and developing my soprano sax into a major voice. On the other hand, being a sideman, I had no other responsibilities, and in a way it represented a shelter from the outside world of business and personal contacts.

My development as a human being paralleled my growth as a musician, and when a new romance presented itself I was ready. Shortly after the formation of the band I met Elizabeth at a New Year's Eve party. She was a striking blond lady and as we danced together it became apparent that there was a mutual attraction. That spring, when the band played for a couple of weeks in Boston, she joined me. Our romance continued through the summer, and when we opened at the Roosevelt Grill that fall she was in constant attendance. The guys in the band used to' call her "Mammy Yokum," after the character in the "Li'l Abner" cartoons, because of her habit of smoking a pipe. Elizabeth was an intellectual, a writer, a very independent-thinking sort of lady. In the summers she lived on an island where the only other inhabitants were the lighthouse keeper and his family. There was no electricity, no telephone – only her motorboat to take her back and forth to the mainland. I used to spend time there when the band wasn't working. As the evenings approached we would run out to her lobster-traps, pick out our dinner, and after boiling the hapless creatures in a pot on the wood-burning stove we'd have our meal, watch the sunset and take turns reading aloud from the latest novel by Saul Bellow, her favorite writer at the time.

It was a very warm, romantic relationship, exciting and passionate, and we were seriously making plans for a future together. The following year, when the band was playing a concert in Saratoga, New York, Elizabeth and I went to the elegant Gideon Putnam Hotel for dinner and quite by chance ran into Pug and John Horton with a party of their friends. They invited us to join them. I looked again at Pug and remembered how beautiful she had seemed to me when I had first met her ten years ago at Condon's. She was the type of woman I had always dreamed of as a kid, and she still looked fantastic. We had exchanged an odd phone call or letter over those years but I had always felt remote from her. She was such an outgoing character and I was such an introvert. Despite my passionate involvement with Elizabeth I felt I wanted to be with Pug more than anything else in the world. As I watched her sitting there with her friends I still couldn't persuade myself that she saw me as anything other than the scared little guy in a raincoat she'd met in 1960. As I looked back and forth between Elizabeth and Pug I couldn't help saying to myself, "Hey, Wilber. What the hell is going on? You're making serious plans with Elizabeth and yet you really want to be with Pug." It wasn't until that confrontation at the Gideon Putnam that I realized how much I cared for this English lady who, in a strange way, had been a part of my life for 25 years. I suppose that meeting with Pug was the beginning of the end of my intense relationship with Elizabeth. She was a recluse, a hermit by nature, who loved the serenity of her island retreat, and here was I, running all over the world, playing my music – too great a difference in life styles to make it work.

In the spring of 1971 the Roosevelt Grill engagement ended and the WGJB went out on the road again with its new backer, Barker Hickox, and a new booking agent, Frank Modica. While playing in Detroit I met Barbara. She was an extrovert, outgoing brunette, totally different from Elizabeth. She seemed to know everybody who mattered in the motor city and she even wangled a job doing public relations work for the band so she could be on the road with us. Her three young boys were delightful little characters, and getting to know them was an important lesson for me in learning to connect with people. It was Barbara who gave me a taste for interesting clothes. Out the window went the conservative pattern of dress that I had kept ever since high-school days; navy blazers, grey slacks, dark suits, white shirts, conservative ties and plain shoes were replaced by casual, colorful clothes, and I let my hair grow longer. I look back and think of those two ladies, Elizabeth and Barbara, with nothing but happy feelings and gratitude. They had taught me the value of human relationships and they showed me how to express myself in ways other than through music – how to be a human being rather than a musical machine. There was still a long way to go but at least I felt I was on the right road.

After leaving the World's Greatest Jazz Band the next big happening in my life was a tour of Russia in 1975. I had always been interested in the roots of jazz and I felt a strong obligation to help preserve the music and its traditions. When the New York Jazz Repertory Company was formed in 1973 I was pleased to be a charter member on the board of directors – along with Jimmy Owens, Stanley Dance, John Hammond, George Wein, Billy Taylor and Robert Wagner, the ex-mayor of New York.

The basic idea of the company was to form a pool of around 50 players whose collective ability covered the full spectrum, from traditional to contemporary jazz, and to draw from that pool different combinations of musicians, depending on the type of music being featured at a particular concert. It was a very loosely structured type of thing. The main problem was always a lack of adequate rehearsal to do the music justice. It was quite a different concept from the one I subsequently developed with the Smithsonian Jazz Repertory Ensemble, which was to form a band of nine musicians capable of playing all the different styles of jazz.

Concert subjects were decided upon at the board meetings and, depending upon the particular project, the musical director for the event was also chosen. One of our best efforts was the "Tribute to Louis Armstrong." Unfortunately I couldn't be part of it because at the time I was committed to a solo tour of Europe, playing with local bands everywhere. Kenny Davern took my place and Dick Hyman was musical director. It was an outstanding success, drawing the biggest crowds of all the Repertory Company's concerts. With the permission of George Wein, it was recorded by a jazz fan from New Jersey and subsequently released on Atlantic Records. I acted as musical director for several other concerts, all of them held at Carnegie Hall. One was called "the Spanish Tinge." It traced the history and explored the use of Spanish rhythms in jazz. The first part of the concert featured the embryo Soprano Summit playing pieces by Morton, "the Lion," Handy and others which had a Spanish flavor. This was followed by the Latin bands of Machito and Tito Puente. A large part of the audience was Hispanic, primarily there for the two big bands. What Soprano Summit did was new to them but they listened attentively and applauded our efforts. Other concerts covered Jean Goldkette, Fletcher Henderson, Bix Beiderbecke, Count Basie, Duke Ellington, John Kirby, Charlie Parker and John Coltrane. The last was an amazing concert put on by Andrew White, who took Coltrane's solos and notated them for four tenors. I didn't get to go but I saw the music – there was more black ink on the paper than white spaces!

Altogether we did about 15 concerts at Carnegie Hall. The first concert of

1975 was the tribute to Armstrong and was broadcast on the Voice of America program. The broadcast naturally was monitored in Russia, where the cultural affairs department heard it and liked it. As a result negotiations were initiated with the State Department to bring our company to Russia to present the music of Louis Armstrong. It was a period when relations between America and Russia were quite cordial and the State Department was interested in promoting cultural exchanges. We were rehearsing at Carrol Studios for the tour when we were visited by a representative of the State Department who briefed us on protocol, what we could and could not do in Russia. We could take cameras but mustn't take pictures of railway stations, bridges, airports and military installations. We had to be careful in our relationships with people we met. We had to be polite at all times – no drunkenness and no fraternizing with Russian women. Some of the musicians were quite fraternal by nature: Joe Newman, for instance, had a marvelous ability to make friends wherever he went, whether he understood the language or not, and inevitably he made many friends in Russia – quite a few of them ladies.

At the end of May 1975 we set off on our trip with Dick Hyman on piano and as musical director. The rest of the personnel comprised Norris Turney, Budd Johnson, Haywood Henry and myself on reeds, Ernie Royal, Bernie Privin, Joe Newman and Jimmy Maxwell on trumpets, Eddie Bert and Eph Resnick on trombones, Art Ryerson on guitar, George Duvivier on bass, Bobby Rosengarden on drums and Carrie Smith, vocalist. After we landed at Moscow Airport we couldn't find Budd Johnson. He had gotten off the plane in an inebriated state and had left all his belongings, including his passport, on the aircraft. When we eventually found him he was surrounded by Russian soldiers and officials. When things were finally sorted out we boarded the bus for Moscow. The Intourist representative was a young girl assigned to accompany us on the whole tour. She was interested in learning more about America – apparently too interested, because after the tour ended she lost her job. There was a curious ambivalence on the part of the Russian authorities about our tour. They were pleased by its success but fearful of close contact between us and our newfound Russian friends. The music of Louis Armstrong was well known to the jazz fans. For years they had listened clandestinely to Willis Connover on the Voice of America broadcasts. To them the music had connotations of freedom and the good life in the western world.

We gave nine concerts in Moscow alone, where we had huge audiences of over 10,000 at each performance. Always, however, police and soldiers were very much in evidence. I remember looking up in the wings of the huge sports arena where the concerts took place and seeing the massive girders supporting the high structure. Standing at regular intervals along the girders were soldiers with their rifles at the ready. This was in addition to the massive security force at ground level consisting mostly of Amazonian women dressed in khaki uniforms with large leather holster belts. As we came out after the concerts the band bus was surrounded by fans, mostly young people with programs they wanted us to autograph. An alarming incident occurred when one youngster tried to indicate to Joe Newman that he too was a trumpet player. Joe reached into his case, took out a spare mouthpiece and, through the open window of the bus, handed it to the boy, who smiled delightedly. In a flash, a police car raced up to the bus and two policemen jumped out, bundled the boy into the car and drove off. We were all shocked and puzzled. When we asked our guide about it, she said, "It isn't what you think it is. The boy was going to take the mouthpiece and sell it on the black market." It seemed that selling on the black market was a very serious crime in Russia, but we really didn't believe her story. We felt that the authorities just didn't approve of young people associating so closely with the Americans. We subsequently found out that the Intourist guide not only lost her job but was forced to move away from Moscow as punishment for being too keen about us Americans.

Getting everybody onto the band bus in good time to go from hotel to concert was always a problem, and we solved it by electing Budd Johnson to be "the Judge." The idea was that anybody who was more than five minutes late would have to buy the band a bottle of vodka, two if he was ten minutes late, three if he was 15 minutes late. Budd was the sole arbitor, but in reality it was a not-so-subtle way of ensuring that Budd was always on time, since he was one of the better drinkers in the band. The one who was consistently buying the most vodka was Joe Newman, but Joe finally figured out a solution by befriending a young lady in Moscow, the wife of one of the American diplomats. From then on she chauffeured Joe to and from all the concerts.

The first time I had direct contact with any Muscovites was in Red Square on our first day in Russia. We were staying in the Hotel Russia, which contains 6000 rooms and is reputed to be the largest hotel in the world. After we had checked in, a bunch of us went out to look around. We met a group of Russian jazz fans in the square, who said that if they could meet us later they'd bring along some of their records for us to autograph. We suggested that they meet us in the lobby of our hotel, but they were obviously reluctant to do that. They suggested we meet at a certain time in the square. It was our first indication that the ordinary man in the street was very apprehensive about showing too much friendliness towards Americans. It was something that happened a lot throughout the tour. One particular feature of all the hotels, I noticed, was that on each floor alongside the elevator was a desk at which was seated a concierge, invariably a woman, who took careful note of all people coming and going on their floor. The food in the restaurants was usually greasy chicken, but there was quite a nice yoghurt that was served either as a drink or on a salad. The salad always consisted of chopped-up scallions. Everybody ended up with bad breath after eating it, and this, combined with the apparently rather infrequent bathing habits of the Russians, made the trip in a crowded Russian elevator a trying experience. The most popular member of the band at meal times was George Duvivier, who had the foresight to bring along a huge bottle of tabasco sauce that was continually being passed around. Russian caviar was something we had been looking forward to, expecting it to be relatively cheap, but it turned out to be just as expensive as it was at home.

After Moscow we flew to Alma-Ata, 200 miles from the Chinese border, and then to Novosibirsk in Siberia. Alma-Ata is a terminus of the Turkistan–Siberia Railway, and it was founded in 1854 as a Russian fort and trading centre. On the first morning a group of us went to the People's Market, where the Kazakhstan peasants came from the countryside to sell their wares. We were amused watching the children, who were fascinated by the black members of the band, never having seen a black person before. They kept touching Carrie Smith's and Haywood Henry's skin and hair, but the two performers, realizing that it was simply the shock of seeing black people for the first time, took it with good grace. The tour was my first experience of life behind the Iron Curtain. It certainly was a different society from the one I was used to. There was a drabness everywhere and the feeling that people were not particularly happy with their lot. On the other hand I could see that everyone took pride in their work. The women you saw late at night scrubbing the marble floors in the hotel were not poor, downtrodden people; they had a genuine pride in what they were doing, polishing the tiles till they absolutely shone. It was not an unusual sight to see women astride the wings of planes, filling the fuel tanks, or operating pneumatic drills on the roads, doing jobs usually done by men in Western society. Quite obviously their system worked – nobody acted as if they were oppressed, or seemed ready to revolt. But without doubt our concerts were a tremendous diversion from, and gave great excitement to, their otherwise drab daily lives. Wherever we played there were jazz musicians and members of jazz clubs who had traveled as much as 500 miles or more to hear our concerts. We were treated with great hospitality at the Cultural Center for the Arts in Moscow, fêted with speeches and toasts, and showered with gifts. Our impression was that, so long as the government was in control of meetings between their people and ours, they would promote and encourage contacts, but when it came to spontaneous meetings they were distinctly worried, as for instance the occasion when some local players invited us to join in a jam session at the Cultural Center. We went there from our hotel with our instruments, all ready to play, but on arrival found that the whole event had been canceled by some official, with no explanations offered or given.

As we moved around the various cities we noticed a profusion of statues of Lenin. We couldn't help but notice the resemblance between Lenin and Bernie Privin, our trumpet player. Every time we passed a statue we'd shout to Privin, "Hey, Bernie, there's another statue of you. How come you've got statues everywhere?" Bernie was not too enamored of Russia, and every time he made some negative comment we used to say, "Bernie, how ungrateful you are. They've erected statues of you all over the country and all you can do is gripe." Something else I noticed was the absence of cats and dogs. I learned that this was mainly due to the great decrease in the animal population during the war, when food was so scarce. The war was still a vivid memory for the Russians – there were memorials to the sacrifices made by the Russian people everywhere we went. We visited the war memorial at Rostov-on-Don towards the end of our tour. It was in a ravine outside the city, where women and children were herded together by German troops and mowed down with machine-guns. Shortly after this horrendous incident the Russians recaptured the city, but it was only when the spring thaws came that the corpses were revealed. Young Russian teenagers with carbines have the responsibility of standing 24-hour guard over this memorial to the dead. It seems the government doesn't want the people to forget the atrocities of the German invasion. It leads me to believe that the Russian people are as sincere as the American people in wanting peace.

After a final performance at the home of the United States Ambassador we returned home laden with gifts that we had bought at the Army and Navy Stores – such things as Red Army belts, boots, caps, blue naval blouses. During our visit, freedom to buy this kind of merchandise was stopped because there were more foreigners walking around wearing these military uniform items than the military themselves! It was a strenuous tour but an enjoyable and educational one. Louis Armstrong, who had hoped to tour Russia but never made it, would have been pleased to see the love and affection with which his music was received by the Russian people. Once again jazz, the international language of peace and goodwill, had triumphed over the barriers erected by governments and opposing philosophies.

In 1976 George Wein decided to reschedule the Carnegie Hall concerts so that, instead of being presented through the fall, winter and spring seasons, he'd bunch them together to coincide with the Newport Festival in late June. Since both projects were run by George Wein out of the same office, the New York State Council for the Arts became dubious about the Repertory Company's claim to being non-profit and decided to withdraw their support, amounting to $90,000 per year. This was a grievous blow to our existence and curtailed our activities drastically. One asset we possessed was a marvelous and extensive library of arrangements which I and other arrangers had been commissioned to write, mostly transcriptions of earlier music taken off the original recordings. The library still exists and is in the custody of the trombonist Al Cobbs, who was our librarian. It was sad to see it come to an end. I had loved being in on the ground floor of the first organization dedicated to jazz repertory and have continued to be active in the repertory field. It was also another step forward in the rebuilding of my confidence. This time I had the responsibilities that went along with being a band member and a musical director. I was beginning to realize that the pleasures of being the top man in charge can often outweigh the pressures of responsibility.

Despite the seemingly impermanent nature of most of my musical ventures I could always count on being invited to play at Dick and Maddie Gibson's Labor Day weekend jazz party. Their soirée in the Rocky Mountains continued to grow until it has become almost a national institution, yet the original spirit of a friendly gathering of musicians and jazz lovers is still very much the essence of the event. The party, first held in Aspen or Vail, subsequently moved to the plush Broadmoor Hotel in Colorado Springs, a beautiful year-round vacation and health resort. Currently it's held at the Fairmont Hotel in Denver. It's a pretty expensive weekend for the guests, costing about $200 per couple, plus travel and hotel accommodation, but Dick still ends up losing money. This is due to the first-class treatment he gives the musicians, which includes the cost of travel from all over the world, accommodation, food and drink, and a generous fee into the bargain. The musicians used to fly into Denver the day before and meet at Dick's large Victorian home on Humboldt Street for a pre-party get-together. They'd stay in various houses up and down the block which Dick and his wife Maddie were able to commandeer for the weekend in exchange for free passes to the jazz party. That evening the jam session at the Gibson home would go on all night. I remember one year leaving the party at 4.00 a.m., having collapsed from sheer exhaustion. As I left, Zoot Sims and Ross Tompkins were playing *There will never be another you*. The next morning, when I came down for breakfast, there were Zoot and Ross still playing the same tune! By now, however, Zoot had sunk lower and lower in his chair until his head was almost touching the floor, while Ross's hands were moving over the keyboard like two lumps of lead. The tempo of the rendition had slowed down to a crawl and threatened to come to a grinding halt at any moment. Right from the start, Dick had the ability to make the wealthy people in Denver feel that it was an honor and privilege for them to accommodate and entertain all these jazz musicians. Most probably they had never heard of them, but when Dick said, "Look, these guys are world famous artists," they believed him and were eager to help out. Over the years they've put up with a great deal of bizzare behavior on the part of some of the more eccentric players, but always they forgive and forget, firm in their belief that these are great artists who are entitled to a certain amount of licence.

The communities in which the parties are held are high up in the mountains. Denver has an altitude of over 5000 feet, while Aspen is higher still at 8000 feet. For anyone not used to the thin air, there are quite a few problems. Until you become acclimatized you experience dizziness, headaches and shortage of breath. You can't sleep for any length of time and you feel high and enervated, full of nervous energy, but not quite thinking straight. The first time I played in Aspen, I flew into Denver and caught the little puddle-jumper plane up to the popular ski resort. As I got off the plane I felt short of breath and had a splitting headache. Nobody had warned me about it and I thought I was having a heart attack or worse. When you drive up from Denver it doesn't hit you as badly, because you're climbing gradually, taking five or six hours on the twisting highway. Those musicians who drink a lot have an additional problem because the effect of the alcohol is greatly increased. Eddie Condon used to be invited every year by Dick to play at the party. He'd arrive in Denver a couple of days before to take part in the pre-party jam session and get-together at Dick's home. The following day, with a king-sized hangover, Eddie would be hustled onto the bus and driven up to Aspen. As soon as the thin air hit him he'd become ill and retire to his hotel room for the whole of Saturday and Sunday. Down he'd come for the last session on Monday afternoon, pale, wan and shaky. This became a regular routine over a number of years, until finally one year, when Dick put in his annual call to Condon, Eddie said, "Dick, please don't invite me to your party any more. I can't take it. Your hospitality is killing me!" On one occasion Gibson invited his favorite drummer, Morey Feld, an easy-going guy who was never bothered by anything. When Morey got up behind the drums on the first set in Aspen the thin air hit him and he collapsed. Dick immediately put in an emergency call to Nick Fatool in Los Angeles, who'd just arrived home from his daily stint on the golf course. Nick immediately flew to Denver and on up to Aspen, grabbing a taxi to the old Jerome Hotel where the party was held. A harried Gibson, having been short of a drummer all afternoon, met him at the door, saying, "Are we glad to see you, Nick. Come on, you're on." Nick climbed up behind the drums and immediately fell off in a dead faint. Dick realized that the thin air was an ongoing problem, so next year he kept some oxygen cylinders backstage so the musicians could take a whiff before they went on. That helped some of them, but many others, including myself, could never quite get used to it. Not only is it difficult breathing, but when you try to hold a high note you think you're about to faint. There is no resonance in the air and it's like playing in a dead studio – you play what you think is a beautiful big note and out it comes sounding small and fuzzy and just plops to the floor. It particularly affects us reed players. The reeds are constantly drying out, resulting in squawks. To get a resonant sound when you blow you have to use a very soft, responsive reed, and that's why reed players are continually looking for a reed that'll play.

The 1972 jazz party in Colorado Springs was coming to an end after three days of continuous music from midday until two in the morning. The guests were just about music'd out and Gibson was looking round for something different to grab people's flagging attention. He suggested to Kenny Davern and myself that we play a soprano sax duet, so we quickly put together an arrangement of Duke Ellington's *The Mooche*. When we hit the last minor chord of the piece, playing in thirds at the very top of our horns, the audience rose to its feet and burst into tumultuous applause. A new sound had been born and it was the beginning of Soprano Summit. Though I was still a member of the World's Greatest Jazz Band, Kenny and I played together on several subsequent occasions, including a party celebrating the fifth anniversary of the band. In fact our first recording was made in December 1973, some time before I left the band, and Hickox put it out on the World Jazz label. We recorded a few more titles four months later, but not enough for an album, and it wasn't until December 1977 that these were combined with some more songs and another album was issued. When I eventually left the band at the end of 1974, we decided to get together on a regular basis as a partnership.

Then there was the time that I worked with the famous Lawrence Welk. It all began one night when the World's Greatest Jazz Band was appearing at the London House in Chicago. After the set the waiter asked me to go to a table where a gentleman wanted to meet me. I recognized him as Welk, whose Saturday night television show had been for many years one of the top rated shows on TV. He invited me to sit down and have a drink, and explained that he was passing through Chicago on a tour to promote his latest book and had noticed from his hotel guide that we were appearing at the London House. He told me how much he loved jazz music and how, through the years, one of his favorite artists had been Johnny Hodges. After telling me how much he enjoyed the sound of my little curved soprano, he went on to say that he liked to feature a top jazz name on his show from time to time, although, he added, "I have to be very careful you know, because most of my audience don't think they like jazz, so I sorta have to slip it in." Our meeting ended with Lawrence saying that one day he'd like to have me as guest on his show. I didn't think he was serious, but a few years later, when Pug and I were living on Cape Cod, we got a phone call. It was Welk himself asking if I remembered our meeting in Chicago and wondering if I'd do a guest shot on his show. He said I could do three tunes, anything I liked. I said he'd have to fly my wife out to the coast too, and that was OK with him. The show only took one day, but he said we should plan to stay for a week at his expense. This all sounded grand, so out we flew to Los Angeles, where we were met by a member of the Welk "family" (anybody who works for Lawrence is part of the Welk "family"). We were driven to the Champagne Towers, a luxurious apartment building overlooking the Pacific Ocean at the foot of Sunset Boulevard, where our suite included two of everything: there were two balconies, two bedrooms, two bathrooms, two walk-in closets. We were asked to be ready in the lobby at 8.30 the next morning, so there we were at the appointed time, expecting to be met by a chauffeured limo. Instead, up drives an ordinary sedan with Lawrence at the wheel. He jumps out, apologizing for being a little late because he had to pick up his secretary, and would we mind stopping on the way to the studio to pick up his clarinet player, Henry Cuesta?

Here was the great Lawrence Welk, the biggest musical attraction on TV, a millionaire many times over with his oil wells and real-estate holdings, running a car service for his staff! We arrived at the studio and Welk helped me carry my instruments and suit-bag containing my tuxedo into our dressing room. After coffee and breakfast at the commissary we had a musical conference with Welk and his arranging staff. I decided to do *Don't get around much anymore* on soprano as a duet with the trombonist, Bob Havens. For the second number I chose an original, *Clarion Song*, which I'd recorded in Sweden with Ove Lind. This was fine, as I could do it as a duet with Henry Cuesta. For the third number Welk said he'd love to hear my alto, and would I be insulted if he picked up his accordion and played a little behind me? When I suggested *My Blue Heaven* he was delighted – it was a song he knew! While his assistant rehearsed my numbers with the band, Welk watched on the monitor in his dressing room, dancing around the room with Pug and making an occasional recommendation over the loudspeaker. The show went forward without a hitch and Pug and I spent the rest of the week cavorting on the beach in front of Champagne Towers. And so it came to pass that on New Year's Eve 1978, at precisely the stroke of midnight, the Lawrence Welk show with Bob Wilber as guest flashed into the homes of 30 million Americans. Probably more people heard me play that night than will ever hear me in the course of my entire career; whether any of them were in any state to appreciate what I was playing is another matter.

What I really wanted to do on leaving the World's Greatest Jazz Band was to form my own group, but I still didn't have enough belief and confidence in myself to assume the responsibilities of leadership. Although the partnership with Kenny was to some extent an easy way out, it was nevertheless a step along the road from being just a sideman afraid to assert himself. I feel in retrospect that I ought to have taken the risk, but on the other hand, Kenny and I had something that was interesting and that worked musically. The way our horns locked together produced a thrilling new sound.

Marty Grosz, whom I had know for many years, joined us on guitar. He was living in Chicago, where his wife had a good job at the university. One night, shortly after we had made the first Soprano Summit album, he came into the London House to hear the World's Greatest Jazz Band. I asked him, "How are things going?" He said, "Man, I play a weekly gig on banjo with a mandolin and a tuba. I have to dress up in short pants with knee socks and a beany hat with a propeller on top. It's awful. No dignity at all." I told him about the record we had made and how we were thinking of going full-time with the group, and I asked him if he was interested. "My bags are packed," was his reply.

We weren't an overnight success. It took a long time for people to notice us, and engagements were few and far between. There was a series of gigs with the Jersey Library System, where we played monthly concerts at different libraries around New Jersey. It was a nice prestige thing but it didn't pay much money. There were a few jazz festivals here and there, but nobody tearing down the door to book the group. The process of moving from an underground interest to even a week's gig in a jazz club is something that can often take years. Unless you're a concert attraction with a big name, the club circuit is basically a solo and trio world. To economize we'd eliminated the piano from the group, but even with five pieces we were out of the budget range of many clubs. The usual casualty would have been the guitar, but we were trying to get a different sound. We knew that Marty's acoustic playing, his humor and his singing were something unique, so the piano had to go.

In July 1975 Soprano Summit was invited to appear at the Nice Jazz Festival. Following the New York Jazz Repertory Company's tour of Russia I joined Kenny and Marty in Nice. From Nice we went to South Africa for our next booking, a short tour covering four or five cities arranged by a Durban journalist who was also a jazz fan. When we went into the airlines office in Nice to confirm our tickets, we were told that, because we hadn't confirmed our bookings within 72 hours before the flight, our seats had been canceled and no alternative space was available. Naturally we were in a panic, but finally we got through to our promoter in Durban, who squared things with the airline. When we finally met him in Durban he turned out to be a great guy who, like so many of the thinking people there, was totally opposed to the South African government's racial policies. He had applied to the authorities for a permit to have a non-segregated audience at our concert in Pietermaritzburg but didn't expect any success, because the order of the day was complete separation of Whites, Blacks and Indians at public gatherings. To everyone's surprise the application was granted, and the concert was one of the very first occasions on which a public event was held without separate sections for the different races. It was quite a breakthrough and we were delighted, even more so when we saw how much everybody enjoyed the show. Another thing that he did was to arrange a joint concert between Soprano Summit and one of the South African coon bands.

This term was not used in any derogatory sense but referred to the street bands, comprising guitar, banjo and string bass, that played a particular style of street music. It was very pleasant with a nice kind of beat, but not really jazz – more like folk music. An annual contest is held in which all these groups compete and the winners get television exposure and a record contract; we were going to play with that year's winner. We met the group's manager, a white guy, and it was agreed that he'd bring the members of his band round to our hotel so that we could figure out what we were going to play. He couldn't bring them through the hotel lobby, however; he had to sneak them in through the kitchen and up in the service elevator, taking great care that they were not seen getting from the elevator to our room. It was an absolutely ridiculous situation, because only a month earlier Teddy Wilson had been a guest artist for the Durban Jazz Society and had stayed in one of the finest rooms in this very hotel, and no questions had been asked. Apparently it was all right for black people from other countries to stay there but not all right for their own black people even to visit.

Anyway, we all sat down and talked about music and played a little. They knew a few old numbers like *Darktown Strutters Ball*, but they didn't swing and couldn't improvise so it wasn't jazz in any sense of the word. Eventually we found some numbers we could combine the two groups on at the three concerts. These were held during the lunch hour in the Students' Union at Durban University. They went down very well. Like young people everywhere, the students were very much for togetherness; seeing the black and white musicians co-operating and playing together was inspiring to them and they loved it. This was the only opportunity we ever had of meeting or playing with black musicians in South Africa. The different drummers and bass players we worked with were all white – they never had any contact at all with the black musicians. We saw all the ludicrous trappings and effects of apartheid, the separate post offices, liquor stores with separate entrances for Black and White (same clerks, same booze), and separate facilities for every conceivable thing. It was ridiculous and obscene. Apart from that, it was a beautiful country. We had the opportunity of driving through the game parks of Durban and Johannesburg, seeing the wild antelopes running across the plain, coming across giraffes standing in the road, or passing a pride of lions just lying there under a tree, sheltered from the hot sun. Very exciting – better than any zoo!

After the success of our World Jazz albums, Hank O'Neal became interested in the Summit and we recorded for his Chiaroscuro label. Then Carl Jefferson came along, invited us to his Concord Jazz Festival and recorded two of our concerts, which he issued on his newly formed label. We found him a difficult person to deal with, however, because somehow he felt that we'd let him down by recording for Hank. As much as we tried to convince Carl that he'd never offered us an exclusive contract and so therefore we considered ourselves free agents, he was still miffed and never gave Soprano Summit or me any further work. Record producers are peculiar people. The musician is very much in their pocket and there is little that one can do about it, but it does get rather hard to take when you know that your career and your livelihood can be at stake. Barker Hickox, for instance, is sitting on a beautiful record we recorded at Vanguard Studios in New York. He won't release it because he never liked Soprano Summit without the piano. It was situations like these that several years later led to Pug and I starting our own label. At least you have your destiny in your own hands.

I was becoming aware of the limitations of Soprano Summit, and within its framework I started looking around for new ways to achieve more variety in the sound. To get more color I encouraged Kenny to play the C-melody sax, and I started playing alto for the first time after the disappointment with my sound at the age of 14. Appropriately enough my first recording on the instrument was an original titled *Debut* on the first record on Chiaroscuro. I had always been an admirer of Johnny Hodges, the epitome of good taste, and I felt that it would be no bad thing if I were to try and follow his example. In the playing of Bechet there had been a majesty, a sweeping grandeur, that so impressed the young Hodges. Johnny combined it, however, with a quality that was not characteristic of Sidney, a peaceful serenity, particularly on ballads. He had this unhurried, relaxed, easy-going way about his playing, even at fast tempos, and it almost seemed as if he threw away phrases in a very casual way. His voluptuous tone on the instrument has never ever been equaled by anyone. It was a tone that could sometimes verge on the edge of being fruity, but it never seemed to cross the line. There was an inner strength that kept it from becoming saccharine. It never had that effeminate quality that annoys me in classical saxophone playing. There was an underlying gutsiness to his playing, no matter how mellow, how beautiful, it got. And then there was his impeccable sense of time, particularly at medium tempos, swinging a band in a marvelously sensuous way that made you want to snap your fingers and move to the music. In later years a note of cynicism crept in, and understandably so, because, like so many of his contemporaries in jazz, he never gained the recognition as a great, comparable to a Heifetz or a Casals. But even with this tough, cynical quality, his playing still had a mesmerizing, hypnotic effect that I've never tired of.

There were many reasons why Soprano Summit broke up. Despite its artistic success we weren't exactly swamped with offers, and the fees we were getting for the group were not comparable to what I could command as a solo artist. The line on my confidence graph was also rising. The four years spent as co-leader had been a natural progression from being just a sideman, but I now felt strong enough to take that final step to being a leader again. I had been choosing the music, writing the arrangements, and running the band in a musical sense, but without ever getting more than 50 percent of the credit. In no way is this a criticism of Kenny, but Kenny's talents rested upon playing the clarinet and soprano, and the musical leadership was left to me. There were also personality problems: Kenny is a volatile person, close to the surface of his emotions, with a

character that is very much Dionysian, whereas mine is Apollonian. I think
before I speak and consider before I play. In retrospect I think it was probably
this contrast that helped to make the whole thing work. Soprano Summit was an
interesting experiment; I liked what we did and I'm glad that we did it. Although
we made an important statement for jazz by showing that there was a way to play
traditional jazz with a fresh sound, the fact remained that for me it had run its
course. In every artistic career, the point is reached where one feels it is time to
move on to other things. There were so many things I wanted to do, and I felt
ready to step out into a more challenging musical atmosphere. Nevertheless,
Kenny and I have remained good friends. We play together a few times every
year at jazz parties and festivals.

While with the New York Jazz Repertory Company I was involved in a series of
four concerts, a retrospective on Ellington. I was given the task of re-creating the
1930s period. We started off with a problem because of my choice of a piano
player. I wanted to use Dick Wellstood but George Wein said, "No, you've got to
have a black player. We don't have enough black players in the band." There was
that old racial bullshit again. It always astounded me because I have never
thought of jazz in terms of color – either you can play or you can't. I've always
listened to jazz with my ears, not with my eyes! I tried to convince George that it
was more important to have a pianist who could do the job better than anyone
else, but he was adamant. The guy who I used did an adequate job, but Dick
would have done it better. I assembled a band of New York musicians, with
Cootie Williams and Vic Dickenson as guest stars. We made transcriptions of
some of the arrangements featuring Ivie Anderson and started looking around
for a singer. What I wanted was someone who could both re-create the ambience
and suggest the elegance of Ivie, but nobody on the Repertory Board could
figure out who to get. We considered Maxine Sullivan, Helen Humes and a few
others, but nobody seemed just right.

Suddenly I thought of Pug. After that first time I heard her at Condon's she
sent me some of her recordings. I admired that warm, throaty quality of her voice
and I knew she would look stunning on stage. Since nobody else had come up
with an idea the board told me to go ahead and see if I could contact her. I
remember the excitement I felt as I dialed her number in Albany and the
disappointment when I was told she was not there but at her summer home at
Saratoga. When I finally reached her, I explained the project and played a tape of
Ivie. Imagine my surprise to hear her say, "I don't think so, Bob, but thank you
for thinking of me." I realized she wasn't playing hard to get, she was deadly
serious. There was I, offering this English lass an opportunity to sing at Carnegie
Hall, the dream of every aspiring performer in music, and she coolly but firmly
turns me down! After further cajoling on my part I got her to promise to listen
seriously to Ivie and told her I'd get back to her in a couple of days. She borrowed
some of Ivie's recordings from a friend and after careful listening finally
accepted my offer – I guess I was developing a persuasive way with the ladies!
She later told me that her Uncle Hank and Auntie Ivy had gone to hear Duke
Ellington on his first English tour in 1933. Auntie Ivy was so enamored of Ivie

Anderson's singing that she changed the spelling of her name! The rehearsals lasted a full week prior to the performance, and it was obvious that our mutual attraction had more to it than mere musical affinity. I found her to be more attractive than ever and somehow I felt she no longer saw me as the frightened little man in a raincoat she had seen at Condon's in 1960. I no longer felt scared of her, and, in line with what was happening to me musically, she made me feel good about myself as a human being. She had a good feeling about herself, an inner strength and confidence, and she was only interested in people who had the same qualities. Something was happening between us – once more, as if pre-ordained by fate, our paths had crossed, and like two magnets we were steadily but surely being drawn together.

The concert was a great success. John Wilson, jazz critic for the *New York Times*, singled out Pug for special praise. With the new confidence, my image began to change. I emerged from behind the mask my glasses had created and started wearing contact lenses. For the first time the world was able to look into my face. I grew a beard, let my hair grow longer, wore sharper clothes and, if all that were not enough, I turned once more to the instrument that had so disappointed me 35 years earlier, the alto sax. The fans saw all these changes and were confused, just like my fans back in the early 1950s had been. They had categorized and pigeon-holed me, and resented changes that they couldn't understand. It was as if they felt they owned me, that I owed them something and that they had the right to protest when I changed.

I particularly remember the year at Gibson's jazz party where one fan had the cheek to circulate a petition that read "Resolved that Bob Wilber shaves off his beard and puts his glasses back on." When it arrived at the piano, where Ralph Sutton was preparing to play, he took one look at it, crumpled it in his great hand and threw it on the floor. Can you imagine that people felt they had the right to interfere in my private life in that way? This kind of criticism from my fans was very hurtful to me. I should have got up on the rooftop and shouted to the world, "Get off my back! Stop interfering and just listen to the music. I changed my image because I wanted to and it's none of your damned business anyway." I was very happy to have found the confidence to be myself. While it's certainly true that a lot of the strength to do it came from my association with Pug, the decisions were mine. It's very difficult to fight back, however. From childhood I was taught the Christian ethic of "turning the other cheek," of thinking well of my fellow human beings. It was hard for me to accept that not everybody in the world was a nice person and that there were those who, usually because of jealousy, would use any opportunity they saw to denigrate another's efforts. It was an aspect of life for which I'd never been prepared by my parents, who preached understanding and forgiveness. The reason I never felt entitled to fight back was buried deep in my subconscious – as that incident with the hot foot demonstrated. All through my life it has hindered my actions when I have been perfectly justified in fighting back, showing resentment or expressing anger. My inability to do so placed an unfair burden on Pug, whom people considered responsible for my new-found assertiveness.

During the seven months following the Carnegie Hall concert Pug and I were practically inseparable. We had a memorable three weeks in Paris, where Soprano Summit was appearing at the Hotel Meridien. This was followed by a three-week tour of England in a cramped bus that Kenny Davern irreverently dubbed "the Turd Wagon." I dreaded the return to the States because I knew it meant Pug would be going back to her home in Albany. It was obvious to me that I couldn't possibly offer her the kind of security she enjoyed, married to a prominent physician, with three wonderful children and a respected position in society that would be the envy of most women. Here was I, an itinerant jazz musician, but I was in love – I knew what I wanted and I wanted Pug. Whatever other opportunities I had passed up in my life, this was one I wasn't going to let slip by. I wooed her with phone calls, letters, flowers and champagne. I wanted this lady and she wanted me, despite the fact that she knew the road ahead was not going to be easy. She obviously cared a great deal for her husband and children and hated the idea of hurting them. She cried a great deal in her efforts to resolve her dilemma. I couldn't cry but I felt.

My total commitment to Pug and our thoughts about getting married bear little resemblance to the agonizing memory I carry of a humiliating and foolish mistake I made when I was 19. I fell for the oldest ploy in the world: I was tricked into marriage by an older and rather plain-looking woman, one of many who used to hang around Bechet when he was playing at Ryan's. Sidney sent me on a date with her. (The old devil subsequently confessed it was his way of getting rid of ladies he no longer cared for.) I was not in love or even attracted to the woman but I was terrified to tell my parents the reason for my urgent pleas for permission to get married – necessary because of my age. Totally bewildered by my jazz-crazed way of life, they reluctantly granted their consent. I feel sure all of us have done things in our youth that deeply shame us and we wish to forget; this was my particular Nemesis. Feeling hopelessly trapped, I sought my revenge by putting on a facade but meanwhile living my life as a single man. That a short correspondence with a schoolgirl from Sheffield would lead to the life I have today is nothing short of a miracle.

It was in February of 1977 that we made our decision to spend the rest of our lives together. I clearly remember that bright, sunny day, driving to Newark Airport to join the Newport All Stars for a tour. Pug flew from Albany and we met in Pittsburgh, where my friend Joe Boughton picked us up and drove us to Meadville, Pennyslvania, where he'd arranged a Soprano Summit concert at Allegheny College. From there we drove to Columbus, Ohio, where we joined the Newport All Stars on the opening concert of the tour. It was an interesting group, with Teddy Wilson on piano, Vic Dickenson on trombone, Joe Venuti on violin, Joe Newman on trumpet, George Duvivier on bass and Panama Francis on drums; I played clarinet and soprano and alto saxes. Although the band had no leader, George Wein asked me to act as spokesman, to co-ordinate the program and to introduce the various numbers. I thought it would be interesting for the audience to have each player talk about their experiences in jazz or the history of their instrument. The former worked like a charm – Pug had a spot on the program where, together with Panama Francis, she demonstrated the dances invented at the Savoy Ballroom in the 1930s. Pug also acted as den mother and kept all the disparate personalities in the group, some of whom had infirmities of one kind or another, from quarreling with each other. In her own special way she made everybody feel loved and wanted.

Later that spring we flew to Sweden with Soprano Summit for a three-week engagement. I had been there before with the World's Greatest Jazz Band, playing at the Atlantic Club. On this second visit I met Anders Ohman. Anders was a leading Stockholm lawyer, a gentleman of great character, taste and wit, and a true patrician. He was also keenly interested in jazz, and besides having been for years a music critic for a major Swedish music magazine he played chamber music on clarinet as a hobby. He was also the owner of a record company, Phontastic Records, dedicated to recording the finest Swedish jazz artists in the swing idiom. He wanted me to make a record with Ove Lind, the Swedish clarinetist. It was an exciting and satisfying experience playing with the Swedish musicians on that date. They were an exceptional bunch, capable of playing very sophisticated tunes and interesting, challenging harmonies, able to play in every key, and all in a very cool, relaxed way. One of Ove's favorite things was to keep modulating up in half steps. As all clarinet players know, it's easy to finger in some keys and fiendishly difficult in others; the thing is to strive for equal facility in every key. Charlie Parker had this total facility in all keys because so much of his playing was involved in false modulations into new keys; he could take a song like *Cherokee* and play it through every key with no problem. They were all the same to him and I admired that. I saw elements in the playing of the Swedish guys that I felt were missing in Soprano Summit, where there was a lot more musical rigidity and more harmonic limitations. I was getting ready to move on to a new musical level.

I was also delighted with Anders Ohman, and a very rewarding association began. Just like Bill Borden, back in 1969, he had faith in my talent and was willing to give me free artistic rein in all the recordings we subsequently made. On each one of them I was able to do something that I wanted to do artistically, and, while there were things that were not perfect about them, every one of them was a record I was proud to have made. The ultimate in recording equipment was used and the discs were pressed on the finest vinyl. Everything in the production was done with loving care and with great attention to detail. It's rather different from the States, where the record business is plagued with problems. Everything goes along smoothly in the studios, where a good engineer with the best equipment can produce a beautiful record, but the moment these records reach the pressing plants things start to go wrong. The quality control must be the worst in the world, with warped records and bad vinyl the order of the day. They employ cheap labor and are controlled by underworld types who have tremendous power because of the limited number of plants. When something big hits the pop field, an immense number of pressings are required in double-quick time. Small jazz companies who need only a couple of thousand pressings have to go down on their knees to beg these people to accommodate them. It was certainly a problem for Pug and me when we went into the record business later.

We returned again to Sweden in 1979 to continue the association with Anders. Right from childhood, classical music had been an important part of my life, and as a teenager I had seriously considered making my career in that field. I've always been influenced and inspired by the great melodists like Mozart, Bach, Beethoven and Brahms, and also by Debussy – although in his case more for his harmony than his melody. I've never been impressed by discordant and purposely dissonant music, which I find to be dry and arid and not expressive of the kind of joy in life that I like to hear in music. The music of Schoenberg after his invention of the 12-tone scale, in fact all atonal music, leaves me cold – neither do I care for the later Stravinsky. The 20th-century composers I like are those that have gone back to earlier music for inspiration – people like Walton, Respighi and Delius, Elgar and Ravel, all of whose music has so much sensuous beauty. I listen to a lot of classical music for inspiration. For instance, Fritz Kreisler's tone on violin has been a model for developing my sound on the soprano. Then there are the great singers like Caruso, and Janet Baker with her marvelous, soaring voice. I love to soar on the saxophone and I'm more concerned with doing that and singing on my instrument than I am with playing many notes or doing things with harmonic complexity. To be able to project your message through tone is one of the greatest ways of doing it. If you can get a beautiful, distinctive sound on your instrument you don't have to rely on playing a lot of notes and impressing people by the complexity of what you are doing. You can play simply and yet communicate by bringing out the beauty of a melody. If you don't have a distinctive, beautiful tone you have to be clever and facile to impress the listener. I've always liked players who used fewer notes, but to do that you have to have tone, tone that says something when you sustain a note. The masters of the sustained sound are the players I'm interested in emulating – people like Armstrong, Bechet, Hodges, Goodman, Teagarden and Hawkins.

Nobody had ever asked me to record classical music, or even expressed an interest in my doing so, but when I told Anders that it was an ambition of mine, he asked me without a moment's hesitation what I would like to do. My first choice had to be the Mozart Clarinet Quintet. At the age of 14 the recording by the Budapest String Quartet with Benny Goodman had introduced me to the magical world of the genius of Salzburg. To help in my preparation Anders gave me unrestricted access to his huge collection of records. His record room was like an Aladdin's cave – in it I found ten different versions of the Quintet. He was also a collector of sheet music and Pug and I spent hours sifting through his huge collection, looking for new tunes.

Anders was a man dedicated to jazz as an art form, but, as in the case of Bill Borden, he fell down in the marketing of his products. He was the head of a successful Stockholm law firm and wasn't concerned with the commercial aspect of his record company. It was a hobby to him, almost a fantasy, in which his greatest dream was to make a beautiful record, put it on his shelf and say, "There, I did it." The fact that it might sell fewer than a thousand copies didn't really concern him. He's the type of guy I have no problem in getting along with, the perfect person for successful collaborations that end up with something of quality but not always financial reward. It seems to take an entirely different type to go out and market the product. Whether we like it or not, this has become the age of big business and profits, usually at the expense of the music, the musician and the listener.

Duke Ellington was one person who seemed to be able to withstand these outside pressures. He believed in his music – a product of artistic creativity and sensibilities of the highest order – but he knew that in order to sell that music, he had to get the audience to like what he was doing. Being a clever man he used every device he knew to achieve that end. No question of turning out any old rubbish just so long as the money was coming in at the box office – his was a dedicated crusade to sell something he believed in, something that was of the very highest artistic quality. The only way he could do it was by keeping his band together through good and bad times. He was able to do this because of his success as a songwriter, which in a sense was another career altogether. It was the success of melodies like *Mood Indigo, Sophisticated Lady* and so on that gave him the financial independence to be his own man. The fact that his success as a composer subsidized his activities in jazz was more than accident. He was a very smart, calculating man, and from the start realized that the only way to support his band was by achieving success as a composer. That band was his great hobby in life, and in later years, when Duke was asked why he stayed on the road with 16 temperamental artists in tow, he had the perfect reply: "I like the luxury of writing music tonight and hearing it played tomorrow the way I want it." Many artists with less determination than Duke would have taken the easy way out by saying, "To hell with it. I don't need to knock myself out trying to keep a band together. Too many problems." Duke could have made a fortune just by being Duke Ellington, performing as a piano soloist or guest artist with symphony orchestras, but he never could do that. It wouldn't be the same to have had other people play his music. He didn't write for instruments like most composers. He wrote for specific people – that's the thing that distinguishes him from all other Western composers and makes him absolutely unique. What he wrote for Johnny Hodges was different from what he wrote for his other alto sax, Otto Hardwick. When a musician joined the band, Duke would listen for a few months trying to figure out what he could write for this new man that would bring out the best in him. It was a creative challenge for Duke to make the musician burst forth, to inspire him to greater heights. The men with Ellington had the finest opportunity ever given to any jazz players to express themselves, to explore the potential in their own playing, because Duke gave them the setting in which they could do the things they did best. That was what the public heard. Any weaknesses in their playing were recognized by Duke, who would downplay those aspects. You'd only hear the flaws when the players left the fold to go out on their own.

To express his musical soul, Duke was absolutely dependent upon being in artistic control. He defied the whole postwar trend in jazz whereby the producers, the A and R (artists and repertoire) men would tell the artist what to record. In the 1950s Duke was turning out one gem after another for Columbia Records, but there were only a few people at Columbia, principally Irving Townsend, who were in Duke's corner. If you read Clive Davis's account of his tenure as president of that company, it's just horrific. All that was important was the bottom line and whether it was black or red. If it was red, get rid – the fact that it was Duke Ellington made no difference. It was a similar story at Victor. The A and R producer for all those magnificent recordings of the 1940s was a supporter of Duke, but as soon as he left, RCA's attitude was one of no profit, no contract. But this is what happens in jazz. It's always that bottom line on the profit and loss account. One particularly worthwhile project that fell foul of the company accountants was the Time Life "Giants of Jazz" reissues. The people in charge of the project, Phil Payne and Jeanne Le Monnier, were very sincere, hard-working people, who were dedicated to doing a good job. They had mapped out a program of 34 three-record albums covering all the leading figures of the golden age of jazz, from 1928 to 1945. The whole thing was done with loving care, with particular attention paid to choice of takes, booklets with fresh, new material about the artists, and photos that had never been used before. The project was a labor of love and a work of art, but half-way through the accountants looked at the figures, saw red ink and that was the end. The producers weren't allowed to finish the project and all the material in the pipeline that was already researched and paid for went down the drain. Marketed properly those albums would not only have pleased the collectors but would have been worthy additions to the shelves of music libraries or universities throughout the world. Corporations are willing to lose money on classical music because it's good for their "image" as supporters of culture, but poor jazz, neither a pop music nor culturally "acceptable" like ballet, symphony or chamber music, is spurned by all when the economic crunch comes.

ELEVEN

On the road

Life on the road is a long-standing tradition in show business and a necessity in the continual search for the audiences that are the only means for the performing artist's survival. It's a tough way to live, even in present day times with modern modes of transport. On the major tours in which I have been involved, travel was generally by means of bus, and because distances in the States are so great it was not at all unusual to spend up to ten hours at a time covering distances of 500 miles or more between dates. It's a very exhausting schedule and after a while you begin to feel you're living in a different world, almost a different dimension from the one you observe through the windows of the bus as you pass through towns and cities. The bus becomes your own self-contained private world and in a strange way you become very attached to it. Your seat on the bus becomes your own little haven and must be respected by your fellow travelers. Each day, as you return to your seat, it develops its own characteristics, different from any other on the bus and reflecting your personality. The other seats are occupied by owners who have their own characteristics too; you can always identify the health-kick guy by the bags of nuts and wheatgerm alongside his seat or the drinker with his stash of booze. Then there are the readers – the lightweight readers with their magazines and the serious readers using the time on the road to study some subject that interests them, anything from astronomy to the works of Chekhov. It's interesting to see how many musicians are intellectuals with enquiring minds, sometimes not formally educated to any extensive degree, but very intelligent and literate people who have read a lot and who have tremendous interest in culture of all kinds. Another group in this self-contained world are the gamblers. There's always a running card game that starts the minute the players get on the bus in the morning and lasts all day long. The bus may travel for eight hours, leaving only a couple of hours to check in at the motel, get a bite to eat, have a quick shower, grab a short nap and rush over to the concert hall to set up. While everybody else is getting off the bus, the gamblers are still deep in their game. It's only after someone shouts, "Come on, guys, we're here," that they look up, totally oblivious of the time that has passed or the miles that have been covered. They reluctantly gather up the cards and troop off the bus to check in, sometimes resuming the game in somebody's bedroom for an hour before the gig – where intermission finds them at it again in the dressing room. If a lot of money has changed hands that day and the losers want a chance to recoup their losses, the game may continue through the night back at the motel. Next morning the gamblers, bleary-eyed from loss of sleep, climb wearily on the bus to collapse in their seats. But not for long – within an hour someone's woken up with a bright idea: "Hey, come on you guys, let's have a game," and they're at it again!

The bus drivers are usually good at their job and really know their way around the country, but I once traveled with one driver who was incredible. He kept making wrong turns, and suddenly we'd find ourselves a hundred miles out of our way. With having to make an eight o'clock curtain at the next venue, every hour on the road counts. We used to get frustrated and angry at this waste of time but eventually realized the guy couldn't read a map, didn't know that south was down and north was up. Not being a gambler nor having to sleep off the effects of too much booze the night before, I was appointed navigator. When we came to an important cross-road out in the middle of nowhere, it was my job to see that the driver turned right instead of left or vice-versa. From then on we saved many wasted hours on the road.

It's such an arduous life that you long for those magic moments in your day that give you a little enjoyment, a respite from the relentless daily grind. While I was never a heavy drinker, my own particular pleasure is an evening cocktail and a social time with one or two of the other musicians before going into the restaurant at the motel for dinner. During the day's travel, as you think of that moment, you get cravings for specific drinks. I particularly favor a nice, cold, dry Martini straight up, about five parts gin and one part vermouth. When you land in a place where they don't know how to make one, where the glass isn't cold, where the proportions aren't right or where it's served with an olive instead of the twist of lemon you've ordered, it's as though your world has come to an end! Other musicians' special moment of the day is a half-hour jog around the motel parking lot in the early morning or a little time to browse around the shopping center down the highway. Whatever your pleasure is, it becomes very important for your peace of mind, indeed for your sanity, on the road.

Usually you stay in motel chains where the food is not the greatest, and if you're served something that's overcooked, too salty or whatever, you get really upset. I guess we "road rats" all over-reacted when things were not quite right because we felt it was the least we were entitled to after getting so little pleasure from the long hours on the road. I remember once having dinner with the road manager in a little town when we realized that there were two separate loudspeakers in the dining room with different canned music coming out of each. We called over the waitress and said, "Don't you realize you got one song coming out of this speaker and another one out of that one?" "Oh yeah," she said, after listening for a moment. "It do sound kinda funny, don't it?" It was probably that way for years – we must have been the first customers to notice it. Then there's the drinking. Sometimes you drink simply to give yourself some energy because the traveling is so exhausting. Then there's the parties after the gig when you're looking for a little fun, listening to records, drinking and socializing. This might continue until 4.00 a.m., with the bus call being for 7.00 a.m. The next morning the guys get on the bus, some still drunk from the night before, carrying their clothes over their shoulders and scuffling about trying to get themselves together. They flop into their seats, fast asleep before the bus pulls away.

Its a tough way to live, and after a while you begin to feel as if you're not working for yourself, you're simply fulfilling someone else's wishes. If it's a full house or a half house or an empty house, so what, who the hell cares? We had one marvelous trumpeter who would play at the top of his form in the little hick towns during the week, but on the weekends, when we hit the big concert halls with big audiences, he'd stagger out on stage, three sheets to the wind. It's as though you lose your sense of what's important. What does make it worthwhile is the fact that you have fans coming to the concert to hear you. It means so much to them, particularly in the small towns in the Midwest where your appearance is a big thing in their lives. The appreciation and adulation you get makes you feel good about what you're doing. Even if you only have a half house, the fact that it's made up of people who know of you, have your records, and want to meet you, means more than playing to a packed house of disinterested, unknowledgeable people. Without those fans I could never envisage undertaking the whole business. Knowing the stresses and strains of life on the road, I feel sympathy for those musicians who tour simply as part of a band behind a big-name singer or playing a musical review. The audience isn't interested in them, only in the singer or the musical; they don't get the recognition that makes a long, tiring tour worthwhile. At least we got the satisfaction of knowing that we personally gave a lot of people pleasure. It's nice to have people come up to you, nice to know that what you've done has meant so much to them, nice to know they're pleased to have you in their home town.

There are other frustrations on the road because people don't realize how difficult your life is compared to their perhaps boring but comfortable day-to-day routine. For instance, when you arrive in town you're met by people who do everything possible to get you to the hall on time, but as soon as you've finished the gig you're on your own. There is always an eagerness to please before the concert, but afterwards the planning of how to get you back to the hotel or airport is something that's not been taken care of. They've had their concert, they've finished with you and they don't want to know any more about you. On other occasions you may arrive dead-beat and desperate for some sleep, but you can't do that because they've got an interview arranged for you with the local paper, followed by a trip to the local radio station to chat with some inane disc-jockey, all for the purpose of promoting their concert. Sometimes when you come off the stage at intermission and find no coffee or soft drinks you are met by the apologies: "Oh, somebody was supposed to attend to that. I really don't know what happened." After the concert you look around for a bar and grill to get some food and they tell you, "Oh no, no food. Kitchen's closed." So it's home to bed at the motel, tired and hungry. Perhaps if you're lucky you find some crummy little place that serves you a plate of unappetizing greasy stuff. I used to get so weary of road food at typical hamburger joints ("quick and dirties" we used to call them) that I'd look around for a supermarket and buy an apple, a banana, some grapes, perhaps a peach and a carton of milk. I just wanted something that was healthy, something that would make me feel better physically, instead of the usual greasy, over-cooked offerings.

The need for female companionship assumed an importance in the lives of most musicians on this treadmill. Different musicians had different styles. In one band we had a guy who looked around the audience at a concert until his eye fell on the plainest and most homely girl sitting by herself or with a girlfriend. He then set about flattering and romancing her, and next morning there she'd be, coming into breakfast with our Romeo. By judicious choosing he didn't have to compete with the other guys. He simply went after the one who would be most flattered by all the attention. Other guys picked out the grateful widows, older women whom they would shower with charm and courtesy. The goal and end result was always the same, a roll in the hay to relieve the boredom of the road. Then there were the women who used to join the tour, girlfriends and ladies met along the way, who somehow or other were able to drop everything and stay with the band and the musician they had picked. The accepted protocol was that when a guy came on to the band bus with a lady, you didn't query it. You were very nice and polite to her in deference to your colleague and you never did anything or said anything that might spill the beans that he was a married man. She might be on the bus for five or six nights going from town to town, but then one morning the man would board the bus and the lady would no longer be there. Nobody would make any reference to the fact – by next day the incident was forgotten, and if the guy's wife came on the bus the next week then naturally the previous week's escapade was totally forgotten by one and all.

One of the hazards that can occur is when you go back to a town and women you have known on previous visits turn up. You can't always plan on who is going to show up where or when, and it leads to some very funny situations. I remember playing at one concert where my current traveling companion, a young lady, was sitting in the audience. As my eyes moved around the auditorium, I was embarrassed to see another girl I'd befriended on a previous visit to the town. I tried desperately to concentrate on my solo and at the time devise a solution to the problem that had cropped up. But suddenly my brain went numb when I spotted a third young lady, a friend of mine from another town who'd heard about our appearance and had driven a hundred miles just to see me. My traveling companion couldn't understand why I spent the whole intermission in the men's room or was in such a hurry to duck out after the concert. On occasions one has to find a deputy and turn a spare girl over to him, and whenever that happens there's always a special affinity. We used to say we were "cousins" because we'd slept with the same girl. Some of the men had understanding wives. I know one wife who used to say to her husband, "I don't care what you do on the road – just don't bring it home with you." Sometimes wives would come along with the band for a while, but nobody would let the cat out of the bag about the girls. That was the unforgivable sin, to say anything, even inadvertently, that would give a fellow musician problems at home.

The *esprit de corps* of the World's Greatest Jazz Band was particularly good.

There were no long-standing animosities within the band. In this respect we were very fortunate – there are known cases of road bands where members haven't spoken to each other for years. With the strain of traveling it's so easy for minor irritations to get blown up out of all proportion. You picked your room-mate gradually until you sifted out the person who would be the most compatible. I usually roomed with Ralph Sutton because we were both quiet and neat people.

Once in a while I'd share a room with Yank Lawson. Within five minutes of his entering, the bathroom would be in a shambles, with crumpled towels all over the place. He'd always buy all the newspapers and stretch out on his bed to read them, a baseball or football game going full blast on the TV. As he worked his way through the papers he'd toss each sheet on the floor, until gradually a huge pile built up alongside his bed. Bud Freeman always roomed by himself because he was such an individualist and so set in his own ways. He was always practicing his saxophone stance in front of the mirror in his underdrawers or working on his book *You Don't Look Like a Musician*. He'd keep his door open and collar the unwary passerby and insist they hear the latest chapter. Bud liked living in hotels – all he needed was his saxophone and a suitcase of clothes. When he got tired of a suit or a pair of shoes, he simply left them behind in the room when he left. Our road manager, Gerry Finningley, an English lad, used to see Bud leaving his clothes in the hotel rooms and finally said, "Look, Bud. If you don't need those things, I sure could use them." Gradually Gerry built up a complete wardrobe of Bud's cast-offs. Bud always dressed immaculately, but hated to be burdened with material possessions. The rest of us in the band used to say that all Bud needed to keep him happy was his saxophone, a room with a mirror, someone to pay his rent and an occasional grateful widow.

The road in the early 1970s was quite different from what it was in the 1950s when I was out with Benny. The civil rights movement in the 1960s caused a tremendous change in people's attitudes. The WGJB, with two or three black members, played towns in the deep South and never had any race problems at all. When things changed in the South they changed radically, more so than in the North, where discrimination was a much subtler thing. What changed the attitude of the southern Whites was money. When the business leaders realized that segregation was bad for the economy, things changed and changed quickly. As a result the atmosphere in the South on our WGJB tours was very different, like another world, from the time down there with Goodman. At that time there was still a lot of segregation and racism in the South and Southwest. Discrimination was a fact of life that the black musician had long been used to, and he usually tried to treat it in a humorous way. When the Goodman band arrived in a town and stopped in the black section outside some funky, run-down hotel, it looked so unbelievably bad that nobody was able to resist laughing. It was sad, but in a very strange way it was funny, and it was only by seeing the comical side that it became bearable. It was the way things were, and you felt there was nothing that could be done about it. Sometimes it made you goddam mad, like the occasion when we played in a large auditorium in Baltimore and were ordered by the police to stay backstage during the intermission because they didn't want the black and white performers being seen together offstage and mingling with the public. It mattered little that we perhaps wanted to get a coke or meet friends from Baltimore who'd come to see us.

Of course, things were even worse for the black musicians in the 1920s and 1930s. I used to talk to colleagues about what it was like on the road in those days and their descriptions were extremely interesting. On the one hand there were the fortunate artists who had their own way of dealing with the situation. In the 1920s, for instance, Bessie Smith was the highest-paid black performer on the TOBA circuit (the Theater Owners' Booking Association, referred to by performers as "Tough on Black Asses"). She could afford to hire a railroad car to accommodate her entire troupe as they traveled around the country, switching from one railroad to another. Duke Ellington's band had the same solution in the 1930s, traveling in a sleeper and a club car. In this way they could travel the whole country without the hassle of finding hotels that would book them and restaurants where they could get served. Duke got many ideas for his songs from life on the rails, the lonely sound of the train whistle and the rhythm of the wheels on the tracks. His finest train piece was undoubtedly *Daybreak Express*, which reproduced all the sounds of a train and was great jazz besides. For a lot of the black bands, however, life on the road was very rough. First of all, they didn't get the great location jobs, the big hotels and the prestige theaters, because those places simply didn't hire black bands. Generally they were restricted to theaters in the black sections of the different cities, places like the Howard Theatre in Washington, or the Oriental in Chicago. In New York it was the Apollo in Harlem, although eventually they began to appear at the Capitol and the Strand in Times Square. The other downtown theater was the Paramount, but that remained exclusively a white province. Other than the theaters, there were some ballrooms that would hire black bands. In the South they would often play in a tobacco warehouse converted to a ballroom for the evening. What with an occasional dance for a black fraternal organization like the Elks or the Freemasons, or a university prom (usually a black college but sometimes a white school), that was the extent of the work opportunities. Faced with a paucity of location jobs, the black bands had no alternative but to stay out on the road in the continual grinding search for work. Finding somewhere to stay for a week or even a night in a strange town was difficult, to say the least. Gradually there developed a nationwide network of boarding houses that would take in musicians. Information about these places would pass on the grapevine between traveling bands. Often the wives traveled with the musicians who were married. Mona, Milt Hinton's wife, described to me what it was like: "When the band arrived in a particular town it was our job to scout around for accommodations. Meanwhile the men would make their way to the theater to set up the stage. In those days it was always a big production with stands, lights and uniforms. All this had to be set up early in the morning because the schedule called for four or five shows each day. The band had to be ready for its first appearance at 10.00 a.m. The shows alternated with the movie throughout the day until the band's last appearance at 11 in the evening, with an extra late show on Saturday night. It was a long, tiring day, and while the men were busy we wives would fix up the accommodations and then go around to the grocery stores and markets buying food, which we took back to the theater and cooked backstage on the portable stoves we carried around. When the men came off stage after the first show we'd have a hot meal waiting for them."

Sometimes there would be babies traveling with the band. The bachelors used to babysit so their buddies could have a little free time with their wives. The relationship that sprang up between the guys in the black bands was a loyal family one which lasted long after the bands had broken up. Colleagues from the prewar bands, like Buddy Tate, Buck Clayton, Dicky Wells and Earle Warren in the Basie band and Milt Hinton, Danny Barker and Doc Cheatham with the Calloway band remained very close friends. When a colleague is in difficulties they all get together to help him out. It was a very close comradeship born out of necessity. The adversities of life made it essential for them to stick together and help each other. The greatest mistake that Lester Young made was to leave the Basie band. It was his family and it protected him. Without that, this insecure shy man couldn't function in the outside world and he fell apart. It's amazing how the musicians survived on the road in those days with no super highways and no big comfortable buses with toilets. A black band wouldn't have dared stop at a service station in parts of the country. You begin to understand all those stories about Billie Holiday and all the embarrassments she suffered. You can see why guys got involved with drugs and alcohol. They lived in a dream world that made it possible for them to survive. I once asked Vic Dickenson what it had been like on the road with the Basie band. He said, "Man, I can't remember anything about it. I was high all the time. Can't remember a thing." That's how Vic got by, just floating along, making himself oblivious to the harsh, cruel world at the other end of his horn. Yet it was an economic fact that the bands had to keep moving to survive. If things went wrong, as they could, dates were canceled or the bus broke down, the leader was blamed. The really smart leader would stay a little aloof from the band and let the road manager take the flak. The road managers were sometimes musicians in the band, but they were always a tough breed; they had to be, dealing with so many different personalities, and musicians by their very nature tend to be temperamental and emotional people. For years Eddie "Lockjaw" Davis was Basie's straw boss, a real tough "don't mess with me" kind of guy. With Duke, Juan Tizol was the musical disciplinarian. According to Rex Stewart, "The reason that Duke's band never sounded as good after Tizol left was because Juan was the only man in the band who insisted on everybody tuning up." He was very concerned about intonation, whereas Duke was more *laissez-faire*.

The 1940s and 1950s were decades of change for musicians and affected every aspect of their lives. The decline of 52nd Street from its height in the late 1930s and early 1940s, when at any given time there were eight or ten jazz clubs on the street, was a sign of the times. During the war there was a lot of sitting-in going on. The club owners, seeing eight or ten musicians on the stand at a time, got greedy and started hiring just rhythm sections, figuring there would always be horn men dropping by to jam. When the union got wind of this they cracked down, forbidding musicians to sit in. The union delegate would tour the clubs every night, asking to see each bandleader's contract and checking everybody on the stand for union cards. Another reason for the decline was the change in the music. With the rise of bebop the music became more difficult for the average person to understand. With business declining, clubs started switching to a strip policy – everybody understands strip-tease!

Interestingly enough the club that survived the longest was Ryan's, the bastion of traditional music. It only came to an end when big business interests bought up the whole block, tore down the old brownstone buildings, and built their new corporate headquarters on the site. Ryan's then found a new home on 54th Street in another old brownstone building, which had once been celebrated as an elegant whorehouse. The new Eddie Condon's followed, and the Half Note also moved up there, hoping it might be the beginning of another 52nd Street, but somehow the dream never came true. Although Ryan's and Condon's hung on for a number of years, the increasing value of real estate in the city dictated that the sites were too valuable for the little three-and four-story brownstones, so once again the property developers moved in with their bulldozers and replaced them with skyscrapers. Ryan's is gone for good, and owners Red Balaban and Eddie Polcer have just about given up trying to find a new home for Condon's. They even thought of taking over the old Nick's in Greenwich Village, which has been empty for years, but the owners wanted too much money to make it economically feasible.

More and more one can see that the days of the nightclub are coming to an end. Bars and restaurants are flourishing, but, with the cost of food and drink on top of an entertainment cover, a visit to a nightclub becomes a pretty expensive evening. People prefer to spend their money on various forms of home entertainment like video machines and CD record players. It makes it hard for jazz musicians to exist, because a whole avenue of work is slowly being phased out with nothing to take its place. Ballrooms, a great bread-and-butter area for musicians, have been replaced by discotheques using records and tapes. The big bands are passé with young people, who will spend millions of dollars on four-piece rock acts blasting away with light shows, smoke bombs, and musical performers setting fire to their guitars or dismembering live chickens on stage. The theater circuit has dwindled away because of television, and the big hotels that had large ballrooms using bands found it far more profitable to use the space for catered affairs and meetings.

The money is there, but it's being distributed in different ways. The record business has become a big money industry. After the war the control and power base of the music business shifted from the publishers to the record companies. The ten or 12 publishers in New York, most of them with offices in the Brill Building on Broadway, virtually controlled what songs the bands would play and what music was heard on the air. Sales of sheet music for use in the home was a lucrative business. After the war hundreds of new record companies sprang up, each with its own "dummy" publishing company, not set up to publish sheet music but merely to collect royalties. Today the old-time publishers with names like Leo Feist, Robbins Music, Bregman, and Belwin-Mills are merely holding companies with a staff of two or three people in their offices whose job it is to see that royalties are paid for performances and recordings of their old tunes. There was also the postwar shift from the band as the main attraction with supporting vocalists to the vocalist as the star with a supporting band. This trend really started during the war, when there was a great desire for sentimental songs. There was also the scientific advance in the means of amplifying and projecting music. In the old days, when amplification was very primitive or non-existent, it was necessary to have a big band in order to project the sound in a ballroom holding a thousand dancers, otherwise the music would not have been heard. Today three kids playing amplified guitars can make more noise than a hundred-piece symphony orchestra. Hard on the heels of amplification came the development of synthesizers which could approximate the sound of all kinds of instruments. Whereas it's perfectly obvious to a musician whether music is being produced naturally or artificially, the average listener is less able to distinguish. Whether the music is live or electronic means nothing to him; if it sounds good he really doesn't care. Technology has had a lot to do with limiting the musician's control and options. More and more, the use of music to help sell commercial products is being made by fewer and fewer people. Advertising companies with an eye on their budgets find that they can produce a jingle with only one or two musicians plus a synthesizer in place of the half a dozen or dozen musicians they might previously have used.

After the war radio was no longer the provider of work that it had been. Being an aural medium, it relied heavily upon music to enhance its programs. There were all kinds of drama and comedy shows that had live bands, in a supporting role maybe, but nevertheless providing regular work for countless musicians. In addition there were those broadcasts that featured music as entertainment in its own right. Dance bands, symphony orchestras and even small jazz groups were all heard regularly on the air in the 1930s and 1940s. The successful shows were heard from coast to coast, and the effect upon record sales and personal appearances was immeasurable. Even the territory bands, who would be heard on local stations only, found that it was sufficient to generate enough work in their area of the country. Radio provided a way for the first time for people over a large geographical area to enjoy entertainment or absorb information simultaneously. There was a magic in the way that it banished the feeling of isolation, in the way that it involved the listener in everything that was happening in the country. It helped bring a smile to the faces of millions of people as they struggled through the Depression years, and it had the immense advantage of being cheap. That all changed with the appearance of television. The technology of television is such that the cost of putting on a show compared to that of a radio show is astronomical. Live music was the first thing to go. Live dramatic shows gradually ceased and were replaced by pre-recorded programs that could be edited and changed as required. Not only were live orchestras no longer required, but it was soon realized that staff orchestras were not even needed for the pre-recorded shows. Service companies started to spring up that had huge libraries of taped music from which they could supply any kind of music to suit any kind of show. Once this music had been recorded and placed in the libraries, it could be used time and time again and remixed in many different ways.

It was a long time before musicians got any real benefit from the recording industry. If you look at old 78 records you will see that they say on the label "for home use only." This was successfully challenged in the courts and musicians lost protection for their product. Records could now be played on radio, but musicians got no payment for the use of their music. More and more disc-jockey shows began to appear, the first being Martin Block with "The Make-believe Ballroom." He had the clever idea of creating the illusion of a ballroom with a band on the stand, ready to go – the listeners could dance around in the privacy of their own homes. The older people liked the sweet music of the Mickey Mouse bands, whereas the kids lapped up the hot music of Goodman, Basie and Crosby. Block gave us kids our own special two-hour show every Saturday morning when nothing but swing music was played.

All this music was going out on radio, but neither the bandleaders nor the musicians were getting any recompense. They were too busy making money from their own radio appearances, plus ballroom, theater and hotel work, and didn't consider records to be important. It was much more important to play the popular songs and get them on radio. They were constantly wooed by the publishers and their staffs of song pluggers, who offered the bandleaders every conceivable inducement to play their tunes on the air. The publishers were the big force in the music business. There were only three major record companies – Columbia, Victor and Decca – and their issue schedules were modest by today's standards. The average band had one release each month, one record with three minutes of music one each side. Not even Benny Goodman was exempt from this leisurely pace. Compare this with the situation today, when more records are released in one week than would have been released in a whole year then.

During the 1940s the musicians' union twice imposed recording bans in an attempt to raise recording fees. The recording companies responded by using singers, who weren't members of the musicians' union, or going overseas to record European musicians. They had so many alternatives available that the recording ban achieved nothing other than hastening the demise of the bands. During a period of a year and a half between 1941 and 1944, when the swing bands were still riding high, the music of Goodman and Ellington and all the other great bands was not documented on record. The public who loved and supported that kind of music were not getting any new product, so they turned to the records that were coming out, the vocal records. The same thing happened again in 1948, when another year-long ban only served to hasten the trend.

The problem with jazz is that it was always a part of popular music. It had a ten-year period, its heyday from 1935 to 1945, when jazz and popular music went along side by side. That was the great era for jazz. It wasn't called jazz, it was called swing, but that was only a different name for the same thing; it was a simple, melodious form of jazz that was accessible to the public. They could dance to it and relate to the rhythm of the music. They were excited by the glamor, by the bandleaders, by the comings and goings of the star soloists. *Downbeat* had a regular column called "Sideman Switches" with items like "Billy Butterfield from Artie Shaw to Benny Goodman," "Charlie Shavers Leaves Tommy Dorsey to Join NBC Staff," etc. Incidentally, the Dorsey band even had a monthly magazine with feature articles about the sidemen, their hobbies, their wives, and their likes and dislikes. Jazz was part of popular music and could thrive in that milieu, but as soon as popular music took other directions after the war, jazz gradually became less and less a part of popular entertainment. It had no place to go unless it was accepted as "culture" alongside symphonic music, ballet, opera and theater, art forms which in every country in the world rely upon society for support. Art is subsidized by government and by the cultural élite, the business and professional leaders in the community who feel they have a responsibility to support the arts. Jazz at present is in a state of limbo, no longer part of popular music but still not accepted by the establishment. To the big record companies, the people who really control the music industry, it is a very small piece of the pie.

Therein lies the big problem: jazz is no longer popular music but it hasn't achieved the status of high culture. The musicians in the swing era were naïvely optimistic in the belief that jazz was finally being accepted as the great American art form. There was tremendous optimism and excitement, a feeling that at long last there was some light at the end of the tunnel and they were going to be recognized as the great artists they were. That feeling of optimism fairly jumps out of the grooves of all the jazz recordings in that ten-year period which started with Goodman's overnight success in 1935. The war changed the whole world and the changes adversely affected the jazz musician. Many great players died in utter disillusionment – people like Coleman Hawkins and Jack Teagarden, who really thought, and had every reason to believe, that the music was going to be recognized as high art. When Hawkins at the very top of his form could make a record like *Body and Soul* and see it become a top-selling hit, he was entitled to feel that it had finally happened and that at last he was going to be celebrated by society as a great artist like a Toscanini, a Caruso. There really was no reason for him to believe otherwise, and when it didn't happen he became totally disillusioned. He was a sensitive, intelligent, cultured man, a great genius in his music, but the eventual realization that white society saw him as just another black man blowing the saxophone destroyed him. He set about killing himself in a very careful, well thought out way by drinking at least a quart of brandy every day and eating only once a week. A very efficient, sure-fire way of achieving his objective, and it worked. It had nothing to do with any suggestion that he wasn't in demand or that he couldn't make money. He could still command $1000 every time he set foot on stage, because he was Coleman Hawkins, a living legend of jazz, but his spirit had been completely broken by the disillusionment.

In exactly the same way, Lester Young was destroyed by society. Poor Pres (Billie Holiday bestowed on him the title "the President," which got shortened to "Pres") was a very sensitive, kind and loving person and there was no way he should have been drafted into the army. He was psychologically incapable of handling it and the psychiatrists should have realized that he was not army material. When he came out he was never the same again. He retreated into his own world of staying high all the time, unable to cope with the lack of feeling and sensitivity of the outside world. He described how, in his later years, he left his home and family and took a room at the Alvin Hotel on Broadway and 49th Street, where he'd sit at his window with a reefer, a bottle of gin and his beloved tenor sax across his lap, just watching musicians going in and out of Birdland. They were all guys who had been inspired to play music by Lester, and as he watched them he drank and drank until finally the end came. Total disillusionment. What was the point in living? Young, who was such an all-pervasive influence on a whole generation of tenor saxophonists, had an ironic sense of humor about the situation. One night he was standing at the bar in Birdland listening to his old boss Count Basie. Paul Quinichette was in his old chair in the sax section, playing Pres's original solos note for note. After listening thoughtfully for a while, Lester turned to his companion and queried, "Is that me or am I me?" It was Lester with his penchant for giving musicians names (Lady Day, his name for Billie Holiday, became known to everyone) who coined the sobriquet for the midget Master of Ceremonies at Birdland. The man was heartily disliked by all the musicians for his annoying habit of mispronouncing their names when introducing the groups unless some monetary compensation was forthcoming. Young referred to him as "Half-a-motherfucker."

Musicians might not openly admit it, but they do feel a sense of security in having around them people who are supportive and who believe in them. It's easy for them to become overwhelmed by the realization of how small this group is in comparison to the rest of the world. This is particularly so if the musician has had a period in his life when he's had a measure of success and adulation – the kind of feeling that Hawkins must have had in the 1920s and 1930s when he was the king of the tenor sax, a figure to be recognized and respected in the close-knit brotherhood of jazz musicians that existed in those days. There's the story of the tenor player from Florida who'd just arrived in New York and was rooming with his home-town buddy, a fellow musician who'd been in town for a while. The first night he goes down to 52nd Street to hear some music. Arriving home at four in the morning he wakes his buddy and exclaims, "Man, I just heard Hawk on the Street – he played so much tenor he scared the hell out of me." His room-mate looked up at him sleepily from the bed and said, "That was Coleman Hawkins. You're s'posed to be scared!"

I remember when Dick Wellstood, Charlie Traeger and I used to go to the Hollywood in Harlem on Monday nights for the piano cutting contests. Some nights there would be someone who knew "positively" that Tatum was coming up after his gig on the Street. The word would spread through the little club like wildfire. When he arrived, the place was bursting at the seams and all the other piano players were shaking in their shoes. Tatum was a musician who commanded tremendous respect in his own world. Maybe it was a small world, but he had a feeling of belonging. Why shouldn't Art Tatum believe that he should have international recognition as a great concert artist just like Horowitz, who, after all, was one of his greatest admirers? Consider too the case of Will Marion Cook, who went to Europe to study violin with the celebrated virtuouso Eugène Ysaÿe and became an accomplished artist. He returned to the States expecting a career as a concert violinist, but was laughed at. In a fit of rage he took his beautiful, priceless violin and smashed it to pieces, never to play again. Here was a marvelous musician, a talented writer and composer who had to endure the indignity of writing coon songs for some white publisher in order to finance his classical studies and then find that it had all been in vain. Why should things like this happen to such people, people who have left statements on records that will last forever?

The swing era also gave me false expectations. When I came up as a kid, wanting to be a musician, I worshiped Benny Goodman, observing his popularity, but also noting how he could switch roles and appear as a guest soloist with the New York Philharmonic or NBC Symphony. I saw my idols, the jazz players, getting recognition for doing what they did best, and a public who were liking and buying it. I realized there were certain restrictions and that many of Benny's recordings of dubious pop tunes were just bread and butter, but there was nevertheless a pride and, seemingly, a future. Many of the musicians who went away to war in 1942 returned in 1945 to the same bands they'd left or, in the case of the staff musicians, to the same radio and film studios. There was a dignified order to it and nobody had any reason to assume that things would not continue in the same way. But after the war the music profession changed, turning into a freelance life with everybody competing, everybody scrambling around to put together a living. It takes a strong person to survive in such an insecure world, to be able to feel at ease, to conduct their life with stability and dignity, to have a normal relationship with a woman, to raise a family and to do all the things that normal people do. In the face of all these difficulties some musicians can't cope and they turn to drugs or booze in order to deal with, or hide from, reality.

Eddie Condon's band on tour, England, 1957: (left to right) Eddie, Gene Schroeder, Wild Bill Davison, myself, Cutty Cutshall, George Wettling, Leonard Gaskin (*photo Denis J. Williams*)

The Six at Ryan's, 1955: (left to right) Johnny Glasel, Eddie Phyfe (hidden), Bob Peterson, myself, Tommy Goodman, Eddie Hubble (*photo Robert Parent*)

A party for Acker Bilk at Atlantic Records, early 1960s: (left to right) Vic Dickenson, myself, Edmond Hall, Bud Freeman, Acker, Sidney De Paris, Leonard Gaskin, George Wein

Bobby Hackett's band, Henry Hudson Hotel, New York, 1957: (left to right) Pini Caceres, Ernie Caceres, Bobby, Buzzy Drootin, John Dengler, myself

At the Gaslight Club, Norwood, New Jersey, July 1963: (left to right) Charlie Queener, myself, Carl Kress

The band at the Uptown Condon's, 1963: (left to right) Eddie Condon, Vic Dickenson, Herb Lovelle, Max Kaminsky, myself, Red Richards

The World's Greatest Jazz Band at the Riverboat Room, New York, 1969: (left to right) Ralph Sutton, Bob Haggart, myself, Bud Freeman, Clancy Hayes, Billy Butterfield, Yank Lawson, Morey Feld, Lou McGarity, Carl Fontana

Bob Crosby's Bob Cats, Chicago, March 1968: (back row, left to right) Billy Cronk, Cliff Leeman, Yank Lawson, Dave McKenna, Cutty Cutshall; (front row, left to right) myself, Crosby, Matty Matlock

Left: Pug and me at Nice, 1978 (with Sinclair Traill)

Below: Soprano Summit playing at Dick Gibson's Jazz Party, Broadmoor Hotel, Colorado Springs, 1974: (left to right) George Duvivier, Kenny Davern, myself, Bobby Rosengarden

Presenting the *Swingin' for the King* album to Benny Goodman, 1979: (left to right) Lars Erstrand, myself, Benny, Anders Ohman (*photo Hank O'Neal*)

"Bob, Dave and Pug" at the Pizza Express, London, 1979 (*photo Max Garr*)

Doc Cheatham and myself during a lecture at Wilkes College, 1986

The Bechet Legacy at Bechet's, New York, January 1981: (left to right) Mark Shane, Chuck Riggs, myself, Glenn Zottola, Phil Flanigan, Chris Flory, Pug
(*photo Jerry Rice*)

Far left: Antti Sarpila and myself, Berne, Switzerland, 1987 (*photo Mark Shane*)

Left: House party at "M'Dina." Bob, Pug, daughter Danielle and friends (*photo Graham Hughes*)

Part IV. Happiness

TWELVE

At last

In between our two visits to Sweden, Pug and I bought our first home in Brewster on Cape Cod, an area I had known all my life. Our first visitor, the widow of artist Man Ray, came into our bare living room, which had no furniture, no rugs, just piles of books and records. Being quite near-sighted, she exclaimed, "How delightfully uncluttered." We found good friends in the McClennens, who owned the Wequasset Inn overlooking Pleasant Bay, the most beautiful inn on the whole of the Cape. It had been a white elephant for many years – nobody could seem to make it pay. Moves were afoot to tear it down and build a condominium in its place. To save it and to preserve the beauty of the waterfront, the McClennens (of whom there was a whole clan owning a string of homes adjacent to the inn) pooled their resources and purchased the property. They were starting their first season running the inn and wanted some music for the evening entertainment. Somebody told them we'd just moved to the Cape and Jamie McClennen gave us a ring. We entertained Jamie and his bride Stefania on our deck, standing up (we had no chairs) with drinks in paper cups, and concluded a deal. We spent that first summer working at the inn with Chuck Riggs, Chris Flory and Phil Flanigan, the talented young trio who came to New York from Providence, Rhode Island, with tenor saxophonist Scott Hamilton. It was an idyllic summer: beautiful sunny days with the sparkling water and warm beaches. But the kids never went outside the elegant house that had been provided for them, other than to go to the inn each night for work; when that summer ended they all went back to New York with the same pasty, white faces they had when they arrived. There was one morning, however, when Chris woke up, looked at his watch, which said eight o'clock, and jumped up in a panic, thinking it was time to go to work. When he was dressed he realized his watch had stopped and it was still morning. Saying to himself, "Aw, the hell with it. I might as well stay up," he walked down to the beach and lay on the sand. That night he came to work red as a beet. That was the only time he was out, so by the time the gig ended he was once more as pale as his colleagues.

Our neighbors in Brewster were the Tuckers, a retired couple from Connecticut. Joe had been an insurance agent all his life, and, although he and his wife Mary were in their mid-60s, they were full of energy and vitality. Joe had passed by our mailbox one day and had seen the name "R. S. Wilber." He wondered whether it might refer to Bob Wilber the musician, and when he found out that it did, he and Mary were the first customers at the inn on our opening night. They made themselves known and we struck up a friendship. They were like second parents to us, counseling us when we had problems and generally looking after our best interests. It was not an easy time for us. I didn't have any real, close friends, only acquaintances from the music business, and Pug chose not to contact friends from her former life. She didn't have any bitter feelings towards John and didn't want to cause any embarrassment by renewing acquaintances with people they'd known together. Gradually, however, her old friends drifted back, glad to see Pug happy in her new life.

In 1978 Pug and I teamed up with pianist Dave McKenna, who'd been living on the Cape for years. We called our group Bob, Dave and Pug. We played on the Cape and in the Boston area, and toured England and Sweden using different drummers and bass players. We made two records for Anders Ohman on Phontastic, one in Stockholm called *Groovin' at the Grunewald*, the other in New York at Hank O'Neal's studios titled *Original Wilber*. *Original Wilber* had Connie Kay on drums and Bill Crow on bass; I played clarinet, soprano and alto sax, and on some numbers, through over-dubbing, you hear five of me or ten of me! It's a record I'm proud of, perhaps the best record I've made yet. More than that I think it offers convincing evidence of my growth as a musician after all those years of searching and doubting. I was playing alongside the woman who had liberated me emotionally and with a pianist who inspired me musically. My alto doesn't sound like Hodges – the influence is there but it's my own sound. All the numbers on the album were originals, some of earlier vintage, some composed since I'd been with Pug. All the lyrics are hers and she sings them with great passion. The tunes all had happy associations and evoked memories of things we'd done together – our feelings about Sweden, our first job at the Waquasset Inn, our love of Brahms and Benny and Billie and King Oliver, and most of all our love for each other. It was all there; we pinned our hearts on that record sleeve.

The association with Dave was another step in my musical liberation. It gave me the feeling that I could now express myself with total freedom because I had a player who had the flexibility and musicianship to follow me wherever I went. I place Dave amongst my favorite piano players to play with, the others being Ralph Sutton, Mel Powell and Mark Shane. They are all great musicians, all different, but all stimulating, exciting and creative. You could throw an original at Dave and, although he'd always protest that he was a lousy reader, he'd read the thing perfectly. He can play any tune he knows in any key and at any tempo, and his repertoire is prodigious. If you called out *Cherokee* in the key of E natural he wouldn't blink an eyelid. I have never yet seen a musical challenge that he couldn't handle. Besides knowing so many songs he knows all the verses and every subtle chord change the composer wrote. If Dave likes a tune, he only needs to play it once and it goes into his computer brain for all time. He is another guy who only recently acquired a piano. When not working he'd go for months without touching a keyboard, but the moment he sits down at the piano, it's all there. "I'm not a jazz player," he says, "I'm just a saloon piano player. Actually I'd really like to be a postman." His two great interests are crossword puzzles and baseball. He makes it a standing rule not to take engagements outside the States during the World Series every fall.

In 1978 Pug and I were married twice, once in June at the little church in Brewster, where we marched out to the sound of King Oliver playing *Canal Street Blues*, and again in July at Nice. The ceremony in Nice took place at the City Hall, where we received the blessing of the mayor. Mona Hinton led our wedding procession along the seafront, with all the musicians following behind playing their instruments. Shelly Manne provided the beat by clapping together his beach shoes. Leonard Feather ran alongside with his tape machine, recording the event and providing a commentary. The procession snaked down the steps onto the beach and picked its way among all the topless ladies, who stood up and cheered. That marriage was a great moment in my life. Over a period of some 30 years fate slowly but surely had drawn us together, not without many obstacles along the way. One amusing hiccup was the letters Pug sent me as a 15 year old; they were signed "Joy Burke." I had always assumed that that was her maiden name, but in actual fact it was a stage name she used touring with stage productions and as a dancer at the Savoy in London. When I came to England with Condon in 1957 we actually met at one of our concerts, but I had no idea that the Pug Horton I was speaking to was the Joy Burke who had written to me. She, in turn, hadn't realized that she was speaking to Bob Wilber because the program had incorrectly described me as Robert Sage (Sage being my middle name), and my appearance was so different from the photograph I had sent her years before. In the crowded mêlée backstage there was little chance to talk, and when I tried to look for her she'd left. It wasn't until years later that we realized we'd actually met on that occasion without each being aware of who the other was! I can't adequately describe the joy I felt about our union. After years of searching for my own identity I'd found a soul mate, a partner to share the hazardous journey through life. From that point on my career blossomed. You can hear it on the recordings, a new confidence and freedom of expression. I owe it all to Pug.

While living on the Cape we got a telegraph from the Polish Jazz Society inviting us to play for them. They'd pay a fee in zlotys, plus transportation, hotel and living expenses. We looked at the Pan-Am timetables and began to get excited, because it seemed to offer the chance of taking in a number of European cities we'd never seen but wanted to. The next telegraph set us straight concerning that idea; we were to fly straight in, and out three days later, on the Polish Lot state airline. When I phoned to discuss the matter I was told in a very Teutonic manner, "You will fly Lot. You will not fly any other way." Still, there would be Poland to see, so we applied for visas. That was an experience in itself. Our engagement was for a television show, a recording session and a concert, but the consul was only prepared to issue a visa for three days. He was unable to appreciate the ludicrous timetable of a transatlantic flight, followed by all that work and then a return flight, all compressed into 72 hours. This was a challenge that Pug couldn't resist. She charmed him into granting us a visa for five days instead. On the day of departure we went along to the airport, not yet having received our tickets. Upon enquiring at the Lot ticket desk, we found they had no record of our booking; the computer wasn't working and they couldn't verify our reservation with the New York office. The plane was due to leave in 30 minutes. What were we to do? Once more Pug put her charm to work and persuaded them to make out two tickets to Warsaw on her say-so. We boarded that somber grey plane and in due course arrived in Warsaw. There was immediately a hassle over my passport because the photograph didn't correspond with my current bearded appearance. This was nothing compared to the hassle the Polish passengers were being subjected to. Their suitcases were being ripped open and they seemed absolutely terrified.

Our guide took us our hotel, where we checked in. There was no opportunity to catch up on sleep because we were taken immediately to a nightclub (at 11 a.m.), where a jazz band was playing and people were sitting round drinking. We were asked to sit in, and, although asleep on our feet with exhaustion and jet lag, felt it diplomatic to comply with the request. That night, after dinner at our hotel, we were asked by the waiter whether we wanted to pay in zlotys or dollars. He explained if we paid in dollars he'd give us an exchange rate of one hundred zlotys to the dollar, as compared with the official rate of 32. Next day out on the street people approached us offering 130 zlotys on a dollar. The taxi drivers had a way of increasing their income. If they heard passengers speaking any language rather than Polish they'd tack a surcharge on the meter. We'd been told by Jazz Club members to keep silent and pay only what appeared on the meter reading. The scenes in the shops were as we had heard, with endless queues of people waiting to buy toilet paper, flashlight batteries, eggs – whatever was in stock that day.

At our first rehearsal we discovered that the different jobs we were hired for were happening simultaneously. We played a one-hour concert with trumpeter Henryk Majewski's radio band (excellent), which was not only televised and recorded but was shown on monitors in various rooms throughout the Cultural Center. Thousands of fans were jammed into the building. That evening, returning to the hotel after our day's strenuous activities, we were crammed in a minuscule taxi riding through the cold, grey streets of Warsaw, keeping very silent as we'd been advised. The driver had the radio on, which featured popular music selections interspersed with comments naturally unintelligible to us. Suddenly we heard Johnny Dodds and the New Orleans Wanderers playing *Gatemouth Blues*, one of our all-time favorites. The music poured forth and filled the little cab with warmth. Pug looked at me and we both started crying with joy. Maybe we were homesick. The taxi driver was perplexed but, seeing our happy faces, he listened to the music too, smiling and laughing.

After three days our free hotel accommodation ceased, so for the remaining two days we stayed with in-laws of an old friend of Pug's from Albany. Majka had married a Polish lad. It was a happy coincidence that she was in Warsaw visiting them while we were there. Her in-laws were two retired architects who lived in one of the few old houses in Warsaw undamaged in the war. It was touching to see the austerity of their lives. In order to obtain food for dinner the night we arrived, Mrs Lamprecht had spent the whole day queueing here and there for a little of this and a little of that. When we went to the toilet we found newspaper neatly cut into sections – toilet paper was in such short supply. Vodka was available in abundance, however: very strong stuff with a kick like a mule. Despite the difficulties, we were received with great warmth and hospitality. The following night we reciprocated by taking our hosts and Majka to dinner at a restaurant in the old town, which had been totally razed by the retreating Germans. After the war an exact replica was built on the same site, every brick and stone the same as the original, even to the indentations in the stone stairs, worn down by the footsteps of millions of people since the Middle Ages. Such tenacity, such courage, you can't help but admire in the Polish people! I couldn't resist wild boar as a main course because of my name. The bill for a six-course meal, including vodka, beer and wine, for five people came to less than ten dollars.

Despite the drabness and austerity, we liked Poland. There was a lot of pretentious Stalinesque architecture in contrast with the picturesqueness of the old town, and the industrial pollution was awesome. Although there were bright sunny days, a thick haze hung over the whole city constantly, practically obscuring the sun. The people were friendly, and more willing to approach us and talk than the Russians I saw in 1975. The presence of dirty snow piled high on all the side streets inspired a joke making the rounds in Warsaw that winter. Question: "What's the Polish word for snow removal?" Answer: "Spring."

My next major project was a result of my continuing interest in the musician who had been my first inspiration, Benny Goodman. Among the players I met and worked with in Sweden was a vibraphone player by the name of Lars Erstrand. He was a disciple of Lionel Hampton. Anders Ohman wrote of him, "Lars plays with a vitality and force, an inventiveness and playfulness which have no equal. He is no plagiarist but an artist in his own right." Benny Goodman's 70th birthday was approaching, and I felt that I wanted to pay my respects. It seemed an obvious step to involve Lars in a tribute to Benny Goodman, and when I mentioned it to Anders he was enthusiastic. We set about planning a record. We wanted to build the whole thing around the clarinet but yet do something different, so we hit upon the idea of a group consisting of four clarinets and rhythm section, plus Lars on vibes. The idea was for me to transcribe some of Benny's solos and arrange them for four clarinets. I called the idea "SuperBenny" after Supersax, the group that played transcriptions of Charlie Parker's solos. We had an excellent Swedish rhythm section, plus Ove Lind, Arne Domnérus and Anders on the other three clarinets. The outcome was an album titled *Swingin' for the King*. After Pug and I returned to the States, Anders asked me to arrange some of the old Hampton classics to feature Lars in a tribute to Hamp. The session took place at Hank O'Neal's studio and the American musicians, all top players (including Hank Jones, Jimmy Maxwell and Frank Wess), were knocked out by Lars, whom they had never heard before. I spent hours transcribing the arrangements from the old Hampton records. A few months later, while out on the West Coast, I visited Benny Carter. I told him about our recording and all the headaches of reconstructing the arrangements. Benny smiled and took me out in his garage. Sitting in a carton in a corner were the original parts, yellow with age, of the things Benny had done for Hamp, including Carter's original *When lights are low*, which we'd just recorded!

The *Swingin' for the King* album was heard by Gil Weist, the owner of Michael's Pub in New York. Liking what he heard, he contacted me with the offer of an engagement. It was a damn good band we took into the pub, although it didn't include Pug, whose singing was an important part of the record. Weist insisted he'd had nothing but singers in the room for a while and wanted a strictly instrumental package. It always rankled with me, and the next time he asked me to bring a group in I turned him down. Along with Lars, I had the kids, Chris Flory, Phil Flanigan and Chuck Riggs, and Mark Shane on piano. I first met Mark in New Orleans when Bobby Rosengarden asked me to join him and Milt Hinton for a two-week gig in the jazz room at the Hyatt Regency Hotel. Mark was a young player around New York at the time, just beginning to get established, but with a really good feel for the music. I liked him immediately, both as a person and as a piano player. Our engagement at Michael's Pub was a great success: four weeks of packed houses and tumultuous applause – including one memorable night when Benny borrowed my clarinet to sit in with the band.

On our closing Saturday night two old friends came in. I had first met Harold and June Geneen when Soprano Summit was invited to play at the Boca Raton Club in Florida at the annual convention of the International Telephone and Telegraph Company. We were flown down from New York, somewhat puzzled as to how we came to get the date, but quite happy as the money was great. After the first set I was ushered over to the table of the Chairman of the Board, Harold Geneen. It turned out that he was a big fan of mine and for a long time had been following me all over town whenever I was playing. His wife June was always urging him, "Go on, Harold. Go up and introduce yourself," but Harold would always say, "Oh no. I don't want to bother him. He doesn't know who I am." This was the man who at that time was the world's highest-paid executive! Anyway, Harold enjoyed our Swingin' for the King group and was interested to know where we were going next. I told him that after that night the group was through, with Lars returning to Sweden on Monday. Harold was aghast. "Do you really mean this is the end of the group? I hope you've made a record while you were here." I had to admit that nobody had even asked us to make one. Harold looked at me, a big smile on his face, and asked, "How would you like to make one now? Don't worry about the cost." There was nothing I would rather do – we'd been playing together for five weeks and were really tight. It took me all of two seconds to say yes. We closed Michael's Pub at 1.00 a.m. on Sunday morning, and nine hours later we trooped into Vanguard Studios and reeled off 21 numbers, with only one re-take. The recording engineer used simple two-track stereo, setting the band up as though we were playing in a club, rather than spreading us all round the studio with individual microphones. What I was trying to get was the kind of sound that Columbia Records used to get at Liederkranz Hall in the early 1940s, my ideal for recorded jazz.

So now we had a record. The next question was what to do with it. Pug came up with the answer. "Let's put it out ourselves. You can write the sleeve notes." It sounded like a good idea, but what name should we give to our label? We thought of our house on the Cape. When I first saw it I said, "Isn't it beautiful? It really bodes well for our future," so we called the house "Bodeswell." That just had to be the name for our record company, so Bodeswell Records was born. We called our first release *Dizzy Fingers* after the Zez Confrey classic we used to open the album. It was to be the first of seven releases over a period of five years. We found the record business to be a lot of fun, a lot of headaches and completely devoid of profits. Last year we threw in the towel and sold the company to our old friend George Buck, who runs the Jazzology and Audiophile labels.

Our second record was made in May 1978. We were living in one room on 12th Street in Greenwich Village, in the apartment of friends of Dick and Julia Hyman. We'd come down from the Cape in January when I went into the Pub with Dick's Perfect Jazz Repertory Group. Dick and Julia suggested we contact their friends the Hanaus, who had a room in their apartment they weren't using. It was a good arrangement, and for as long as we lived on Cape Cod we had a place to stay when we came to town. We recorded that second record shortly after our album with Dave McKenna. I told Pug that, although she was a lovely singer, the world didn't really know it. The only records she had made besides the Phontastic sides were with the mediocre dixieland bands, and didn't show the way she could sing. She was known as a blues singer and was in fact one of the few non-Americans with a picture and a bio in the *Blues Who's Who* by Sheldon Harris. She has a wonderfully intimate way of singing ballads, and I wanted that side of her talent to be presented on record. Having prevailed on another well-heeled friend of ours to foot the bill, we decided she'd record with just piano and bass. Our first choice on piano was Dave McKenna, but unfortunately Dave had just signed an exclusive contract with Carl Jefferson at Concord, so that ruled him out. Pug suggested Don Ewell because she always felt comfortable with him, but I felt Don's style was a little old-fashioned. I favored Hank Jones, but Pug was worried that he'd be too modern. Almost simultaneously we came up with the idea of using Roland Hanna – modern, yes, but a pianist who took chances and was exciting. The bass spot gave us no trouble. It had to be Mister Reliable, Milt Hinton. Having picked the group, we chose an interesting program ranging from Jelly Roll Morton's *Sweetheart o'Mine* (the first vocal recording ever) to the contemporary hit song *If*, and including some of our originals. We again chose Vanguard, the best studio in New York, with a Steinway concert grand considered the finest in the city. Our engineer was Fred Miller, who'd done the Summit records for Hank O'Neal and also our first Bodeswell record. The tape was made with Pug, Roland and Milt right in the middle of the huge studio. When we listened to the playback it sounded great but it also sounded a little empty. I started wondering whether there was anything I might be able to do to give it more body. I evolved a whole part adding either soprano, alto or clarinet, interweaving it with Roland's improvisations. I took Roland's piano lines and doubled them on my horn so that it sounded like an arrangement, something that was pre-conceived, whereas in reality Roland was improvising. We then dubbed in my part after we'd mixed and edited the original tape. It was a beautiful job of engineering by Fred Miller, because it's difficult to over-dub without it being obvious to the discerning ear. You invariably get a different ambience, and you can usually tell its been grafted on, but to my knowledge no critic or listener has ever cottoned on to the fact that my part was inserted later. It emerged as a perfect record, one that we're really proud of having made. The sound of the LP is exquisite: Roland plays superbly and Milt's bass is as good as anything I've heard him do. On top of all that there's Pug's singing, which is an absolute joy. Even the art work is great. The cover photograph was taken by Tim Motian on one of our engagements at the Pizza Express in London and catches Pug peering out into the dimly lit jazz cellar. It gave us the feeling that the people sitting there in the dark were saying to her, "Don't go away," hence the title for the record.

In 1980 we heard about a new club called Bechet's that was opening on Third Avenue. I was pleased with the idea that Sidney was at last going to get some recognition in his own country. One of the owners was a man I knew, Bernie Brightman, who had a small jazz record company, Stash Records. When I called him he told me he had two partners, one a business man and the other a French chef. In looking for a name for the club they had initially thought of Beiderbecke's, but that seemed too long, so they settled for the shorter Bechet's. I told Bernie that I thought it was a great idea, but what was the actual connection with Bechet? "Well," said Bernie, "I don't really know. It's just a jazz room where we're going to have jazz." I suggested to him that I do a tribute to Bechet at Bechet's. Bernie thought for a moment and then said it was a fine idea, but the club was small, big enough only for a trio, maybe a quartet at most. Without a moment's hesitation Pug came up with the answer. "The Bechet–Spanier Big Four. Let's use trumpet, guitar and bass. We can use the kids, Chris and Phil, and on trumpet we'll use Glenn Zottola from our Smithsonian group, and a few vocals from me."

So that is what we did. We got a little extra money so we could hire Chuck Riggs on drums on the weekends. We decided to record the proceedings one night, so we drafted in Mark Shane to make up a full band and Fred Miller brought in his portable gear. My mother and father were there, as also were some new acquaintances of ours, Andrew and Susan Sordoni. The resulting album was the third on our Bodeswell label.

When we made the booking we were living on the Cape and had to come into town. Seeing that we were going to be at Bechet's for four weeks we wanted a little more space than the single room at the Hanau's. Pug thought it would be cheaper to look around for an apartment we could rent rather than stay in a hotel. She found an advert in the *New York Times*: "East Side studio apartment overlooking East River. Occupant moving South for Winter." When she contacted the owner, he gave her a glowing description of the beautiful apartment, its glorious view of the river and all the valuable silver and the *objets d'art* that were in the place. It sounded great, just the kind of place we were looking for, so my nephew Tim Jenson concluded the deal and signed the agreement. We flew into New York, loaded with luggage – all Pug's gowns, my horns and music – and took a cab to the address. The first impression was a favorable one. It was a large apartment building on the upper East Side with a doorway and elevator. We left the luggage with the doorman and took the elevator up. I opened the door and stepped inside, but in the darkness bumped into something large and solid. When I found the light switch and turned it on, we were astonished to find the whole place absolutely filled to the rafters with large pieces of furniture, books and packing cases, with the smallest amount of open space imaginable right in the center. It was like picking your way through a maze as you moved around the corridors formed by the packing cases. When I eventually found my way to the window and opened the curtains, which were bright yellow oilcloth, I looked for the promised view of the East River. I found it to be the merest glimpse, only to be seen if one looked at the right angle between two tall adjoining buildings. All the contents of the apartment were covered with a thick layer of dust, and it was obvious from the odor that permeated the room that the occupants kept cats, probably a whole family of them. We looked at each other and wondered how on earth we were going to manage there. I was for staying, cleaning the place up and making the best of a bad deal, but Pug was adamant that it wasn't for us. We went downstairs to speak to the superintendent, and when we told him that we were the people staying in the apartment, he said, "What do you mean? He's not allowed to sub-let. It's against the law. You'll have to get out." So we were out on the street with all our luggage, on a bitterly cold February day with the temperature below zero. We sat in a coffee shop trying to get warm, waiting for the phone while a young man argued interminably with his boyfriend. We called everyone we knew in New York, but nobody was home.

By now it was getting dark and we contemplated checking into a hotel, which we could ill afford. Suddenly Pug remembered that a sister of a friend of hers from Boston had married some guy and they were living across from Carnegie Hall. But what was his name? She thought she remembered it, so I looked in the phone book, and sure enough there was the name with an address on 57th Street. Pug called the number, made known our plight in her typically persuasive manner, and ten minutes later we were heading downtown in a taxi. Pug started calling rental adverts in the *New York Times* and eventually found a lady whose son, a jazz trumpeter, was away at school in Boston and who was delighted to have a famous jazz couple occupy her son's room for a month. I've described this incident in detail because it's so illustrative of Pug's resourcefulness in dealing with crisis situations.

After the engagement at Bechet's ended we thought about trying to keep the group, which Pug named the Bechet Legacy, together. We got a trip to England set up, but almost immediately ran into difficulties. Some of the guys wanted more money, and gave us an ultimatum of pay up or else. Taking a newly formed group overseas can be a tricky financial operation and our first priority was to get the band established. There was only so much available and that was it. Rather than give up the tour we sought out replacements. We brought in Mike Peters on guitar. The first time I had met Mike was when we were working at the Maryland Inn in Annapolis with Swingin' for the King. He was passing through town and sat in with us and made a great impression. That left us with the problem of a drummer. I knew that Glenn Zottola was a friend of Butch Miles and that they had a little group of their own, so I asked Glenn if he would sound out Butch about joining our group. Butch agreed and we got ourselves a great drummer, a marvelous showman, and a beautiful guy. On bass we got our English friend we'd worked with before, Len Skeat. Our original guys were rather taken aback by the firmness of our stand, but we had no alternative: either replace them or no tour. As it turned out, the English fans, with their typical respect for jazz tradition, loved the idea of the band and we got rave reviews in all the papers and magazines. Typically for us, we didn't make any money. Maybe it was the economic situation in England at that time but our agent couldn't get enough money to cover salaries, transportation and hotels. We began to build a following, however, and over the next three years we toured England again, played Belfast two years in a row and played at the Cork, North Sea and Nice festivals.

Our furthest trip was to India. The founder of the Indian Jazz Convention, known as the Jazz Yatra, was Narajan Jhavari. He'd masterminded a complex deal with Air India and leading hotels whereby free travel and accommodation would be provided. There were no fees for the musicians, but the prospect of a trip to India had attracted many top players, including Stan Getz, Dizzy Gillespie, and Sonny Rollins. Narajan used to come to New York to book the musicians, and on one trip heard the Legacy at Condon's and offered us a deal. On the face of it, it was non-profit, but if you could tie it in with other gigs in the Far East it made sense. The promoter would fly you from New York to Bombay and back. Alternatively, if you had a booking in, say, Japan, he would fly you from Bombay to Tokyo instead of back to New York. In turn, all the Japanese promoter had to do was to fly you back to New York. In this way the musicians got from Bombay to Tokyo and back home at no cost, and picked up an engagement fee in Japan as well. All the established groups used it as a means of getting out to the Far East. Unfortunately we were not known in Japan, so we couldn't take advantage of the arrangement. We just looked at it as an opportunity that we otherwise wouldn't have of seeing India. The first week we played in New Delhi and the second in Bombay.

We loved New Delhi with its stately government buildings, a holdover from the days of British rule. Our first night there we were entertained by Solly Sorabjee and his wife. Solly was by all accounts India's number one jazz fan and gave us a rousing send-off for our stay in India. He had covered the garden of his stately home with a tent and laid beautiful oriental rugs on the grass. Besides the élite of New Delhi society, the Sorabjees had invited a few of the old-time Indian jazz players still living who had worked with the pianist Teddy Weatherford in Bombay in the 1930s. We had some leisure time in Delhi to sightsee and shop. One day our promoter organized a bus for the band to travel to Agra to see the famous Taj Mahal. The night before, we'd had a big Indian meal at the hotel. In the restaurant was a three-piece orchestra playing two sitars and a tablā. Mike Peters was fascinated by their music and asked them if he could sit in. They graciously acceded to his request, and Mike, who thought the music sounded quite easy, ran upstairs for his guitar. Once he started playing it was a different story. Not being able to figure out where the first beat of each measure was, he was simply lost from beginning to end. His respect for Indian music increased one hundred-fold. He bought a sitar and a set of tablās to take back to the United States to study. That night Len Skeat had too much rich Indian food and next morning he felt deathly ill. Determined to see the Taj Mahal, he joined the rest of us on a bumpy four-hour ride along the dusty two-lane highway to Agra. By the time we reached our destination poor Len was positively green, and while we trooped in to marvel at the beautiful palace built by an Indian prince for his wife as a token of his undying love, our bass player lay in the back of the bus in a comatose state. He then had to face the four-hour return journey. Obviously Len's memory of the Taj Mahal is rather different from that of the rest of us!

We saw much more of India's legendary poverty in Bombay. Outside our hotel was a sign reading "Barbecue around the pool every Saturday – 5 p.m." Directly across the street from the hotel was a large vacant lot taken up with squatters, who had built low hovels out of mud and straw to live in. Imagine these poorest of the poor waking up each morning to gaze at that sign across the street. One day Mark Shane, who was very distressed to see such poverty, bought a basket of apples at a fruit stand and, standing at the edge of the squatters' settlement, offered apples to several children standing there. Suddenly, as if they sensed what was going on, hundreds of children started to appear, descending on Mark like vultures. As the children surged around him, Mark threw the rest of the apples down in a panic and ran across the street to the hotel. He was very shaken by this experience and still has nightmares about it.

Our big concert in Bombay was the last night of the festival. The concert featured Ronnie Scott's group, the Woody Shaw band, the Vienna Arts Ensemble and the Bechet Legacy, and finished with a large band from the Soviet Union. We never did hear the Russian band because we had to leave for the airport immediately after our set. The large Austrian ensemble went on interminably, mostly squeaks and squawks, with a girl making chirping and clicking noises at the mike. I can only describe their music as a study in schizophrenia – the fast numbers manic, the slow numbers depressive. The audience, 3000 strong, sat in the large sports stadium and applauded politely, totally mystified by most of the music up till that point. By this time we were getting worried that we'd miss our plane, so we set up quickly, asked our friend Phil Schaap, a New York jazz disc-jockey who'd gone over to MC the concert, to keep his comments to a minimum, and roared into our usual opener, *Down in Honky Tonk Town*. This time the applause was more than polite, and, sensing the audience warming to our efforts, we continued with *Promenade aux Champs-Elysées* and *Dans les rues d'Antibes*, two of Sidney's best numbers from his later years in France. By now we could feel the excitement rising in the audience. I stepped up to the microphone and announced, "And now, ladies and gentlemen, Joanne Horton." Pug swept out, dressed in a beautiful sari with a bindi, a traditional Indian beauty-mark, on her forehead. She went into *St Louis Blues*, and as it gathered momentum the audience began to clap, freely at first, but as the pulsing rhythm got to them, in time to the music. As Fats Waller would have exclaimed, "the joint was jumpin'." When we hit the last chord the audience, all 3000 of them, jumped to their feet and roared out their approval – this was what they'd been waiting for, this was what jazz was all about! As the fans surged towards the stage, hoping to get autographs, we rushed backstage, packed our gear, jumped into the waiting bus and sped to the airport, where they were holding the plane for us. It was an exciting climax to an unforgettable experience.

The Bechet Legacy made three records in all. The second was made in England while we were on tour and was called *On the Road*, and the third was recorded at the Vanguard Studios in New York with Vic Dickenson as guest artist; we titled it *Ode to Bechet* after one of my originals. Vic was a marvelous player and I was so delighted to have him. He'd been very tight with Sidney, played with him many times, and blew on some of Bechet's best records on Victor and Blue Note. Sadly it was his last recording date – he died the following spring. It was the most exciting album we made with the Legacy and it contains some of the finest soprano playing I've done on record. All the hurt, all the problems, everything I had gone through in my life, I poured into my horn, warts and all. I wasn't playing as beautifully and as mellifluously as before. I was doing a lot of growling, no longer the Grace Kelly of the soprano sax, more like Wallace Beery. Vic and I had known each other for many years and I have a great many happy memories of him. I once owned a parakeet that could talk. When Vic came round to my apartment he was intrigued with the bird and developed a way of communicating with it. Vic used to wear patent leather shoes. He discovered that when he rubbed his feet together the shoes made a squeaking sound that somehow meant something to the bird. It would then start talking to Vic, who replied by rubbing his shoes, and in this ridiculous fashion they used to carry on conversations for hours at a time. I always smile when I remember the time when I was playing at the Savoy and doing some Christmas shopping at Filene's, the famous bargain basement store in Boston. Seeing a crush of women scrambling over one another to take advantage of a record sale, I wandered over to see what all the fuss was about. I saw that the store had 200 copies of *Jingle Bells* by Leo Watson and the Spirits of Rhythm and was selling them for ten cents apiece. Braving the crush, I bought one. When I played it back home I discovered the craziest whacked-out version of the number imaginable. There was Leo doing his surrealistic scat vocal, with very obscene gutteral comments from Vic's trombone. I tried to imagine all those mothers taking their copies home and playing them on Christmas morning with dad and the kiddies around the tree, expecting some sort of traditional rendition but getting instead this crazy, but wonderful, version.

Over the years the record companies, always mindful of public disapproval, have made ridiculous attempts to edit the vocals of various jazzmen, who can be very spontaneous and free in their utterances on record. There is, for example, the recording of *Sweet Hunk o'Trash* by Louis Armstrong and Billie Holiday. On the original version Billie is singing the blues with Louis rumbling and grumbling in the background. After one particularly salubrious stanza he offers the comment, "fuck 'em, babe." On a subsequent issue of the record it comes out as "uck 'em, babe." The company had simply deleted the letter "f"! Perhaps the most famous example is the recording of *Barnacle Bill the Sailor* by Hoagy Carmichael's orchestra featuring Bix Beiderbecke. While most of the inane lyric is sung by the band, the final line, "For he's Barnacle Bill the Sailor," is given to Venuti as a vocal break. Joe, whose voice was very deep anyway, growls it out at the bottom of his range, a true basso profundo. It wasn't till years later, when the recording was reissued in a Beiderbecke collection, that the listener, with the benefit of greatly improved fidelity, could actually hear Joe saying, "For he's Barnacle Bill the shithead."

What a character Joe was! Stories of his practical jokes are legion – one of my favorites is about when he reduced the orchestra conductor to a bag of nerves. They were in the radio studio rehearsing for a broadcast that was due to go out live, coast to coast, at 9.00 p.m. While the conductor went out to confer with the producers, Joe advanced the studio clock by five minutes and explained in a whisper to his fellow musicians what he had in mind. The conductor came back into the studio, called the orchestra to order and stood on the podium, baton raised, watching the second hand go round. When it hit nine o'clock he gave the downbeat. Nothing happened. The musicians just sat there and looked at him while the hapless fellow, his arms flailing in the air, sweat pouring off his brow, glared at his musicians with his mouth forming obscene but silent epithets. Joe played with Paul Whiteman's orchestra in its heyday, when the jazz wing included such luminaries as Frank Trumbauer, the Dorsey brothers, Eddie Lang and Bix Beiderbecke. He eventually got fired for the incident involving Mike Pingatore, the banjo player. Mike had been with Whiteman from the beginning, when the band consisted only of five pieces. He was a cripple, a small hunchbacked man who walked with a cane. This didn't bother Venuti, but the fact that Pingatore was getting paid more than he, the great Joe Venuti, really rankled, so one day he went out and purchased a small saw. That night, while Pingatore was engrossed in conversation with another musician, Joe sneaked up behind him, grabbed his cane, sawed a quarter of an inch off the end, and carefully replaced its rubber tip. He repeated this caper on each successive night, and poor Mike sank lower and lower as he complained of the terrible time his back was giving him. One night Whiteman caught Venuti sawing away and fired him immediately. Joe, who figured he was just having a little innocent fun, was incensed and determined to get revenge for this gross injustice. So he went out and formed his own band. One of his first dates was on the same bill as

Whiteman's orchestra at the Texas State Fair. Each band would come out and play their set, and the revolving bandstand would then carry them off while bringing on the next group. Paul's classic opening for his concerts was a darkened stage, with a little pin-spot of light gently moving to and fro as the band played its opening theme, *Rhapsody in Blue*. As the lights gradually came up, the audience would see Whiteman, resplendent in white tie and tails, conducting the orchestra with this long baton with a little light on the end of it. Venuti had it fixed so that his band followed Whiteman's. Paul finished in a blaze of glory to tumultuous applause. As the stage slowly revolved, the audience observed a light bulb on the darkened stage swinging about to the strains of *Barnacle Bill the Sailor*. As the lights came up, there was Venuti, conducting his band with a broomstick; the light bulb was tied to the end with a long electric wire trailing conspicuously off into the wings. Joe, a great player until the day he died in 1978, refused to take life seriously.

The Bechet Legacy was an exciting little band, and it represented a continuation of the efforts I have made over the years to do something that was musical and of superior quality, something that was unique, original and presented with dash and flair. Throughout the swing era, the public was thrilled by the exciting presentation of the music, each band with its own distinctive opening theme followed by a well-structured program that combined excitement with showmanship, with the result that the audience was given maximum value for its money. I always tried to give the public that value, right from the very beginning with the Wildcats, the Savoy and Storyville bands, and the Six. As I emerged from my years of confusion and self-doubt I realized I still believed in this concept. I couldn't have had a better example to follow than Bobby Hackett, who believed in an organized group and the idea of putting together something of real quality. As I gradually found my own feet again, it was with the World's Greatest Jazz Band and Soprano Summit where a premium value was placed on musicianship, presentation and good taste. I never deviated one inch from this line when I resumed my career as a leader with Bob, Dave and Pug, Swingin' for the King, the Smithsonian Jazz Repertory Company, the Bechet Legacy and my current group, Bob Wilber and Friends. I set out certain things that I want to do artistically with my music and try to come reasonably close to achieving what I want. With the Bechet Legacy my goal was to celebrate one particular man, both as a musician and as a composer, and to bring the maximum possible attention to his music. The group was not intended to produce a carbon copy of his recordings but to interpret Sidney's music in its own way. It didn't have a dixieland sound, but neither did the bands that Sidney led. Some traditional jazz fans don't believe the music is authentic unless they hear a banjo, a tuba and a tailgate trombone. I call this the "Sacramento" mentality, after the Sacramento Jazz Festival in California, which attracts thousands of fans every year. They listen in delight to hundreds of banjo-and-tuba bands chugging away with great enthusiasm but very little swing or invention. Although the bulk of their repertoire is taken from the recordings made in the 1920s by Oliver, Armstrong and Morton, the music they produce is light years away from the source. The intensity and seriousness of purpose of the original is replaced with a kind of frivolous "isn't this great fun?" spirit. Ironically, this music, based for the most part on the contributions of black pioneers, is played by white bands for white middle-class audiences. Black people simply don't relate to this "good-time" music – they prefer sterner, tougher sounds that reflect the realities of life. With the trad audiences the subtleties and intricacies of authentic jazz are completely wasted. With the Bechet Legacy we worked to capture the spirit of Sidney's music, not to play in any categorized "traditional" style.

Groups like mine, which celebrate jazz music's past by bringing attention to or re-creating earlier styles, run into a particular criticism which usually goes like this: "That music you're playing is a part of jazz history and well-documented on record, so what's the point of playing it today? You'll never sound as good as the original." Musicians playing classical music of earlier eras do not face this same kind of criticism. The music of Bach, Mozart, Beethoven and Brahms is "re-created" every day of the year all over the world and nobody thinks it shouldn't be. So why not re-create or celebrate the music of King Oliver, Sidney Bechet, Duke Ellington or Benny Goodman? It won't be better than the original but it will be different, because, as in classical music, the music changes according to who is playing it. Every musician, jazz or classical, brings his or her own experiences and feelings into the music. I believe all great music from the past should continue to be played by live musicians. As the world evolves the music will evolve also.

THIRTEEN

Jazz education

The Smithsonian Jazz Repertory Company was a project very dear to my heart. In the 1970s Martin Williams, for many years a respected jazz critic, approached the Smithsonian Institution in Washington, DC, with the novel idea that jazz music was an important part of American culture and perhaps it was time that the Smithsonian took note of this fact. He succeeded in getting a job there and gradually built a jazz program, which included concerts, reissues of important recordings and finally an organized group, as part of the Smithsonian's Performing Arts Program. Martin used to call on me to help him present concerts at the Baird Theater in the Museum of Natural History in Washington, featuring the music of different figures. These included Jelly Roll Morton, Bix Beiderbecke, Duke Ellington, James P. Johnson, Fats Waller and others. Some of these concerts were recorded and released on the Smithsonian label. In 1977 the Smithsonian Institution of Performing Arts concluded a deal with Harold Shaw, a prominent booker of classical music, whereby Shaw would book four groups playing different kinds of music under the aegis of the Smithsonian. One of the groups was to be a jazz repertory ensemble, which Martin Williams was delegated to organize. Martin asked me to select the musicians.

The Bechet Legacy was just getting started, so I used the players in that group, plus Tom Artin on trombone and Bob Kindred on tenor and baritone saxes. For the next three years we did two tours a year for Harold Shaw, for audiences that were used to Shaw's usual attractions – a chamber group, an opera singer, a ballet company, etc. Since we were playing jazz for the uninitiated, we devised a program that gave a capsule history of jazz in two hours. We started out with me, standing in a pin-spot on a darkened stage, telling of the origins of jazz, with Pug's voice offstage singing Bessie Smith's *Backwater Blues*. Two hours later, having guided our neophyte audience through 60 years of jazz history, we were into the music of Parker, Gillespie, Monk and Coltrane. When the Reagan administration came to office in 1980 they cut back funding for the arts, and the Smithsonian could no longer afford to sponsor the performing groups. The Shaw organization's response to our group had been overwhelmingly enthusiastic, so they kept us on with the name the Bob Wilber Jazz Repertory Ensemble. Without the Smithsonian stamp of approval, however, they found it difficult to get bookings, and after one year we threw in the towel.

One particular project on which I worked long and hard during our tenure with the Smithsonian was the re-creation of the music of King Oliver and the Creole Jazz Band. I used to listen to the original recordings and wonder what the band really sounded like in person. The opportunity of trying to answer that question presented itself with the inclusion of King Oliver in the Smithsonian program. With the help of a talented young composer, Mark Tucker, I made an analysis of the music by studying the old records. By very careful listening we figured out the inner parts of the music – what Lil Hardin played, what Baby Dodds played, all the things you hear only vaguely through the surface noise of the records. From this painstaking work we were able to re-create original performances note for note. The new interpretations weren't intended to replace or improve on the originals – they are perfect in their own way – but rather to allow people to hear the music in hi-fidelity sound in all its glory. We recorded the King Oliver re-creations at a concert at the Smithsonian in 1981. Included in the program was an experiment that I had done to prove my theory about improvisation. I wrote an original piece called *Lincoln Gardens Stomp*, with every part written out note for note in the style of the Creole Jazz Band. The band played it exactly as I wrote it and the record sounds like an unissued recording of the Creole Band. There wasn't a note of improvisation, yet it contained all the elements of the group's sound, the polyphonic texture, the characteristic style of each player in Oliver's group.

How this actually came about was interesting. Pug and I were sitting out on our deck on the Cape one morning when she said, "You know that *Lincoln Gardens Stomp*? You've got the Smithsonian concert coming up where you'll be recording the King Oliver music. You told me it was written with the Creole Band in mind. So do me a favor, write it out and play it at the concert." I looked at her and said we were leaving for New York to rehearse next day – there was no way I could possibly do it in time. "Do it," said Pug. At four o'clock that afternoon I told her I'd finished it, but didn't know whether it would work. In any event it did work and we included it in the concert. You can create new music in any style. A style never becomes dated because it belongs to a certain era. One of the common misconceptions about jazz history is that a style which started in a certain era is then superseded by another style which makes the first one obsolete, and then that style is superseded by a third, and so on. What really happens is that each style starts and keeps on going – all the styles go forward in parallel with each other. The Preservation Hall Band's music is just as contemporary in the 1980s as Cecil Taylor's, because New Orleans music has never stopped evolving. So long as a musician keeps creating I don't care how old he is or what style he plays in, he is still a contemporary jazz performer. Americans tend to think that the latest thing in any field is the best. Scientific progress is a measurable thing, but to take that idea and apply it to the arts is not a valid proposition.

To illustrate my point, let's compare the following bass players – Pops Foster, Walter Page, Ray Brown and Scott LaFaro. Each of them was a style setter, a major influence on the instrument. But was each musician's playing really an improvement on the player of the generation before? Pops Foster's way of playing roots and fifths with a big booming sound was exactly right for Luis Russell's band in 1929. It was still exactly right in 1947 with my band at the Savoy, although by then Walter Page and Ray Brown had changed bass players' thinking about their instruments. Scott LaFaro played many more notes than any of the musicians before him, but to do this he had to sacrifice volume, relying totally on his amplifier to project his sound. He would have been virtually inaudible, therefore totally ineffective, playing in Pops Foster's place in 1929. So was his playing really better than Foster's? Similarly, Walter Page's walking style, with its repeated notes, was perfect for Count Basie in the 1930s, but would not have complemented Dizzy and Bird's playing the way that Ray Brown's did in the 1940s. Would Basie's rhythm section have sounded better with Ray Brown? I don't think so. The best example of the fact that good playing is never dated is Milt Hinton. Hinton's first influence was Bill Johnson of the Creole Band. In the 1980s Milt is still a major voice on jazz bass, and I'm sure he'll continue to be so right into the new century.

On all instruments styles and disciplines change. The emphasis goes from projecting melody to demonstrating harmonic sophistication. The importance of tonal qualities was paramount in players of the swing era. Then with bebop the emphasis changed to technical mastery and linear movement. The emphasis changes but there is not improvement. *West End Blues*, made in 1928, is a perfect jazz performance. There is no way to make it better; it's perfect and you can't improve on perfection. Nobody ever played the opening cadenza like Louis played it. Nobody has ever played it better – in fact I've never heard anyone play it as well, though many have tried. I don't care what Freddie Hubbard or Wynton Marsalis might play, nothing they ever do is going to be an improvement on *West End Blues*.

Because of internal rivalries at the Smithsonian, the Oliver tape sat on their shelves for an interminable length of time. I felt quite sick about it because the project meant so much to me. Finally we persuaded them to sell us the master tape and we issued it on Bodeswell. Eventually I'd like to record all the Creole Band numbers and also publish the music, so that musicians can listen to the originals, listen to my re-creations and have the music to play from. The music is being played, of course, but in most cases poorly albeit with much love and sincerity, by amateur bands all over the world. Our re-creation is far from being the definitive one. It would take months of playing together for a band to achieve the cohesion and unity of the original. It does demonstrate, however, that re-creating jazz music is just as valid as re-creating classical music. One of my projects for the future is to present Bach's Brandenburg Concertos in concert, followed by the music of the Creole Band. The polyphonic texture and rhythmic drive of both musics is so similar that we should be able to combine the two for a grand finale!

To help with the Oliver project I applied for a grant to the National Endowment for the Arts in Washington, DC. This process is not quite as simple as one might imagine but posed no problem for Pug, who had studied the technique of applying for grants in her Masters program. (She subsequently

helped me get three more grants.) During the course of the preliminary research
we learned a lot about the NEA jazz panel. First we found that it was dominated
by black musicians working in contemporary jazz idioms who had very little
interest or knowledge of earlier forms; there were very few grants being given to
white musicians or anyone working in traditional areas of jazz. Despite these
handicaps, we pressed ahead with our application because we believed we had a
project that was unique, in the sense that it was a re-creation of very important
American music, the first really great jazz group. It was quite a struggle. With
Pug's tenacity we finally succeeded in securing an appointment with the deputy
chairman of the NEA. Most of the people in the working echelon of the
organization had little interest in our proposal, but the man in charge was a very
patrician English gentleman named Hugh Sothern, who just happened to love
the music of King Oliver. I wasn't aware of this fact until we got to Washington
for the conference at which I was to present my case. It had taken a lot of
persistence on Pug's part to get us even that far. When I went into the room to
meet the committee, Mr Sothern said, "I'm very pleased to meet you. Do you
know where I was last night? I was at the Brooklyn Academy of Music watching
the Twyla Tharp Dancers dancing to the music of Jelly Roll Morton. Do you
know who was leading the band?"

I said, "Yessir, I was." He then told me that he thought the show was
marvelous. It was very kind of him to put us at ease in this way.

The presentation of my project impressed the committee and we got our
grant. We happened to be successful and lucky, in contrast to many other
deserving people who have been turned down for projects involving earlier jazz.
A spokesman for the Jazz Centre Society in England, a body which organizes
government-funded jazz concerts, turned down our request for help for the
following reason: "You people in traditional jazz have an audience out there who
love your music. We've got to fund those people who play music no one wants
to hear." Incredible reasoning, but very common to arts councils all over the
world.

The Smithsonian Repertory Ensemble mirrored my ideas about the
preservation of jazz and its history. My idea of teaching is to present jazz as a
great American tradition, with important music and legendary heroes from
Buddy Bolden on. The study of classical music is founded on the analysis of the
old masters, starting with the Gregorian chants of the Middle Ages, moving up
through Monteverdi, Bach, Mozart, Beethoven, Wagner, Brahms, and into the
20th century with Debussy, Ravel, Stravinsky and Schoenberg. The jazz studies
programs don't apply that method. To them jazz is all about today and tomorrow.
Aside from the pioneering work at Berklee and North Texas State, most jazz
studies programs started in the 1960s with the growth of the militant black
movement in the States. Civil rights leaders demanded that recognition be given
black people for the unfair way in which they had been treated over the past
300 years. They demanded equal opportunity for black people to advance
themselves scholastically. In response the major universities all over the States
set up black studies programs. It seemed logical to incorporate jazz departments

within the black studies programs and staff them with prominent black jazz musicians. Initially the black studies programs had great success, but it was soon discovered that the black students' interests in their cultural roots were quite superficial. Basically, what black students wanted were the tools and skills to make it in the white man's world, to be a part of that upwardly mobile American middle class. They really wanted to forget the past and be part of the American Dream – a wife and kids, two homes, two cars and a pocketful of credit cards. As far as jazz studies was concerned the big drawback was that many of the programs gave a false picture of jazz, presenting it as the black man's music, totally ignoring the white musician's involvement right from the beginning. Jazz history was rewritten to ignore or minimize the contributions of the Original Dixieland Jazz Band, Bix Beiderbecke, Jack Teagarden, Eddie Condon, Benny Goodman and postwar figures such as Stan Getz, Lee Konitz and Dave Brubeck. Even the contributions of the great black pioneers, Morton, Oliver, Bechet and Bessie Smith, were studied only in a superficial way. As a result, to today's black student of jazz, Miles Davis and Wynton Marsalis are much more important figures than Louis Armstrong, whom he or she may remember vaguely from their childhood as some black man with a handkerchief and a lot of teeth singing *Hello Dolly*. Would a student of classical music have the same attitude towards Bach or Beethoven? Of course not. They would have studied their music in depth and would have a real understanding of their greatness. While the educators, like of a lot of black people in recent years, were certainly interested in their roots, to them those roots were African, almost mythological.

Oberlin was the first school I was connected with. Situated in a small town in Ohio, it is very proud of its tradition of liberal education, of being one of the first colleges to admit and encourage black students, long before they were able to attend other than a few specifically black schools. It is also famous for its music school. I was asked to be artist-in-residence there in 1982. I found that the jazz department created there in the 1960s during the black studies craze was looked on as a poor relation by the rest of the music department. The building they were given to rehearse in was practically off-campus, and most of the instructors were part-time professional musicians who drove down from nearby Cleveland once a week. As a result of this second-class treatment the head of the jazz department, a black man, felt like a pariah in his own community. His hostility towards his classical colleagues and his general disillusionment with his job affected his teaching, and I found interest and morale among his students very low. When I asked him why no jazz history course was offered, he replied, "I don't have time for that, and, besides, they don't pay me enough money." This dismal situation may be rectified shortly, however. The new president of Oberlin, Fred Starr, is a jazz clarinetist with an interest in traditional jazz. He is the author of a fascinating book that traces the history of jazz in the Soviet Union. He is also the organizer of the Louisiana Repertory Orchestra, which plays a lot of rags and early jazz, and I'm sure that under his guiding hand jazz at Oberlin will take on a new lease.

Rutgers is another school where I've taught. The jazz studies department came into existence at about the same time and in the same way as at Oberlin, but again the whole direction of the jazz courses seemed to be towards contemporary jazz, with little recognition or appreciation of what had gone before. I did two artist-in-residence courses, separated by an interval of several years. The second time there I spent a full week working with the students on Ellington. At the end of the week the student band played a concert of Duke's music dating from 1926 to 1956. It was a great experience for them, exploring areas of jazz they had little knowledge of and which they found fascinating. I don't suppose there could be any better example to support my case for the preservation of jazz. What would life really be like if the music of Ellington, more than anyone else, was allowed to fade away, never to be heard again in live form? Yet this is the direction in which so many of the jazz studies programs are moving. Most of the instructors are from the bebop era and are not interested in earlier jazz. The opportunity to study jazz history at Rutgers is greatly enhanced by the presence of the Rutgers Institute of Jazz Studies, an archive of records, tapes and memorabilia under the care of critic and author Dan Morgenstern. However, because of the teachers' attitude, little use of the facility is made by the students. Morgenstern started the Hall of Fame at Rutgers, commemorating all the great names of jazz. He asked me to organize the music to be played at the first induction, and for each musician the band played an appropriate selection. The band consisted of myself and the faculty members of the jazz department. None of them knew the music of Louis Armstrong and Bix Beiderbecke, which I had to teach them for the occasion. They knew virtually nothing about jazz before Charlie Parker; they were strictly musicians from the post-Parker era and that was what they taught their students.

A teaching appointment that I've really enjoyed has been at Wilkes College in Wilkes-Barre, Pennsylvania. My first stay there was as artist-in-residence, and I became Director of Jazz Studies in 1982. I was introduced to the college by Andy Sordoni, whom I met when we opened at Bechet's with the Bechet Legacy. Andrew has been a lover of Sidney's music all his life and was interested in me because of my connections with the maestro. He is a successful business man, a patron of the arts, and Wilkes-Barre's leading citizen. I started out at first by simply giving record lectures on specific aspects of jazz, such as comparative studies between Bessie Smith and Billie Holiday, or Coleman Hawkins and Lester Young. These lectures were aimed at a fairly wide spread of people, the high-school students, the music majors, area educators and the general public. Usually they would be concluded by recollections of my own musical career and my connections with many of the great names of jazz who have passed on. Subsequently I widened the scope of the lectures by bringing in guest speakers who could give the students the benefit of their experience in the music business and some idea of the lifestyle of a professional musician. Fred Miller, who engineered so many of our record dates, talked about the techniques of recording, while John Glasel, my former colleague in the Wildcats and now President of Local 802, discussed career opportunities available to students after graduation.

An interesting talk also came from Doc Cheatham, who traced his phenomenal career from his early days in Tennessee, through his years in Chicago playing with Ma Rainey and his big-band days, to his present career as a globe-trotting jazz soloist. When, at the end of his lecture, Doc, who is in his 80s, took out his trumpet and popped out a high C, clear as a bell, the students, particularly the trumpet players, were flabbergasted. Doc told about the time when he was living in Chicago in 1927 and met his idol, Louis Armstrong, at the union. A few days later he got a call from Louis asking Doc to sub for him with Erskine Tate at the Vendome Theater while Armstrong made a record date at Okeh. "You seen me at the Vendome, Pops. Jus' get up there and do what I do, 'n' you'll kill them cats." Doc, in seventh heaven at being called by his hero after a few days acquaintance, trooped along to the theater, introduced himself to Tate and took his place in the pit. After playing the opening overture and accompanying several vaudeville acts, Doc climbed on the darkened stage, trumpet in hand, while the orchestra struck up the introduction to *Heebie Jeebies*. As the spotlight brought him into view, Doc remembers this long groan, a sigh of disappointment, from the packed house, who were expecting the great Louis Armstrong and instead saw this spindly kid standing there. Cheatham went ahead anyway, charming the audience with his playing and singing. He's been doing it ever since.

Another popular visitor was Milt Hinton, who spoke about the history of the string bass in jazz and provided an inexhaustible fund of stories about his career. He told of being with the Cab Calloway band for ten years and how it came to break up because there were no places left for them to play. He was standing one afternoon on a corner in Times Square, with no work, no prospects, a young baby and another on the way, when his old friend from the Calloway band, Danny Barker, came by. Danny could see that Milt was down in the mouth, so he told Milt to meet him at the same spot at five o'clock with his bass. Milt went home, got his bass and came back, and together he and Danny took the subway out to Jersey City to a really low-life place, a sailor's hang-out with cheap booze, a lot of smoke and hookers at the bar. Danny got out his guitar and Milt his bass, and they set up in a corner and started to play. Pretty soon the sailors were dancing over with their chicks, dropping money into Danny's open guitar case. By the end of the night they had made a few bucks, enough for a hot meal and car fare home. Within a few years of that experience Milt was one of the busiest musicians in New York with all the dates he could handle.

An interesting aspect of Milt's lecture was the exhibition of his photographs covering 40 years of his life in music adorning the walls of the lecture hall. This unique departure led to two more presentations at the college in conjunction with the Sordoni Art Gallery. These were celebrations of music and art, the first presenting the music and paintings of Bob Haggart, while the second presented the music and paintings of Pee Wee Russell and George Wettling. The paintings were hung in the gallery while the concerts were presented at the Music School. For Haggart's concert I assembled a group of my young repertory musicians from New York. We played many of Bob's originals and things he'd arranged for the WGJB. The concert included a section called "The Musician Meets the

Painter," in which Bob set up one of his paintings on an easel in front of him and composed an extemporaneous piece on his bass. It was really a bit of hokum, but it was fun and the audience loved it. For the Russell–Wettling affair I recommended Kenny Davern, a great admirer and friend of Pee Wee, to put together the band. Their different styles of painting were interesting to observe. Wettling was a student of Stuart Davis the contemporary American painter, and his technique was quite sophisticated. Russell, on the other hand, was a true primitive who took up painting only after his wife brought a paint-kit home and ordered him to do something besides watching television. Pee Wee's squiggly lines and bright colors are as fiercely individualistic as his clarinet playing. His paintings add a new dimension to this important jazz artist.

The jazz program at Wilkes continues to flourish and grow, mostly due to the dedication and enthusiasm of Andrew Sordoni. In the 1986–7 season we presented Sammy Price, Dick Hyman and Slam Stewart in concert, plus a special program hosted by Pug Horton entitled "Ladies of Jazz." In the fall of 1987 we are presenting the music and art of Mel Powell. The concert will feature Powell's chamber works in the first half and the second half will present Mel Powell, the jazz soloist, plus a re-creation of the Benny Goodman Trio. The Sordoni Art Gallery will be showing Mel's paintings, a little-known aspect of this great artist's talent.

Another important part of my work at Wilkes is the jazz archives which I started by contributing my entire music library, gathered over the past forty years. During the past five years I have built up an extensive collection of transcriptions from the original recordings of King Oliver, Jelly Roll Morton, Sidney Bechet, Duke Ellington, Count Basie, John Kirby, Benny Goodman, Artie Shaw and Lu Watters, to name a few. The archives also houses copies of the arrangements and originals I have written for various groups, including the WGJB, Soprano Summit, the Bechet Legacy and Swingin' for the King. In conjunction with the jazz archives at Rutgers and Tulane University, New Orleans, we are working out ways and means of making these scores available to music students and jazz historians for study and performance.

Jazz musicians are always complaining about the lack of acceptance by the cultural establishment, but until we in jazz, both black and white, study our traditions closely, teach our students the whole history, the way it really happened, and celebrate the contributions of our great creators with well planned concerts, we will not really be taken seriously. Jazz will forever be known as "light" as opposed to "serious" music. The people, businesses and government who support and subsidize symphony orchestras, chamber music, opera and ballet own the ball park. If we in jazz want to play on their field it would behoove us to study their ground rules!

FOURTEEN

The Cotton Club

The Cotton Club was a club in New York that opened in the mid-1920s. It was Harlem's most famous night spot until 1936, when it moved downtown to Broadway. It was never as successful there as it had been in Harlem – part of the excitement was going uptown to hear the music. The Cotton Club was the great center, the sounding board, the place to get exposure for the black artists of that period. It was the making of Duke Ellington, who went there from the Kentucky Club in 1927 when King Oliver turned down the job because the money wasn't good enough. Duke was there for five years, with a radio remote every night. When he went out to Hollywood in 1930 to make his first movie, *Check and Double Check*, the management brought in a young singer and dancer by the name of Cab Calloway. It was also the making of Cab. Up and coming songwriters of the day wrote the shows for weekly salaries of $75. The first team was Dorothy Fields and Jimmy McHugh and after them came Harold Arlen and Ted Koehler, and later, Rube Bloom. Ethel Waters introduced *Stormy Weather* at the Cotton Club; Lena Horne started her career there at the age of 16 as a chorus girl. Bill Robinson danced there, as did the Nicholas Brothers, who started there as kids. It was the place for black talent to be seen and heard, but there was an irony about it. The place was run by white gangsters, and, although the club featured all-black entertainment, it was impossible in the earlier years for a customer of darker color to get through the front door. The chorus girls all had to be light-skinned, or "paper-bag brown," as it was called. The first girl to break this color line was Lucille Wilson, who later became Mrs Louis Armstrong. She was such a sensational dancer that Harold Arlen persuaded the management to bend its rules and hire the dark-skinned entertainer.

In 1982 I heard rumors that a picture was being planned about the Cotton Club. I had read Jim Haskin's book *The Cotton Club*, which had given producer Bob Evans the idea for the film. My eventual involvement came about in a very circuitous way. It started out with a phone call from a man I had known for many years, Jerry Wexler. Wexler and the Ertegun brothers, Ahmet and Nesuhi, founded Atlantic Records in the 1940s. It started out as a small jazz label, got into black soul music after the war and prospered through the 1960s and 1970s, finally joining forces with Warner Brothers Communications to become one of the giants of the recording industry. Jerry, like the Ertegun brothers, became a big wheel but never lost his basic grass-roots enthusiasm for jazz. He is still a jazz buff who likes nothing better than to sit around and talk about Red Allen. In the formative stages of the movie he was asked by Evans to be musical adviser. Jerry felt that I was the ideal musician to do the Ellington re-creations. He told me that most of the people in the movie business don't know beans about jazz and hadn't heard of me. He suggested that I put together a tape of stuff I had done in the Ellington vein with examples of my alto playing à la Johnny Hodges. He played it for Greg Hines and Evans, who were impressed. At the time, we were working at Condon's Monday nights with the Bechet Legacy. Jerry started bringing in various people connected with the movie to hear the band.

The producers sent me a copy of the script by Mario Puzo, author of *The Godfather*. It seemed kind of phony, but when did Hollywood ever treat jazz realistically? One night Jerry came in with an executive from Paramount. As we sat around talking, the conversation turned to a compelling book that Jerry and the other guy were currently reading, *Ironweed* by Bill Kennedy. Pug joined in, saying that Bill was one of her dearest friends from Albany – someone she'd known for 20 years. Jerry's ears pricked up and he asked if Pug could arrange for Bill to meet him sometime with a view to discussing a movie option on another of Kennedy's books, *Billy Phelan's Last Chance*. After that I didn't see Wexler for a few weeks. One day I read in the paper that Francis Ford Coppola had been hired to direct *The Cotton Club* and had fired Jerry Wexler, bringing in Ralph Burns to write the score. Well, I figured, that's it for me, so I forgot about it and concentrated on getting gigs for the Bechet Legacy. Later I heard that Coppola had said, "What's this about Bob Wilber? He's a dixieland clarinet player. I want Ralph Burns – he knows jazz and knows movie scoring."

A few months later the Legacy had a concert at the Village Gate, part of the annual Greenwich Village Jazz Festival. Pug got a call from Bill's wife, Dana, saying they were coming to town with their son Brendan, and could we get together. Pug said we were playing at the Gate that night – we'd leave three tickets at the box office and meet for supper after the concert. Dana and Brendan showed up, saying that Bill was busy. After the concert, which was very poorly attended, we went to a Chinese restaurant across the street, where Bill joined us. He'd just come from the Sherry-Netherland Hotel, where he'd been closeted for the last 18 hours with Francis Coppola, working on a new script for *The Cotton Club*. I was flabbergasted. Already feeling down because of the meager turnout for that night's concert, this latest news was a bitter blow. I'd lost the opportunity to break out of the jazz world into a world of high exposure and big money. Here was Pug's old friend, who had struggled for years to gain recognition, now the writer of the year, with offers coming in from every direction. Bill, sensing my disappointment, took Pug aside and said, "Don't worry, Pugalla. Bob is so talented he's going to get the recognition he deserves. Someone's going to notice."

We took a three-week engagement at Jaylin's Club in Berne, Switzerland, with the Legacy. On our second night there we got a phone call from New York. It was Bill Kennedy, who had been trying frantically to track me down. He told me they were having problems with the movie. Ralph Burns had written and recorded a complete score for it. When Coppola, who had immersed himself in the sounds of 1928 Ellington, heard the tapes, he exclaimed, "That's not what I want at all – it sounds like a Pontiac industrial." In truth, Burns, a brilliant arranger and composer, who wrote the beautiful *Summer Sequence* I'd heard premièred at Carnegie Hall by Woody Herman in 1946, had written a highly professional score and recorded it using the top New York studio musicians. As well written and played as it was, it didn't have that distinctive sound of early Duke. If it did at times sound like Ellington it was like the 1940s band, a very different sound from the Cotton Club band. Bill described the scene out at Astoria Studios, the old silent films studio where Charlie Chaplin, Doug Fairbanks and Mary Pickford got started. They were in the midst of filming the big production numbers, with singers, dancers and hundreds of extras playing the part of the audience at the Cotton Club, but no musical director. The film was way over budget, and the backers, tough business men with interests in Las Vegas, gambling and Arab oil, were getting itchy. When Coppola discussed the problem with Kennedy, Bill said to him, "Francis, you had Bob Wilber – he really knows the music. If you want, I'll try to contact him." Bill said to me, "Bob, this is a golden opportunity. You should drop everything and come back to New York." My immediate reaction was that I would love to do so, but we had contracts for five weeks of work in Europe that we had to honor. Bill's proposition just didn't seem feasible, so I said, "Thanks for thinking about me anyway, Bill," and the conversation ended.

I hung up and told Pug what it was about. Pug immediately called Bill back, who said, "I can't believe it! I spend the whole day tracking down your husband, finally locate him in Switzerland, and when I offer him the opportunity of a lifetime he turns me down because of five weeks' work in some lousy nightclub!"

I discussed the matter with Pug on the way to dinner. At the restaurant we talked with the guys in the band about our problem. I asked Jimmy Woode, our bass player and senior member of the band, for his opinion. Jimmy's immediate reaction was that, if he were in my place, he'd do both the film and the band's gigs! We thought about Jimmy's reply, and Pug said, "He's right. You can do both." When we got back to the hotel I put a call through to Bill and asked him if he could get the producer to phone me. Shortly afterwards one of the co-producers, Fred Roos, called me back. I said I understood they had problems. I didn't know what I could do for them, but it they'd fly me over on my day off I'd sit down with him and try and figure something out. "Fine," said Fred. "I'll book a flight on the Concorde for Sunday. Meet me at my apartment at nine Monday morning."

That Sunday afternoon I took the train to Geneva, flew to London and boarded the plane for the three-and-a-half-hour trip to New York. When I arrived at Fred's apartment the next morning I found him pacing the floor. The problem had become serious. He thought from all he'd heard about me that I was probably the right guy for the job, but they needed somebody immediately on the set that day. He asked, "How can you possibly do it with your European commitments?" I thought quickly and replied, "If I can find an assistant he can start today, I'll keep close contact via phone from Berne, and fly over each week for two days to be on the set." I didn't really know whether my boss at Jaylin's, Hans Zurbrugg, would let Pug lead the band for a night so that I'd have that extra day in New York, but knowing Hans to be the reasonable chap he is, I was prepared to take that chance. When he asked me who I could get I thought of Sy Johnson. I'd met Sy when I was rehearsing for the Ellington concert at Carnegie Hall in 1975. He'd done some excellent transcriptions of early Ellington and seemed to know the music of that period. It was a long shot. I hadn't heard of Johnson for years – he might have moved to the West Coast, might have been dead for all I knew. I found his number through the musicians' union and called him. His wife answered; he was in the shower and would call back. Roos continued pacing – the day's shooting had already started out at Astoria. Five minutes later Sy called back. He wasn't doing anything particular at the present time. I explained to Fred, who said, "Have him meet us out at Astoria in half an hour." We grabbed a taxi, drove out to Queens, met Johnson at the door and went up to co-producer Barrie Osborne's office. In 30 minutes we'd concluded a deal. We met music editor Norman Hollyn, who took us on a tour of the set. It was a madhouse. The studio covered a whole city block and was equipped with the largest indoor sound stage in the world. Branching out in all directions from the sound stage, like the tentacles of an octopus, was a myriad of corridors, which would suddenly ascend or descend to another level with seemingly no rhyme or reason. Rushing through the corridors were hundreds of men and women, many in tuxedos and evening gowns, on their way to or from sound stage, dressing rooms, makeup and costume department, dance studios and offices. Still suffering jet lag from my flight over, I was totally bewildered by it all. My office, which contained a piano, phonograph and tape decks, was right off the entrance; at least I wouldn't get lost when I came to work.

That evening Johnson and I shared a taxi back to Manhattan, bade each other good luck and good-bye, and next morning at nine I was on the Concorde, on my way back to Berne. I arrived in London and took the plane to Geneva, where I boarded the train to Berne. Arriving at 10.30 in the evening I rushed across the street to the hotel where Pug was waiting in the lobby, clarinet in hand. She took my coat off and I rushed down the stairs into Jaylin's and onto the stand to join the band. Every week this was my regular journey – Berne, Geneva, London, New York, work a day, and then back to Berne on Tuesday night. Every morning at 2.00 a.m. after the gig I'd talk to Sy Johnson in New York to find out what had happened on the set that day. There were also the daily calls to my lawyer in New York, who was trying to work out a contract with the film company's lawyers in Hollywood. Every week when I went back to New York I'd find all kinds of problems awaiting me; by the end of our European tour I was a basket case. We finished our tour at the Cork Festival in Ireland and on November 2nd we flew home to New York, where I plunged into full-time work on the picture.

The backers were exerting tremendous pressure on Coppola to finish shooting by Christmas. A couple of them had ensconced themselves on the set, either prowling about the studio or closeted away with the producers, who were trying desperately to save a penny here and there. One day, while passing the producers' office, I saw one of these gentlemen, still sporting his Las Vegas tan after weeks in New York, standing on a chair behind Barrie Osborne's desk and circling December 15th on the calendar with a large black marker. "Dat's it," he screamed. "Dat's when we finish shootin'! You unnerstan', Barrie?" The gentleman was not kidding. Production costs had been soaring daily. Estimates of the final cost of the film had risen from the 20 million dollar expenditure originally envisaged to over 50 million, making *The Cotton Club* potentially the most expensive picture ever made.

Coppola is a genius, but he drives everyone nuts because he directs a movie like a jazz soloist, improvising all the way. When he comes onto the set, he doesn't know exactly what he's going to do – he prefers to rely on the inspiration of the moment. He shoots every scene from every possible angle in order to have the maximum number of choices when editing. His most characteristic expression on the set is, "Don't worry. We'll fix it in the mix." If necessary he'll spend a whole day on a three-minute sequence to get it right. As a result, shooting schedules go out the window. The average day on the set found hundreds of extras sitting round on call waiting to discover what Coppola had in mind for that day. I got the impression that Coppola actually enjoyed working in an atmosphere of chaos and tension. I think he feels he'll get more exciting performances out of the actors if they are constantly on edge, never knowing what each day will bring. This tension inevitably led to many shouting matches involving Coppola, the actors, choreographers (there were five of them!), producers and backers. They usually ended with Coppola storming off the set, vowing to quit. He'd retire to his office, lock himself in and practice his tuba for the rest of the day, while thousands of dollars were going down the drain each hour. On another occasion, with the day's shooting called off because of a financial crisis, I wandered onto the empty set to find Coppola, sleeves rolled up, with a bucket of suds and a mop, happily washing down the aluminium body of his beloved "Silver Bullet," a large trailer outfitted with every electronic gadget imaginable. Coppola was so enthused when he first acquired his new "toy" that he directed a whole picture without ever leaving the trailer, watching the proceedings on numerous television monitors and barking out his orders over a microphone.

We actually finished shooting on 23rd December 1984. To give the picture a rip-roaring finale with music and dancing but also to tie up the loose ends of the main plot and various sub-plots, Coppola devised a phantasmagorical scene using Grand Central Station. The Cotton Club dancers become railroad porters, Owny Madden is escorted off to Sing Sing Prison, Dutch Schultz's coffin is placed on a train to go to the cemetery, Gregory Hines and Lonette McKee leave on their honeymoon, and, in the final shot, Richard Gere and Diane Lane embrace on the rear platform of the Twentieth Century Limited as they disappear in the distance, heading for Hollywood, fame and fortune. The whole Cotton Club company assembled at 6.00 p.m. on Friday evening, December 16th, at the station. The lower level at Grand Central had been roped off. In the center on the huge marble-floored hall were chairs and long tables, where uniformed caterers were busily serving up coffee, tea, sandwiches, beer, soft drinks, fruit, cakes and pies. It was going to be a long night. Hundreds of people were milling about – actors, extras, sound crew, the producers and the backers, who'd brought along their long-legged bleach-blond girl friends in spike heels, skin-tight slacks and silver fox furs. The only people from the music department were myself, Sy Johnson and music editor, Norman Hollyn, since all the dancing was to be done to pre-recorded music. In the midst of this chaos Coppola was running about, his camera crew in hot pursuit, devising ways to utilize the whole cast, to gather up the strands of the long, confusing story, hoping to send his audiences out of the theaters not totally bewildered by what they had just witnessed.

The shooting continued through the night, with actors and extras slouched in their chairs or stretched out on the long tables taking cat-naps until they were called. The seemingly indefatigable director continued to run about, discovering new locations for shots and improvising wildly off the top of his head as the cameras reeled off roll after roll of film. The last scene with Gere and Lane embracing on the rear platform of the train took over an hour to shoot. The two actors, numb with fatigue and asleep on their feet, kept missing their cues as Coppola, pleading with them one moment and angrily remonstrating with them the next, attempted to eke out one more "last shot." On Saturday afternoon at 1 p.m., 29 hours after we'd started, Coppola yelled "Cut! OK, that's it – we got a picture." I crawled wearily home to bed, having lived through the most exhausting, exasperating, nerve-racking, but exciting and stimulating two months of my career. Little did I realize the most difficult part was yet to come.

Work on the picture for the post-production phase was scheduled to resume again in April. That meant putting all the footage into place, synchronizing sound and action, and actually recording the score. Whenever music had been needed in the shooting stage, we used a small cut-down band playing a skeletal version of the big-band arrangement. In movie language these were known as "temp tracks" (temp for temporary). This was done in order to save money – $100,000 had already gone down the drain on Ralph Burns's score and the producers were becoming very cost-conscious. My biggest problem was that most of the song and dance footage had been filmed to Ralph's score. The company had neither the time or the money to reshoot the sequences using my score. I had to separate Ralph's music from the footage and substitute music that would be authentic to the period but which would fit the visual action already shot. This was a very difficult thing to do. With *Creole Love Call*, for instance, the singer you see in the film had long gone. She'd done her job, done it well, and moved on, but there she was on the screen with Burns's arrangement behind her. Working with her vocal track, I had to insert another score underneath that would fit with what she'd sung. Instances like this were numerous. One of the most difficult things to figure out was the opening sequence at the Cotton Club when all the dancers come out onto the floor. The musical background in Burns's score was *Heatwave*, a flag-waver piece recorded in 1934 by Jimmie Lunceford's band. Coppola objected because *Heatwave* was from a later period and from the wrong band. He absolutely insisted the music be authentic for the period, so I had to search for something of Ellington from that period that would fit the action. *Heatwave* was a very fast number, faster than anything Ellington played in 1929. What was considered very fast in the 1920s was perhaps only medium fast by the standards of the 1930s. The pieces that I considered would all have needed speeding up. The problem with that was most of the Ellington flag-wavers of the period had very complex solos by Bigard, Hodges and the others. The soloists seemed to play as many notes as possible, and to speed up the music still faster to synchronize with the dancers would have sounded ridiculous, like cartoon music. One day I chanced on a piece of music that worked. It was *Cotton Club Stomp* – not the *Cotton Club Stomp* from 1928 but a later one by Rube Bloom. It was confusing having two pieces with the same name. The publisher, Belwin-Mills, had both compositions filed together, not realizing they were two separate pieces. It was a nice, simple little riff tune with no complicated solos. Halleluja! I could speed it up and it still sounded authentic. I breathed a big sigh of relief and went on to the next problem.

Synchronizing the soundtrack with the film caused all sorts of headaches. If the film showed a trombone player taking his trombone away from his mouth, I had to ensure that the trombone on the soundtrack also stopped. Even when a movement such as this is in the background, it will be spotted and the illusion of reality destroyed. Because there was no corresponding trombone solo in the piece I'd transcribed from Duke's original record, I had to insert a solo to match what the viewer saw on the screen. One of the most difficult and frustrating scenes to co-ordinate was the sequence at the Hoofers Club with the tap-dancers' jam session. The scene was actually recorded with Henry Le Tang, the tap-dance choreographer, playing piano. It was a half-ass kind of stride piano and just right for the sequence. However, the song he chose to play was off the top of his head and wasn't from the Belwin-Mills catalogue. The producers had bought the rights to the whole catalogue because it contained most of the Ellington and a lot of the Calloway music of the period, plus a lot of popular songs. Faced with footage already shot, I was told to take out the piece Henry played (*You're driving me crazy*) and substitute a Belwin-Mills tune. I hired my old pal Dick Wellstood to play piano. Talk about driving me crazy, that little assignment drove us all crazy. In the film Lonette McKee starts to clap to the music as she watches the dancers. We found that when Dick played the piece I'd substituted, Lonette appeared to be clapping on the first and third beats, making it look like a Western hoe-down rather than a swinging jam. Somewhere Dick had subtly to skip a beat so that the clapping was again on the off-beats. We later had to synchronize the breaks to correspond with the Hines brothers' cutting contest. That little Hoofers Club sequence, which lasted about three minutes on screen, took three hours to record and another three hours to synchronize in the editing room.

Coppola was fascinated by Ellington's train piece from 1932, *Daybreak Express*. In fact the whole idea for the Grand Central Station finale stemmed from Francis's desire to include *Daybreak Express* in the film. The record of the piece is about three minutes long, but the Grand Central scene required at least ten minutes of music. I kept on asking myself how on earth I was going to extend *Daybreak Express* and still make sense musically, because you couldn't just keep repeating it. When I realized that the melody of the number was based on *Tiger Rag*, a solution presented itself. Many of Duke's fast numbers of the early period used *Tiger Rag* as a basis – I suspect that it was because his soloists were comfortable with the chord sequence. Barney Bigard used to eat up *Tiger Rag* – he found so many different things to do with it. I examined all the different pieces from that period based on *Tiger Rag*, and I ended up with Duke's two-part arrangement of *Tiger Rag* itself, *Slippery Horn*, *High Life* and also *Wall Street Wail*, which was not quite *Tiger Rag* but similar. Then I put them all together in a big montage. The next thing to do was to look at the footage and, by cutting and clipping, put the new arrangement together to fit it. It wasn't, however, just background music for the finale, because Coppola wanted it closely synchronized with what was happening on the screen. So it became a huge scissors-and-paste operation, with six bars from here and two bars from there, until finally I emerged with this long piece of music that had started out with *Daybreak Express*. I'd really wanted to start it with Duke's opening, which depicts the train pulling out of the station, but it wouldn't fit with the screen action. The opening section, which is like a verse or a build-up to the chorus, starts in tempo and then the chorus beings with the amazing three saxophone passage. I repeat this, and then interpolate sections of *Tiger Rag*, *High Life*, *Slippery Horn* and *Wall Street Wail*, reverting to the original with Lew Soloff doing the Cootie Williams trumpet part on top, and finally ending with the train pulling into the station (although this never seemed right to me because on the screen the train is pulling *out* of the station). There had been so many things going on in the film, with plots, counterplots, gangsters, love affairs, the sociological thing of black versus white, the singing and the dancing – it could leave the audience thoroughly confused. I have a feeling that the music department was asked to produce some really exciting music at the end of the picture to send the audiences out of the theaters in a happy frame of mind.

The film was originally envisaged as a very long one, running to over three hours – there was certainly enough footage to justify the unusual length. When the first version was completed Coppola followed his usual practice of taking his film around the country for trial screenings to test out public reaction. He invited different sections of the public to these screenings and stood at the back of the theater closely watching the response. One of the first showings of the long version was out in California with a lot of young people in the audience. Coppola sensed that they were becoming restless and immediately decided to cut the film. Eventually he emerged with a version that ran about two hours and ten minutes, but in doing so he cut out a lot of good stuff and made the editing very choppy. There was, for instance, a confusing scene where Gregory Hines goes into a church hall to look for Lonette McKee, who's been decidedly cool to his advances. The next thing you see them coming out together, hand in hand and very much in love. What you don't see is what took place inside the church hall.

In the scene that was cut you would have seen a dancing class in progress. As Greg enters he keeps telling himself how much he loves the girl and wondering how he can impress her. Having spotted Lonette, he goes over to the pianist and asks her to play *Tall, Tan and Terrific* for him. He begins to dance and sing so amusingly and charmingly that Lonette's heart is melted. It was a marvelous scene with Greg at his brilliant best, but it ended up on the cutting room floor.

There was also a musical sequence representing a re-creation of the popular Peters Sisters that disappeared. They were three sisters, all very large ladies, who originally started out at the Cotton Club and subsequently gained a great deal of fame in Europe during the 1930s and 1940s. Coppola got three girl singers, led by Patti Bown, who did a wonderful version of *Truckin'* which never made the picture. Another scene of the customers dancing at the Cotton Club to *Rockin' in Rhythm* was also cut out. The original version of the film, instead of starting at the Cotton Club with *The Mooche*, began at night on a rainy, windswept street in Harlem to the ominous strains of *Black and Tan Fantasy*. I thought it was an exciting opening, but Francis felt it was too solemn a way to start the film.

Coppola came to our first recording session and listened very carefully to everything. I told the musicians that our task was to reproduce the sound of the Ellington orchestra in the 1920s, the sound that we would actually have heard if we had been there in the Cotton Club in 1928. I didn't want to improve on it or to make it sound better. If the Ellington band played out of tune, we'd play out of tune. "Yeah, yeah," said Coppola, "that's what I want. I want all the roughness, even the mistakes, but I want it in hi-fi state of the art sound." On each tune I first of all played the original recording several times over, pointing out to the guys the different things that were going on, and then we started rehearsing. As his excitement grew, Francis kept saying, "It's almost there. It's getting close. Let's try it again."

When my contract was originally drawn up I was a virtual unknown in the movie industry who, in effect, was being hired on trial. The producers wanted the option either to renew my contract so that I could work on the post-production phase if they were satisfied, or to find someone else if they weren't. Although Coppola liked my work, he wasn't sure I was capable of handling the underscoring for the dramatic scenes. I knew I was capable of doing it and even submitted a theme for the picture, entitled "This was Harlem," for Coppola's approval. Some of the backers wanted a name that would mean something in the film industry, and they had never heard of Bob Wilber. So the decision was made to bring in John Barry to underscore. John had over 70 films to his credit and had worked with Coppola before. In effect I was no longer musical director. I had the option of either bowing out or working with John and sharing credit with him, knowing full well that the bulk of the music in the film would be mine. What John had to do was to provide background music for emotional dramatic scenes that would provide a bridge between my re-creations of period music. I told myself, "Look, you can be silly about this and get all disgruntled, letting your ego take over, or you can use it as a learning experience 'cause you've never done a picture before. You'll be working with a guy who's got

186 / MUSIC WAS NOT ENOUGH

70 films under his belt. You can learn a lot from him. So I buckled down to the job, got along well with John, and learned a lot from him, too.

There has always been a great mystique about writing movie scores, probably started by the prewar Hollywood composers, who wanted the field to themselves. Without any previous training or experience, here was I writing the music for a major film in which music was a prime ingredient. I soon found that there were certain techniques one has to learn and the rest is common sense. Both Norman Hollyn and John Barry were tremendously helpful to me in learning the procedure. I can honestly say I'll be able to accept another movie assignment with no qualms whatsoever. One technique is the use of click tracks to integrate music and sound with visual images. The click track is a tempo track, like a metronome click, which you follow with earphones when you record the music. Sometimes it can be very tricky, particularly when the integration has to be meticulous and subtle changes in tempo are necessary to stay in synch with the visual. If you're playing something with a jazz beat and you have to keep speeding up and slowing down, but in a way that's not noticeable, it can be quite a challenge. When we did the slowing down of the train at the end of *Daybreak Express*, it had to be accomplished within a specific time frame. We kept doing it over and over again, because we'd either finish too soon or over-run. Gradually we got closer, until finally we got it right. There I was, standing on the podium with earphones on giving me the variable speed click track. Before me was the score of *Daybreak Express* which I had to follow, turning pages with one hand while I conducted the orchestra with the other. I was also keeping my eyes on two other things – the TV monitor showing the visual action and a large clockface with a moving second hand. The music had to take a specific number of seconds and finish exactly when the scene ended. To start the music at precisely the right moment a vertical guideline is superimposed on the screen image. It moves slowly across the screen from right to left. You start the music the second the line reaches the left edge of the screen. In the same way you have a moving line telling you when to stop at the end of the scene. I could have used several sets of eyes as I watched the clock, the screen, the score and the orchestra – and I also had to listen to the click track and the music. After doing this for six hours, running back and forth into the control booth to listen to playbacks, I'd get my clarinet and alto out. Sitting in the middle of the now empty studio with earphones on, I'd overdub the Bigard and Hodges solos, doing them over and over again until they were exactly right. It used to be midnight or one in the morning before I'd leave the recording studio, – but the next morning at nine I'd be back in the control booth, a cup of black coffee in hand, discussing the day's recording schedule with Norman and John while observing my musicians warming up through the glass window.

I was given full authority regarding the choice of players, and, although I worked with the contractor, I had the ultimate choice. The contractor was Emile Charlap, a leading figure on the New York music scene who contracts for movies, theaters, television and jingles. Emile has his own stable of musicians whom he keeps busy, and naturally he wanted me to use them as much as possible on the movie. I pointed out to him that, although they were all good musicians, we'd simply end up with the same band and the same sound that Coppola had rejected. Many of the players I wanted to use weren't from Emile's stable but were specialists who had studied the old records. After the film was released I received a number of poison pen letters criticizing me for not using allblack musicians. I was similarly taken to task in an article in the *Village Voice* entitled "The Rotten Club," the theme of which was, "Why did they use a white cat to play our music?" I was shocked. I'd hired who I thought were the best musicians for the job regardless of color. To use the old-timers, the original players, wouldn't have worked, because they no longer had the energy or chops to re-create the music – in any case most of them were either retired or no longer living. I had to get young guys, but it just so happens that practically all the young musicians who are interested in going back and studying early jazz are white! Young black players are into music since Charlie Parker. Even so, there were about ten black musicians I used on the score. Naturally the band that was assembled for the visual shots had to look like the Ellington and Calloway bands of the period. They were young black musicians in their 20s and 30s who freelanced around New York. They looked right, but they just couldn't play that music. They didn't have the knowledge or dedication that the players I hand-picked had to have in order to get the authentic sound of the period. Each player on the soundtrack was assigned a corresponding player in the Ellington band to emulate. For instance, in the trumpet section all the Cootie Williams and Bubber Miley solos were played by Lew Soloff, all of Arthur Whetsol's solos by Randy Sandke, all of Freddie Jenkins's solos by Dave Brown. Similarly, in the trombones, Britt Woodman played Lawrence Brown's parts, Joel Helleny played Tricky Sam Nanton's book and Dan Barrett captured the unique sound of Juan Tizol on valve trombone. To re-create the power and authority of Wellman Braud's bass, young John Goldsby set up his instrument with heavy gut strings and high action. Jazz bassists today use metal strings, set very low on the neck. They pick the string very gently, and the note is amplified and projected through a speaker. In Braud's day amplifiers weren't invented – he had to pluck the thick gut strings with tremendous force in order to project the sound. The only way John could get Braud's sound was to play the instrument in exactly the same fashion.

Because the Cab Calloway band was not the polished musical miracle that Duke's group was, but mostly a background for Cab's singing, I instructed the musicians purposely to play with less finesse and precision than in the Ellington re-creations. With the various small jazz groups that appear throughout the picture I tried to convey the feeling of the passage of time by changing the style of the music. For instance, in the Bamville Club scene laid in 1927, the band's sound suggests New Orleans players newly arrived in New York. Later, when Richard Gere sits in on a jam session playing *Indiana*, the sound is of the Chicagoans like Goodman, Krupa and Sullivan, who all migrated to New York around 1928. In the *Crazy Rhythm* scene, in which the feuding Hines brothers are reunited, the flavor is Harlem in 1930, the sounds of Red Allen and Coleman Hawkins.

Our leading man, Richard Gere, turned out to be quite a jazz fan. He was familiar with Armstrong and Beiderbecke's records and wanted to get as many re-creations of their solos in the movie as possible. (We ended up with Louis's *Big Butter and Egg Man* and Bix's *In a Mist*.) He was determined to record his own cornet part. To help him get the solos right we hired Jimmy Maxwell and Warren Vaché as coaches. The other solos which were not re-creations, such as *How come you do me* and *Indiana*, were composed by Warren, who spent many hours working with Gere. Incidentally, in the few scenes where Gere plays a piano, it is actually himself; Richard worked as a pianist in bars during his lean years.

Despite the hassles, working on the film was an extremely rewarding experience. The film's reviews were mixed but it did tremendous business all over the world, and, with the one exception of the *Village Voice*, the music reviews were overwhelmingly favorable. I tried to do the best job I could to make the music authentic and right for the picture. I met many delightful people, none more so than Gregory Hines. He's a fine actor but doesn't take it seriously because it comes so naturally to him. His tap-dancing is his big thing, and he works very hard at it. He has the charisma of a star, but he's an unassuming, natural guy, without the overweening ego that so many stars have. It was a pleasure to work with him. The film took me out of the limited category of a traditional jazz clarinet player and allowed people to see me in another light. My name is more widely known because of the film than it ever was as a jazz musician, which is not surprising in view of the tremendous publicity and exposure the picture had, even before its release.

In 1986 Pug and I returned to New York from our home in England to find the soundtrack album had won the Grammy Award for the best big-band jazz record of 1985. My Grammy statue sits on the piano in the living room of our home in the Cotswolds. It's really Pug's Grammy too – she gave me the courage to tackle the impossible. You never know, it might just work!

FIFTEEN

Hope fulfilled

As Pug and I got our life in order it seemed as if I was riding high on the crest of an artistic wave; things were happening to me that had never happened before. One such event took place in the summer of 1984 at Waterloo Village, a park two hours west of the city in New Jersey, about the time that work on *The Cotton Club* was drawing to a close. I had been approached by Jack Stine, a jazz promoter and a good friend, who was on the board of the Waterloo Concert Series. His committee was planning its Saturday night summer concert series, and Jack suggested I do a 75th birthday tribute to Benny Goodman. He wanted me to put together a band, and hoped to get Benny to assist in the planning and be the honored guest. Benny was flattered – he was genuinely enthusiastic and surprisingly co-operative, even to the extent of making available his library to choose the arrangements from. I used the Cotton Club band. We'd been recording the soundtrack for three weeks, often two sessions a day, and it had the cohesiveness and spirit of a real band – not the usual pickup group you hear nowadays. We rehearsed for nine hours, and by concert time on August 23rd the band was raring to go. Even the weather co-operated. It was a beautiful warm night, the one Saturday evening of the whole summer on which there was no rain. The program covered Benny's work from 1935 to 1945, and featured the arrangements of Fletcher Henderson, Deane Kincaide, Jimmy Mundy, Mary Lou Williams, Eddie Sauter and Mel Powell.

Benny helped with the program, suggesting numbers that were his favorites. He had donated a large number of arrangements to the Lincoln Center Music Library and had his lawyer send me a letter allowing me to have the parts photocopied. I spent hours poring over scores at the library, including a considerable number that had never been recorded. Fletcher's scores were written in a very precise, beautiful hand; he utilized both sides of the score paper, obviously an economy measure. There was one score, and one score only, by Harry James, called *Peckin*, which we used in the concert. Written in a laborious style by someone not used to writing music, the various parts were labeled with the players' names: thus the trumpet parts read "Chris, Ziggy, Harry," and the rhythm section parts read "Gene, Jess, Allan (Reuss) and Harry (Goodman)," etc. Fascinating business, this research! I even discovered 16 bars on Eddie Sauter's *Benny Rides Again* which had been cut from the original recording, presumably because of time limitations (it was a 12-inch record, unusual for those days), but which I restored in our version. I planned the concert in chronological order, ending the first half with *Sing, sing, sing* from 1937. When Benny saw the program, he said, "You can't end the first half with *Sing, sing, sing* – everybody'll go home. The only number you can play after *Sing, sing, sing* is *Good-bye.*" Of course, he was right.

Benny wanted to invite his family and friends, so the whole first row at Waterloo had been set aside for his entourage. Motel reservations were made for the whole party, the press was alerted and the committee even planned to read out a birthday telegram from the governor. It was all too perfect to be true. Benny, never having been known to act in a predictable fashion, was true to form. He canceled his appearance two days before the event. His lawyer, an amateur clarinetist, was there, however, and recorded the whole event on his small tape recorder. He must have called Goodman first thing next morning and played a little of the tape, because by noon Benny was on the phone congratulating me. When I asked him why he had decided not to come, he replied, "Aw, with all those reporters and people I thought they might ask me to play. I haven't been playing lately, ya know." In truth Benny had been plagued by health problems in recent years. In addition to his recurring back problem (celebrated in 1944 with the sextet's *Slipped Disc*), he'd had a pacemaker installed for his heart and was advised to take life easy. He'd even invited guitarist Bucky Pizzarelli by one day, and after a couple of hours' jamming said to Bucky, "That's enough. Jazz is terribly boring, don't you think?" Given the foregoing scenario, nobody would have predicted what happened in Benny's last two years, but if you knew Benny it made sense.

It was an electric atmosphere at Waterloo that night with a wildly enthusiastic audience of over 4000 people, young and old, cheering every number. When we hit the last chord of *Sing, sing, sing* the audience rose to its feet and clapped, stamped and roared for ten minutes. A large amount of the credit for our success has to go to producer Jack Stine, a guy of great integrity with a knowledge of classical music every bit as extensive as his knowledge of jazz. He has none of the ego of the typical producer, whose idea of a Goodman tribute would be to assemble as many of the original sidemen as possible and shove them on stage, trusting to luck they'll recapture some of the former glory. That, fortunately, is not Jack's style. He believes in the ability and integrity of the artist and appreciates the care and planning necessary for artistic success. As a result I was inspired by the way I was treated and worked my ass off – most musicians will do the same if they feel they're really appreciated. Why this lesson is so hard for jazz promoters to learn will forever remain a mystery to me.

Jack had arranged, with permission from Waterloo Village, Goodman, the musicians and myself, to have the concert recorded professionally. His appetite having been whetted by his lawyer's modest recording, Benny couldn't wait to hear the real thing. Every day I'd come home to a message on my answering machine: "Benny here. When can I hear the tapes?" I wanted to go in the studio with the engineer and edit out some extraneous dialogue but still leave all the music intact, so it wasn't until two weeks later that I rushed the finished product up to Benny's apartment. The scene had changed dramatically from just one month before when I'd been there planning the program. In place of the neat, well-ordered living room we'd sat in, there was now a chaotic scene. There were clarinet reeds everywhere – on the piano, on the desk, on the coffee table and scattered all over the rug. The antique music stand I'd read duets off many times was in the middle of the room, the Klose exercise book open, other clarinet studies scattered about the floor. Benny, clarinet in hand, thanked me for the tapes, muttered that he was very busy but would give me a call, and ushered me out. What was going on? I was mystified by Benny's behavior until I remembered a comment he'd made when he phoned me after the Waterloo concert. I'd suggested that the incredible response the night before showed what a demand there still was for Benny's music, and wasn't it a shame to have it just existing on old records. His brusque response was, "Well, I'm here, aren't I?" I realized that the fierce competitive spirit that made him "King of Swing" 50 years before was still burning brightly. The old fox wasn't finished yet! I never got another phone call from Benny but I began to hear stories via the musicians' grapevine: first, Benny was inviting musicians up to the apartment to play; then he was rehearsing a big band using many of the young musicians who'd worked with me.

Benny had agreed to play a benefit at Yale University for nothing, just expenses for the band. What's more, he was calling the musicians himself and booking dates personally. Exactly one year after I'd been at Waterloo Village Benny was there with his new band. Other concert dates followed, still more were planned for the future and a new album was recorded. On 13th June 1986, while busily practicing for an upcoming recital, Benny's ticker threw in the towel. Was he inspired by my successful concert at Waterloo Village or was he just bored with life, wanting to be back in the spotlight again? Whatever it was, I'm convinced he bowed out doing what he liked best – blowing that clarinet with a big band swinging behind him. It was only an echo, a shadow of the glory of the old days, and Benny knew it. But it was a damn good try. After all, he'd done it better than anybody had before or anybody is likely to do in the future. The King of Swing's crown is secure forever.

Among those present that night at Waterloo Village was my English friend Derek Webster, without whose patient cajoling and long hours spent burning the midnight oil this book would never have been finished. Derek was one of a committee of six who organized the Duke Ellington Conference in 1985, an annual affair attracting Ellington lovers from all over the world. It was England's turn to host the conference, the first time it had ever been held outside the United States. It was to be held at Birch Hall, a hotel outside Oldham in Lancashire, where for years host Ray Ibbotson has been presenting all the great names in jazz. Ray was also on the committee, and after due deliberation they decided to offer me the job of musical director. Their brief to me was clear and concise. "We're not interested in jam sessions. We've heard enough Ellington tributes with 'All Stars' stumbling through *Take the 'A' Train* and *Mood Indigo*. What we want is a structured presentation: three concerts that will cover various periods of Ellington and demonstrate the beauty, timelessness and universality of Duke's music. You're the man for us. We've complete faith in your ability to do this and know you won't let us down."

Here once again was the Bill Borden, Anders Ohman and Jack Stine syndrome. The freedom they were giving me to put the thing together was, as always, a great stimulus to my creative juices. Because I was being given the opportunity of doing something I could be proud of, I felt a great responsibility to do it right. The guest artists were Jimmy Hamilton, whose 68th birthday fortuitously fell during the event, and Willie Cook, a superb but often overlooked trumpet player from the postwar Ellington band. The guest singers were Pug, who could be counted on to re-create the ambience of Ivie Anderson, and Herb Jeffries of *Flamingo* fame. Alice Babs, the lovely Swedish lady whose soaring voice contributed so much to Duke's Sacred Concerts, was guest of honor. She'd come from her home in Majorca on the understanding that she wouldn't be asked to sing. As it turned out, Alice was so carried away by the emotional atmosphere of the conference she couldn't wait to join in.

The first evening's concert featured a band from Coventry called Harlem that specialized in Ellington of the 1920s and early 1930s. Willie and I were guest soloists. I was impressed with their enthusiasm and dedication and it made me think about the music education scene. They were all part-time players who wouldn't claim to be top-class musicians, but they had a love, a dedication and a knowledge of jazz music that enabled them to play it with conviction. Sure, there were rough spots, a few wrong chords, but they really got the message of the music across to the audience. I couldn't help contrasting them with the general run of the jazz studies stage bands where the musicians really know their instruments, know every scale and all the chords, but really know nothing at all about jazz. Why are the worlds of Harlem and the stage bands so far apart? Why is there no interaction between those worlds? It should be just as easy for the college kids to listen to the jazz reissues that the guys in Harlem listen to, to transcribe the music, to study the solos, to get inspiration. In fact it might be easier, because they're full-time students – not like the Harlem musicians who have to hold down a job during the day. For my money, Harlem was a much more meaningful jazz experience than the stage bands because they got into the music rather than playing a lot of glib flagwavers with screaming trumpets and a million notes. You don't hear many bands in the world that sound like Harlem, but you hear hundreds of stage bands and they all sound the same. The Harlem musicians didn't learn about jazz at college, they studied it by listening to old records. The whole history of jazz is documented on records. It's all sitting out there in the record shops waiting to be heard. Harlem got the message and Willie and I had a ball playing with them.

The second evening's concert featured my seven-piece group – four horns, three rhythm – presenting the music of the Ellington small bands led by John Hodges, Cootie Williams, Rex Stewart and Barney Bigard. It included some of England's leading jazz musicians. Danny Moss was on tenor and baritone, Roy Crimmins on trombone, Bobby Orr on drums, Len Skeat on bass, a first-class

Manchester pianist, Chris Holmes, plus Willie Cook and myself. Pug handled the vocal spot along with sitters-in Herb Jeffries, Alice Babs and June Norton, another former Ellington singer. A non-musical highlight during the evenings proceedings was a hilarious 15-minute monologue by Herb Jeffries concerning his love–hate affair with *Flamingo*, the song that made him famous. He started with the comment, "Why would anybody name a song *Flamingo*? Ugliest bird I've ever seen – stands in a puddle all day on one leg scratching itself!" He went on to describe the first recording: "The band was winding up a three-hour record date, five minutes left; guys yawning, starting to pack up. Duke says, 'Herb, let's do that *Flamingo*. We got time for one take.' We do one take – guys tired, sight-reading mistakes and all. I figure they'll never issue it."

Jeffries went on to describe how he'd left the band, not able to get a raise from his $75 a week salary. He's scuffling around Los Angeles and one day hears Duke's record of *Flamingo* on the radio: "I went down to the record store next day and they got the record in the window. There it was! *Flamingo* by Duke Ellington and his Orchestra with Male Vocalist. Suddenly I'm hearing it night and day all over the radio – people walking down the street whistling *Flamingo*. It's a hit. Here am I without a dime in my pocket, hearing myself everywhere. I figure I'll cash in on it and change my name to 'Male Vocalist'. Can you imagine it – Walter Winchell announces on his radio show, 'The top crooners in America today are Bing Crosby, Frank Sinatra and that sensational newcomer, Male Vocalist'."

Jeffries gets a telegram: "Please come back – stop – all is forgiven – stop – Duke." Duke woos Herb back into the fold with the words, "How much ya need? Look, I'll pay ya $150."

Herb is flabbergasted – twice the money! He blurts out, "One hundred and Fifty?"

"OK, OK," says Duke, "I'll give ya $200."

After a stint back with Ellington Herb goes out on his own, singing *Flamingo* in nightclubs, theaters and concerts and on TV around the world. "Every time I go with a new record company they say, 'We gotta find another *Flamingo*. Come on, Herb, we need a hit.' Well, I've never found another bird like that one. I've made five recordings of it – figure I've got four more to go."

The conference concluded on Sunday night with my big band playing Duke's classics of the 1940s. In the second half we presented selections from *Such Sweet Thunder* and the *New Orleans Suite*, including the *Portrait of Sidney Bechet* restored to its intended solo instrument, the soprano sax. Jimmy Hamilton was featured in *The Tattooed Bride*, Willie Cook paid a tribute to the late Shorty Baker in *All Heart*, and pianist Chris Holmes played *Single Petal of a Rose* from *The Queen Suite*. The concert ended with an extended version of *Stompy Jones* with everybody participating.

During the daytime hours the conference presented lectures, symposiums, films and recordings covering every aspect of Ellington. A particularly touching event occurred Saturday afternoon, when all the participants were bussed to a small village nearby where the town brass band saluted the conference with a short concert on the village green, concluding with their own arrangement of *Mood Indigo*. Interest was so high that a major television company produced a 60-minute documentary, which was subsequently shown in Europe and the United States. The whole event covered four days, with musicians and fans sequestered together under the same roof. The atmosphere of togetherness, the idea that we were all dedicated to honoring a great musician, was unique and moving. It will long remain a model for this type of event. The more that we in jazz can present these tributes with care and planning, the more the cultural establishment around the world will start to take jazz seriously. Most jazz festivals are circuses, not serious cultural events. It's my hope that the annual Duke Ellington Conference will take its place alongside the Mozart Festival at Salzburg and the Wagner Festival at Bayreuth as an international musical event of major importance.

These two events, the Waterloo Village Concert and the Duke Ellington Festival, have been two of the most satisfying experiences of my career. They embraced everything I believe to be important in presenting jazz. The music was on a very sophisticated level, but presented with flair and showmanship that communicated to a wide audience. As I listen to jazz today I hear more notes per bar being played on every instrument, more chords being altered in different ways. Some times the tremendous complexity seems to be just for the sake of complexity. As a musician I admire technical accomplishment, the ability of players to cover their instruments with tremendous agility and speed; I also admire musicians with great harmonic knowledge, extended range, razor-sharp reflexes. Too often, however, when I hear players possessing all these attributes I find myself left with the question – "So what?" All I hear is musical knowledge and technical expertise. They haven't touched my emotions; they haven't made me sad, or happy, or excited, or set a mood that's made me feel richer for the listening experience. A lot of jazz music today reflects a scientific approach to life, as if the human being is just another form of computer. It seems as if the structures the musicians set up are not designed to express feelings, but to represent a sort of maze through which they work their way. I hear so many pieces of music set up like mathematical problems – chord changes every bar, unusual time signatures, incredibly fast tempos. One has to concentrate so much on surmounting the obstacles set up by the complex structure that there is no opportunity to think about saying something. The only excitement the music generates is our awe at the musician's virtuosity. You can admire something that requires tremendous practice, such as the high-wire acts at the circus, but is this what we listen to jazz for? I hear John Coltrane's dedication in his playing and the work he put into it, but it doesn't give me a warm feeling; it just doesn't seem to express any joy. Maybe different people look for different things out of jazz, but I look for the pure joy of being alive that you get from Fats, from Louis, from Sidney and Duke. I enjoy listening to George Lewis's recording of *Burgundy Street Blues*. I'm perfectly aware that he plays some wrong notes – he doesn't hear all the changes. I also hear he's out of tune and his technique is limited, yet I come away from listening to that simple blues performance with a feeling of

"What beauty. How moving! What feeling the man had." It's primitive and crude, but the man had something to say and said it beautifully. This is the kind of music that never wears out its welcome. Not the wrong notes, the bad intonation, the crudities – to imitate a musician's faults is usually to ignore his virtues. I'm talking about saying something that is meaningful in a way that the listener doesn't have to be a walking encyclopedia of music to get the message. I don't want to hear music that represents an attempt to show what a fantastic master of the instrument a musician is, what range he has, how clever he is, what a brilliant mind he has. These facts are all part of the listener's experience, but when there's nothing else there, it's "so what" music. I'm reminded of the visiting musician who comes up to the bandstand after hearing a particularly fast, technical piece, brilliantly executed. He addresses the tenor man: "You cats were really burning."

The tenor man replies enthusiastically, "Yeah, man, we were really saying something."

The listener immediately responds, "I didn't say you were saying anything, I said you were burning!"

Singers are equally guilty. There are those with a five-octave range, but five octaves of what? In all the swoops, the groans, the trills and the affectations, the poor song is forgotten. The thing I love about Pug's singing is her reverence for the melody. She sings the melody the way it was written – every note exactly right on the button. Singing can be such a beautiful non-egotistic art when you concentrate on the beauty of the song, but some people don't even think that's jazz singing! Just to sing the melody with a beat is regarded as nothing. I'd like to hear young players concentrate on just that basic feat, playing the melody with a beat. It's a hard thing to do. You've got to make a sound that means something; you've got to sustain notes and make them sing. Louis Armstrong's 1929 recording of *When you're smiling* should be required listening for every aspiring jazz trumpet player. What he does, playing the melody an octave up with perfect control, majestic phrasing and a deep emotion that seems to express all the sufferings of the human race, is so difficult to do that it would have been regarded as impossible if Louis hadn't done it. I remember once playing a duet at a jazz party with a young alto player regarded as one of the new stars. As everybody before us had played fast numbers, I suggested a ballad. I realized right from the beginning that my partner was in deep trouble because of all the long notes. He couldn't sustain them or do anything with them; he just didn't know what to do except to go into double time. Although he went back to the safety of flying eighth-notes, I think he learned something from that experience. The more I play, the more I look for simplicity, for tunes with fewer changes and big wide spaces – just open, free music where you can swing and say something.

Take modern bass players, for instance. You hear them playing all the substitutions, all the extra notes, doing the "stumbles" (a descending triplet figure bass players love) and the double stops. I always say to them, "Listen to Milt Hinton." There's nobody better in the world than Milt – only different. The strong point in his playing is that he knows his roots. He plays a bass line which is also a foundation, and he plays it with a big, gorgeous, warm sound. Sometimes he plays slap-bass, a technique developed by early New Orleans bassists like Bill Johnson, Pops Foster and Wellman Braud, and is, I think, the only top professional bassist in the world who still plays that way. Milt himself gets a tremendous kick out of it, the audiences love it and I as a musician love it. Nothing upsets Milt as much as the fact that there are so very few young black musicians coming up who are interested in earlier styles. When he comes across any promising young players he puts them in touch with me, because I always like to encourage them. Sadly, when we were putting the Smithsonian Jazz Repertory Ensemble together, we didn't get any young black players coming to the auditions. The music we were playing was not of any particular interest to them. The soprano players want to emulate Coltrane, not Bechet; trumpet players Marsalis, not Armstrong. It's like aspiring classical composers ignoring Bach and Mozart. In jazz, like classical music, you have to acknowledge traditions. You have to achieve a fine balance of emotion and intellect. You have to organize feelings into thoughts. Bach and Mozart did it and so did Armstrong and Bechet. To reach emotional ecstasy without losing control, that's the trick! Bach achieved it in *Sleepers Wake*, Mozart in the Clarinet Quintet, Louis in *When you're smiling* and Sidney in *Blue Horizon*. Music desperately needs more musicians like them as we approach the 21st century.

The significant thing about my career is how different it has been from those of most players. In the majority of cases, players achieve their success and make their definitive statements at a comparatively young age. Thereafter, if they're lucky enough not to die from booze or drugs, they continue to repeat their early statements, some more successfully than others. Bix was dead from booze at 31, Bird from drugs at 34. Benny continued to repeat his early musical statements with diminishing success, while Doc Cheatham at 82 seems to play his stuff as well as ever. Although my career had a start that had a lot of publicity, I spent the next 30 years in a state of suspended animation, and it's only in the last ten years that I've begun to achieve my goals, the things I spent my whole life training to do. The catalyst was Pug, who restored to me the confidence and belief I'd lost. With such a totally encouraging and supportive helpmate I knew I could do everything that I'd ever done throughout my life better than I'd done it before.

Pug had a colorful childhood. She left home at the age of 14 to go on stage. Her education suffered during those war years in England, but in the early 1970s she went to night school, got her high-school diploma and went on to college to study sociology and psychology. In due course she obtained her Master's degree. This gritty determination, plus an intuition I refer to as her "gypsy vibes," make her a good business woman. She has a natural talent for banking transactions and real-estate dealings – in short she's an ideal foil for my own dreamy, Piscean nature. In the field of music we're a partnership in every sense of the word. On the artistic side her talents as a singer and lyricist have complemented my own musical efforts; together we've composed many songs and produced some records we're proud of. On the business side, her efforts have continually advanced my career. She convinced Anders Ohman that he should let me record some chamber music on his classical label, thus fulfilling a lifelong ambition of mine. Similarly, after our discovery of Scott Hamilton, she sat on Hank O'Neal's desk and persuaded him to record Scott's group with me without him having heard them. Pug was the driving force in setting up our own publishing company, Chalumeau Music, and our own record company, Bodeswell. She urged me to take up the challenge of *The Cotton Club* and, most recently, to renew my acquaintance with the tenor sax. She has never known the meaning of the word "can't" and refuses to take "no" for an answer.

There are so many ways in which Pug has influenced me. My degree, for instance, was entirely due to her urging. It was a project I had never felt confident of tackling, always convincing myself that I didn't have the time and that it wasn't necessary anyway. Pug's educational experience should have showed me the way. It turned out to be something that I really enjoyed doing and I'm proud to be a Bachelor of Arts. It certainly pleased my father tremendously; the fact that his son had a college degree meant a lot to him. I know he was bitterly disappointed when I dropped out of school all those years ago, though he never said so. When I graduated from college Pug organized a reception, and with her usual thoughtfulness and sensitivity arranged to have it at the Gramercy Park Hotel, directly across from One Lexington Avenue, where Mother and Dad had set up their first home together. At the height of the celebration my father rose to his feet and proposed "a special toast to the lady who made this occasion possible. Without Pug, all this wouldn't have happened."

One year Pug gave me the birthday gift of a concert at Carnegie Recital Hall. She set the whole thing up and produced the event, getting all her friends to help out, including Joe and Mary Tucker, who came down from the Cape. Pug was busy ushering people into the Recital Hall while Mary was in the box office selling tickets. Pug's cousin Kate looked after the food, while my nephew Tim organized the wine for the reception. It was a real family affair with everybody involved under Pug's direction. The first half of the concert consisted of trios by Beethoven and Brahms. Cellist Leo Winland, who'd played on the recording for Anders Ohman, flew over from Stockholm to join us. In the second half an all-star band played our original compositions, and Pug sang. Many important and distinguished people were in the audience, including critic John Hammond, Stanley Drucker, Leon and Penny Russianoff, Anders Ohman and our old friends Harold and June Geneen. Two years later Pug arranged and produced another concert, which featured three facets of jazz. We opened with the Bechet Legacy, then Major Holley's group paid tribute to Louis Jordan, and, to conclude, both groups combined to play the music of John Kirby.

The energy and drive of Pug is everywhere to be seen, but perhaps her finest quality is her ability to make friends everywhere she goes. People warm to Pug easily and are willing to go out of their way to do things for her and help in any way they can. It is something that has opened my eyes, to see how rewarding life can be when you give of yourself. Friends and social contacts mean so much more to me than they did "BP" (before Pug). To have meaningful and sincere friends, not just professional associates, has been an absolute boon in my life. Pug's credo is to think of the other person; not to be selfish and say, "What's in it for me?"

An added bonus has been a marvelous relationship with Pug's three children. Russell is a trial lawyer in Atlanta who destroys me on the tennis court with ease. Her younger son Nick, a computer wizard and a devoted Quaker, has just graduated from Harvard. Danielle, her daughter and the youngest of her children, is studying at Brown University in Providence, Rhode Island. They're all out-going, giving, warm-hearted people who enrich our lives.

Pug is very open and frank and she expects people to be the same way with her. I've tried to emulate this attitude – a big improvement on my old "peace at all costs" ways. This has resulted in a much closer, realistic relationship with my mother, and with my father while he was alive. We have big family get-togethers where there is much genuine love and emotion displayed – so very different from the gatherings during all those years when everything seemed so superficial. Pug's presence in my life has made me a complete person, no longer just a music-making machine. The best part is that when I look into the mirror I'm beginning actually to like what I see. The anger I felt when I looked at myself on my 50th birthday is no longer there. It was a difficult but rewarding experience finding out that, indeed, music was not enough. Without love, friendship, and all the give and take involved in human relationships, life's not worth a row of beans, is it?

Pug and I have found our own oasis in England, in the little village of Chipping Campden. We're in the very middle of the country, in an area known as the Cotswolds, about ten miles south of Stratford-on-Avon. If it eventually turns out there's nobody out there who wants to hear my kind of jazz (which may happen considering current trends) then I'll have ended up in a beautiful environment with a loving wife and true and trusted friends such as the swinging guitar duo, Alan and Diane Carter. Like Dave McKenna, I could be a postman and be happy! All these things outside music have become important to me. They're all here, right on my doorstep. If my musical activity consists of get-togethers in the living room playing for friends, I'll still be alive and communicating. I've lived and worked in a world where for so many people the order of the day is ambition, jealousy and greed; the big thing is to be successful, to make it. They're not happy people, nor do they make others happy, because their primary aim is to take, not to give. I don't want to be like that. I've got Pug, a loving family and dear friends. I don't need to be a success; I don't need to make it. I already am and I already have! As an added bonus I have a student, Antii Sarpila from Helsinki, Finland, who plays clarinet and tenor sax like a fiend. He's 23 years old, been studying with me since he was 16 and he's one helluva player! I'm grateful to this kid for coming along, kicking my ass all the way.

In 1985 I received a letter from Philip Larkin, the eminent English poet. He wrote: "I heard you in the flesh twice, once with Eddie Condon in the City Hall in Hull back in the fifties and again when you visited Hull University with Kenny Davern. Both occasions have stayed vividly in my memory. I sat through both houses for the Condon concert and your Soprano Summit concert had me stamping and shrieking . . . I wish you would write a book yourself. You have been pretty well through it all and your views would be of enormous interest. It is good to hear that you are making your home in England and I hope that we may one day meet, although I am an aged, infirm invalid unable to visit or receive." Not longer afterwards Philip Larkin died.

Well, I've written my book and I've told my story. I wish Philip Larkin were here to read it.

Selective discography

arr	arranger	fh	french horn
as	alto saxophone	g	guitar
bcl	bass clarinet	p	piano
bj	banjo	perc	percussion
bs	baritone saxophone	ss	soprano saxophone
c	cornet	t	trumpet
cl	clarinet	tb	trombone
cond	conductor	ts	tenor saxophone
d	drums	v	vocals
db	double bass	vib	vibraphone
dir	director	vn	violin
flhn	flugelhorn	*	composition by Bob Wilber

1947
Feb 22   New York
Bob Wilber and his Wildcats – "New Orleans Style Old and New"
John Glasel (c); Bob Wilber (cl); Dick Wellstood (p); Charlie Traeger (db); Denny Strong (d)
A-4903-1 Willie the Weeper   Commodore XFL 15774
A-4903-2 Willie the Weeper
A-4904-1 Mabel's Dream
A-4904-2 Mabel's Dream
A-4905-1 Wild Cat Blues
A-4905-2 Wild Cat Blues
A-4906-1 Blues for Fowler
A-4906-2 Blues for Fowler (*)

1947
July 14   New York
Bob Wilber's Wildcats with Sidney Bechet – "The Sidney Bechet Story"
John Glasel (c); Bob Mielke (tb); Sidney Bechet (ss, cl); Bob Wilber (ss, cl); Dick Wellstood (p); Charlie Traeger (db); Denny Strong (d)
CO37999 Spreading Joy   CBS 88084
CO38015 I had it but it's all gone now
CO38016 Polka Dot Stomp
CO38017 Kansas City Man Blues

1949
April 28   New York
Bob Wilber and his Jazz Band
Henry Goodwin (t); Jimmy Archery (tb); Bob Wilber (cl, ss); Dick Wellstood (p); Pops Foster (db); Tommy Benford (d)
NY87 Sweet Georgia Brown   Jazzology J-44
NY88 The Mooche
NY89 Coal Black Shine
NY90 Limehouse Blues
NY91 Zigzag
NY92 When the saints go marching in

1949
June 9   New York
Same personnel as session of 28 April 1949, plus Sidney Bechet (ss, cl)
NY93 I'm through, goodbye
NY94 Love me with a feeling
NY95 Waste no tears

NY96 Box Car Shorty
NY97 Broken Windmill
NY98 Without a Home

1954
April   New York
The Six
John Glasel (t); Porky Cohen (tb); Bob Wilber (cl, ts); Tommy Goodman (p); Bob Peterson (db); Eddie Phyfe (d)
Porky's Blues   Norgran MGN 25; Verve MGV 8155; Clef (E) 33C9028
St James Infirmary
A Foggy Day
Little Girl Blue
Riverboat Shuffle
Music to Sin By
Between the Devil and the Deep Blue Sea

1955
July   New York
The Six
John Glasel (t); Sonny Truitt (tb); Bob Wilber (cl, ts); Bob Hammer (p); Bill Britto (db); Eddie Phyfe (d)
Tasty   Bethlehem BCP 28; London (E) LTZ-N15042
As far as we're concerned (*)
Shifty
Serenata
Pink Ice (*)
Strange Diet
Old Folks
Itchy Fingers
Two Kinds of Blues (*)

1956
Jan   New York
The Six – "The View From Jazzbo's Head"
John Glasel (t); Sonny Truitt (tb); Bob Wilber (cl, ts); Bob Hammer (p); Bill Britto (db); Jackie Moffitt (d)
Giggles   Bethlehem BCP 57; London (E) LTZ-N15066
Phweedah (*)
Over the Rainbow
The View from Jazzbo's Head
The Troglodyte
Blue Lou
Our Delight
My Old Flame

1957
June 28   New York
Eddie Condon and his All Stars – "The Roaring Twenties"
Billy Butterfield (t); Cutty Cutshall (tb); Bob Wilber (cl); Gene Schroeder (p); Eddie Condon (g); Leonard Gaskin (db); George Wettling (d)
CO58207 What-cha-call-'em Blues   *Columbia CL1089;*
                                             Phillips (E) BBL.7227
CO58208 Heebie Jeebies
CO58209 Chimes Blues
CO58210 My Monday Date

1957
Aug 19
Same personnel as session of 28 June 1957, but Wild Bill Davison (c) and Vic Dickenson (tb) replace Butterfield and Cutshall
CO59524 Wolverine Blues
CO59525 China Boy
CO59526 St James Infirmary
CO59527 That's a Plenty

1957
Sept 24
Same personnel as 'session of 28 June 1957
CO59867 Put 'em Down Blues
CO59868 Davenport Blues
CO59869 Apex Blues
CO59870 Minor Drag

1958
Nov 15   New York
Benny Goodman – "Happy Session"
John Frosk, Allen Smith, E. V. Perry, Benny Ventura (t); Rex Peer, Hale Rood, Buster Cooper (tb); Benny Goodman (cl); Herb Geller, Jimmy Sands (as); Bob Wilber, Arthur Clark (ts); Pepper Adams (bs); Russ Freeman (p); Turk Van Lake (g); Milt Hinton (db); Shelly Manne (d)
Happy Session Blues   *Columbia CL1324;*
                                             Phillips BBL7318

Nov 18   New York

King and Me
What a Difference a Day Made
Batunga Train
Clarinet à la King
Macedonia Lullaby
NB: Wilber is not present on four further tracks included on this album.

1959
Sept 14, 15   New York
Lou McGarity – "Blue Lou"
Doc Severinson (t); Lou McGarity (tb); Bob Wilber (cl, bcl, ts); Dick Cary (p, t); George Barnes (g); Jack Lesberg (db); Don Marino (d)
Blue and Broken Hearted   *Argo LP(s) 654*
Blue Moon
Blue Prelude
Blue Again
Blue Champagne
Blue turning grey over you
Blue Lou
Born to be Blue
Blue Skies
Black and Blue
I get the blues when it rains
Under a Blanket of Blue

1959
Late 1959
Bob Wilber Quintet, Septet – "Spreadin' Joy"
Bob Wilber (cl, ts, bcl); Dick Wellstood (p); Barry Galbraith (g); Leonard Gaskin (db); Bobby Donaldson (d)
Spreadin' Joy   *Classic Jazz CJ5*
Where am I
Who'll chop your suey when I'm gone

Quincy Street Stomp
Georgia Cabin
Blue Horizon
Dick Cary (t); Vic Dickenson (tb); Bob Wilber (cl, ts, bcl); Dick Wellstood (p); Barry Galbraith (g); Leonard Gaskin (db); Bobby Donaldson (d)
Polka Dot Stomp
Ghost of the Blues
When the sun sets down South
Little Creole Lullaby
Black Stick

1959
New York
Bob Wilber All Star Jazz Band – "The Dixie Do-it-Yourself"
Buck Clayton (t); Vic Dickenson (tb); Bob Wilber (cl); Bud Freeman (ts); Dick Wellstood (p); Ahmed Abdul-Malik (db); Panama Francis (d)
Basin Street Blues   *Music Minus One MMO1010*
Chimes Blues
High Society
Milenberg Joys
Wild Man Blues

1960
New York
Bob Wilber – "New Clarinet in Town"
Bob Wilber (cl); Dave McKenna (p); Charlie Byrd (g); George Duvivier (db); Bobby Donaldson (d)
Benny Rides Again   *Classic Jazz CJB*
Django
The Duke
Upper Manhattan Medical Group
Bob Wilber (cl); Charlie Byrd (g); Dave McKenna (p); George Duvivier (db); Tony Miranda (fh); Jessy Tryon, Peter Dimitriades (vn); George Brown (viola); Sidney Edwards (cello); Deane Kincaide (cond)
Swing '39
Blame it on my youth
All too Soon
Clarinade
Lonely Town

1962
June 4, 6   New York
Jack Teagarden
Bobby Hackett (c); Jack Teagarden (tb); Bob Wilber (cl); Bud Freeman (ts); Hank Jones or Gene Schroeder (p); George Duvivier (db); Ed Shaughnessy, George Wettling (d)
Johnny   *Verve V-8495*
Moon River
All the Way
Gigi
The last time I saw Paris
Learnin' The Blues
Dame Blanche
Never on Sunday
Time after Time
Secret Love
The Atcheson, Topeka and the Santa Fe
High Hopes

1967
Various dates, Jan–May
Bobby Hackett – "Creole Cookin'"
Bobby Hackett (c); James Morreale, Rusty Dedrick (t); Bob Brookmeyer, Cutty Cutshall (tb); Bob Wilber (cl, ss, arr); Jerry Dodgion (as); Zoot Sims, Joe Farrell (ts); Pepper Adams (bs); Dave McKenna (p); Wayne Wright (g); Buddy Jones (db); Morey Feld (d)
High Society   *Verve V/V6-8698*
Tin Roof Blues
When the saints go marching in
Basin Street Blues
Fidgety Feet
Royal Garden Blues

Muskrat Ramble
Dixieland One-step
Lazy Mood
Do you know what it means to miss New Orleans

1968
Dec 10   New York
World's Greatest Jazz Band
Yank Lawson, Billy Butterfield (t); Lou McGarity, Carl Fontana (tb); Bob Wilber (cl, ss); Bud Freeman (ts); Ralph Sutton (p); Bob Haggart (db); Morey Feld (d)
Sunny   *Project 3 PR5033SD;*
                                          WRC(E) ST1091
Panama
Baby won't you please come home
Up, up and away
Ode to Billie Joe
Honky Tonk Train Blues
A Taste of Honey
Limehouse Blues
Big Noise from Winnetka
This is all I ask
Mrs Robinson
Bugle Call Rag

1968
Dec 19   New York
World's Greatest Jazz Band – "Extra"
Yank Lawson (t); Billy Butterfield (t, flh); Lou McGarity, Carl Fontana (tb); Bob Wilber (cl, ss); Bud Freeman (ts); Ralph Sutton (p); Bob Haggart (db); Gus Johnson (d)
Love is Blue   *Project 3 PR5039SD;*
                                          Parlophone PCS71
I'm prayin' humble
It must be him
59th Street Bridge Song (Feelin' Groovy)
Alfie
Wolverine Blues
What the world needs now
Savoy Blues
Wichita Lineman
Do you know the way to San Jose
The Windmills of your mind
South Rampart Street Parade

1969
Jan 24, 31, Feb 3   New York
Bob Wilber – "The Music of Hoagy Carmichael"
Yank Lawson, Bernie Privin (t); Lou McGarity, Buddy Morrow (tb); Bob Wilber (cl, ss, bcl, arr); Bud Freeman (ts); Bernie Leighton (p); George Duvivier (db); Gus Johnson (d); Maxine Sullivan (v)
Riverboat Shuffle   *Monmouth Evergreen MES6917;*
                                          Parlophone(E) PCS7137
Georgia on my Mind
One Morning in May
Skylark
Washboard Blues
Stardust
In the cool, cool, cool of the evening
Jubilee
The Nearness of You
Rockin' Chair
Lazy River
I get along without you very well
Ev'ntide
New Orleans

1969
Feb 16–19   Aspen, Colorado
Ralph Sutton Trio with Bob Wilber – "The Night they Raided Sunnies"
Bob Wilber (cl, ss); Ralph Sutton (p); Al Hall (db); Cliff Leeman (d)
Lulu's Back in Town   *Blue Angel Jazz Club BAJC504*
Stumblin'
Give me a June Night

As long as I live
I'll be a friend with pleasure
I believe in miracles
I'm always in the mood for you
Just Friends (without Wilber)

1969
June 11, 13   New York
Bob Wilber, Maxine Sullivan – "Close as Pages in a Book"
Bob Wilber (cl, ss, arr); Bernie Leighton (p); George Duvivier (db); Gus Johnson (d); Maxine Sullivan (v)
As long as I live   *Monmouth Evergreen MES6919;*
                                          Parlophone (E) PCS7123
Gone with the Wind
Rockin' in Rhythm
Darn that Dream
Ev'ry time I fall in love
Harlem Butterfly
Loch Lomond
Too Many Tears
Jeepers Creepers
Restless
You're driving me crazy
Close as Pages in a Book

1970
April 17, 18   New York
World's Greatest Jazz Band – "Live at the Roosevelt Grill"
Yank Lawson (t); Billy Butterfield (t, flh); Vic Dickenson, Lou McGarity (tb); Bob Wilber (cl, ss); Bud Freeman (ts); Ralph Sutton (p); Bob Haggart (db); Gus Johnson (d)
That's a Plenty   *Atlantic SD1570;*
                                          ATL/Polydor 2659-006;
                                          ATL(E) 2402037
Five Point Blues
My Honey's Lovin' Arms
Black and Blue
That D Minor Thing
Royal Garden Blues
Come back sweet papa
Under the Moonlight Starlight Blue
Constantly
New Orleans
Jazz me Blues

1973
Dec 17, 21, 23   New York
Soprano Summit – "Soprano Summit"
Bob Wilber (ss, cl); Kenny Davern (cl, ss); Dick Hyman (p); Bucky Pizzarelli (g, bj); George Duvivier (db); Bobby Rosengarden (d)
Swing Parade   *World Jazz WJLP-S-5*
Egyptian Fantasy
Johnny was there (*)
Penny Rag (*)
The Mooche
Where are we
Please Clarify (*)
Song of Songs
Milt Hinton (db) replaces George Duvivier
Oh sister ain't that hot
Stealin' Away
The Fish Vendor
Meet me tonight in dreamland

1976
March 3   New York
Soprano Summit – "Chalumeau Blue"
Bob Wilber (cl, ss); Kenny Davern (cl, ss); Marty Grosz (g, bj); George Duvivier (db); Fred Stoll (d)
Nagasaki   *Chiaroscuro CR148*
Chalumeau Blue (*)
Black and Tan Fantasy
Grenadilla Stomp (*)
Danny Boy
Everybody loves my baby
Linger Awhile
Slightly under the weather (*)

Wake up Chillun
Ol' Miss
Debut (*)
Some of these days

1976
Summer   Concord, California
Soprano Summit – "In Concert"
Bob Wilber (cl, ss); Kenny Davern (cl, ss); Marty Grosz (g); Ray Brown (db); Jake Hanna (d)
Stompy Jones   *Concord CJ29*
The Grapes are Ready (*)
Doin' the new low down
The Golden Rooster (*)
Moxie
Brother, can you spare a dime
All by Myself
Swing that Music

1977
Spring   New York
Bob Wilber and the Scott Hamilton Quartet
Bob Wilber (as, cl, ss); Scott Hamilton (ts); Chris Flory (g); Phil Flanagan (db); Chuck Riggs (d)
Riff (*)   *Chiaroscuro CR171*
Rocks in my Bed
Between the Devil and the Deep Blue Sea
Time after Time
I never knew
Jonathan's Way (*)
All too Soon
Freeman's Way (*)
Treasure (*)
Puggles (*)
Taking a Chance on Love
144 West 54th (*)

1978
Nov 15, 16   New York
Bob Wilber – "Original Wilber"
Bob Wilber (cl, as, ss); Dave McKenna (p); Bill Crow (db, 1); Connie Kay (d); Pug Horton (v, 2)
Movin' 'n' Groovin' (*)(1)   *Phontastic 7519*
BG (*)
Treasure (*)(2)
Land of the Midnight Sun (*)(1)
Don't go away (*)(1)
Wind Song (*)(1)
Wequasset Wail (*)
I've loved you all my life (*)(2)
Hymn: In Memory of Joe Oliver (*)
I can't forget you now (*)(2)
Crawfish Shuffle (*)(1)

1979
Feb 21, 22   Stockholm, Sweden
Wilber, Winland, Solyom – "Beethoven and Brahms Trios"
Bob Wilber (cl); Janos Solyom (p); Leo Winland (cello)
Beethoven: Trio in B Flat Major, Op.11
                                       Artemis ARTE 7107

1979
Feb 26, 27   Stockholm, Sweden
Bob Wilber and the Phontastic Swing Band – "Swinging for the King"
Collective personnel: Bob Wilber, Ove Lind, Anders Ohman (cl); Arne Domnerus (cl, as); Lars Erstrand (vib); Lars Sjösten (p); Karl-Erik Holmgren (g); Arne Wilhelmsson (db); Rune Carlsson (d); Pug Horton (v)
Let's Dance   *Phontastic 7406/7*
It's been so long
Changes
Goodnight my Love
The best things in life are free
I had to do it
Bach Goes to Town

By Myself
Silhouetted in the Moonlight
Jubilee
Why do I love you
Seven Come Eleven
Jersey Bounce
Deep Night
All the things you are
We'll meet again
Keep your sunny side up
Rachel's Dream
Lullaby in Rhythm
Miss my Lovin' time (*)
Somebody else is taking my place
Lovely to look at
Stealin' Apples
Good-bye

1979
Feb   Stockholm, Sweden
Bob Wilber – "Mozart Clarinet Quintet and Trio"
Bob Wilber (cl); Gert Crafoord, Willie Sundling (vn); Lars Jonsson (viola); Lars-Olof Bergström (cello)
Quintet for Clarinet and Strings in A Major (K581)
                                       Artemis ARTE 7109
Bob Wilber (cl); Björn Sjögren (viola); Janos Solyom (p)
Trio for Clarinet, Viola and Piano in E Flat Major (K498)

1979
May 30   New York
Pug Horton – "Don't Go Away"
Pug Horton (v); Bob Wilber (cl, as, ss); Roland Hanna (p); Milt Hinton (db, 1)
If   *Bodeswell BW102*
Breezin' Along (1)
I can dream
Send a little love my way (1)
Melancholy
Don't go away (*)(1)
By Myself (1)
Sweetheart of Mine
I'll string along with you
I Found A New Baby (1)
Miss My Lovin' Time (*)
Tipperary (1)

1979
May 30, 31   New York
Bob Wilber and the American All Stars – "In the Mood for Swing"
Jimmy Maxwell (t); Bob Wilber (cl, ss, as); Norris Turney (as); Al Klink, Frank Wess (ts); Lars Erstrand (vib); Hank Jones (p); Bucky Pizzarelli (g); Michael Moore (db); Connie Kay (d)
I'm in the mood for swing   *Phontastic 7526*
It's the talk of the town
Dinah
I'm Confessin'
When lights are low
Ring dem bells
Memories of you
Bei mir bist du Schön
Yours and Mine
Chinatown, my Chinatown

1980
Aug 24   New York
Bob Wilber with Lars Erstrand and Pug Horton – "Dizzy Fingers"
Bob Wilber (cl); Lars Erstrand (vib); Mark Shane (p); Chris Flory (g); Phil Flanagan (db); Chuck Riggs (d); Pug Horton (v, 1)
Dizzy Fingers   *Bodeswell BW101*
Poor Butterfly
Airmail Special
Foolin' Myself (1)
Soft Winds
Jumpin' at the Woodside

Clarinade
Rose Room
Royal Garden Blues
What a little moonlight can do (1)
Memories of you
The world is waiting for the sunrise

1981
May 10   Washington
The Bob Wilber Jazz Repertory Ensemble – "The Music of the King Oliver Creole Jazz Band"
Bob Zottola, Glenn Zottola (t); Tom Artin (tb); Bob Wilber (cl); Mark Shane (p); Chris Flory (bj); Phil Flanagan (db); Chuck Riggs (d)
Canal Street Blues   *Bodeswell BW107*
Mabel's Dream
Alligator Flop
Krooked Blues
Chattanooga Stomp
Camp Meeting Blues
Dipper Mouth Blues
Lincoln Gardens Stomp (*)
Snake Rag
Riverside Blues
Froggie Moore
Jazzin' Babies
Buddy's Habits
Wa-wa-wa
I ain't gonna tell nobody

1982
Aug 5, 6   New York
Bob Wilber and the Bechet Legacy – "Ode to Bechet"
Glenn Zottola (t); Vic Dickenson (tb); Bob Wilber (ss); Mike Peters (g, bj); Mark Shane (p); Reggie Johnson (db); Butch Miles (d); Joanne (Pug) Horton (v, 1)
Margie   *Bodeswell BW104*
Blues in the Air
I can't believe you're in love with me
I get the blues when it rains (1)
The Mooche
I ain't gonna give nobody none of my jelly roll (1)
When my dreamboat comes home
Ode to Bechet (*)
Quincy Street Stomp
A Sailboat in the Moonlight (1)
High Society

Bechet's Fantasy
Shake it and break it

1983
June 8, 10   New York
Bob Wilber with the Bodeswell Strings – "Reflections"
Bob Wilber (as, ss); Mark Shane (p); Mike Peters (c); Todd Coolman (db); Butch Miles (d); plus strings (Harold Cohen, cond)
All Alone   *Bodeswell BW106*
Deep Purple
I'll be seeing you
Bess you is my woman
Treasure (*)
Bossa Losada (*)
One Morning in May
Song of Songs
Clarion Song (*)
In the wee small hours
Body and Soul
Memory

1984
June, July   New York
Soundtrack Recordings – "The Cotton Club"
Collective personnel: Dave Brown, Marky Markowitz, Randy Sandke, Lew Soloff (t); Dan Barrett, Joel Helleny, Britt Woodman (tb); Bob Stewart, Tony Price (tuba); Bob Wilber (cond, arr, as, ss, cl); Frank Wess (as, ss, ts, cl); Chuck Wilson (as, ss, cl); Lawrence Feldman (ts, ss, cl); Joe Temperley (bs, as); Mark Shane (p); Mike Peters (g, bj); John Goldsby (db); Chuck Riggs, Brian Brake (d); Danny Druckman, Gordon Ruttlieb, Dave Samuels, Ronnie Zito (perc)
The Mooche   *Geffen GHS 24062 E*
Cotton Club Stomp, no. 2
Drop me off in Harlem
Creole Love Call
Ring dem Bells
East St Louis Toodle-o
Truckin'
Ill Wind
Cotton Club Stomp, no. 1
Mood Indigo
Minnie the Moocher
Copper Coloured Gal
Dixie kidnaps Vera
The Depression Hits
Best beats Sandman
Daybreak Express

Index

Wilber, Bob [contd]
——, and Friends, 166
——, Jazz Repertory Ensemble, 169
Wilber, Gonka [grandmother], 10
Wilber (née Alder), Margaret
    [stepmother], 1, 4, 5, 10, 18, 24, 79,
    160, 198
Wilber, Mary Eliza [mother], 3, 5
Wilber, Mary Margaret [sister], 1, 3, 4, 5,
    10, 18
Wilber, Robert (Ardie), 90
Wildcats, 17–19, 31, 34, 45, 54, 59, 60,
    78, 92, 166, 174
Wiley, Lee, 70
Wilkes-Barre, Pennsylvania
——, Wilkes College, 174–6
Williams, Cootie, 39, 73, 83, 132, 184,
    187, 192
Williams, Gene, 47, 48
Williams, John, 8
Williams, Martin, 169
Williams, Mary Lou, 23, 189
Williams, Sandy, 35
Williams, Tennessee, 44
Wilson, John, 133

Wilson, Lucille, 177
Wilson, Teddy, 8, 54, 70, 73, 110, 130,
    134
Winchell, Walter, 193
Windhurst, Johnny, 14–15, 16, 47, 53
Winland, Leo, 197
With Strings Attached, 68
Wolverine Blues, 68
Woode, Jimmy, 179
Woodman, Britt, 187
Woods, Phil, 85
World's Greatest Jazz Band, 69, 106,
    111–18, 119, 120, 121, 125, 127, 128,
    129, 135, 142–3, 166, 175, 176

Yaged, Sol, 95
Yancey Special, 7
Young, Lester, 43–4, 48, 55, 56, 90, 97,
    145, 149–50, 174
Young, Trummy, 38
You're driving me crazy, 183

Zottola, Glenn, 160, 162
Zurbrugg, Hans, 180